**BLOOMSBURY
TEACHER
GUIDE**

ANITA AND ME

Zara Shah
and
Kerry Kurczij

BLOOMSBURY EDUCATION
LONDON OXFORD NEW YORK NEW DELHI SYDNEY

BLOOMSBURY EDUCATION
Bloomsbury Publishing Plc
50 Bedford Square, London, WC1B 3DP, UK
29 Earlsfort Terrace, Dublin 2, Ireland

BLOOMSBURY, BLOOMSBURY EDUCATION and the Diana logo are trademarks
of Bloomsbury Publishing Plc

First published in Great Britain, 2024

Text copyright © Zara Shah and Kerry Kurczij, 2024

Zara Shah and Kerry Kurczij have asserted their rights under the Copyright,
Designs and Patents Act, 1988, to be identified as Authors of this work.

Extracts from *Anita and Me* by Meera Syal, Flamingo, 1997, copyright © Meera Syal, 1996.
Reprinted by permission of HarperCollins Publishers Ltd; and Curtis Brown Group Ltd on behalf
of Meera Syal.

Bloomsbury Publishing Plc does not have any control over, or responsibility for, any third-party
websites referred to or in this book. All internet addresses given in this book were correct at the
time of going to press. The author and publisher regret any inconvenience caused if addresses
have changed or sites have ceased to exist, but can accept no responsibility for any such changes.

All rights reserved. No part of this publication may be reproduced or transmitted in any form or
by any means, electronic or mechanical, including photocopying, recording, or any information
storage or retrieval system, without prior permission in writing from the publishers.

A catalogue record for this book is available from the British Library

ISBN: PB: 978-1-8019-9362-3; ePDF: 978-1-8019-9360-9; ePub: 978-1-8019-9361-6

2 4 6 8 10 9 7 5 3 1 (paperback)

Text design by Marcus Duck
Typeset by Marcus Duck

Printed and bound in the UK by CPI Group (UK) Ltd., Croydon, CR0 4YY

To find out more about our authors and books visit www.bloomsbury.com and
sign up for our newsletters

CONTENTS

Acknowledgements v
Foreword vi
How to use this book 1
› Why, what and how 1
› Pit stops 7
› Dual coding 9
Introduction to *Anita and Me* 11
› Tracking the text 11
› Assessment objectives 12

Chapter 1 of *Anita and Me*
At a glance 14
› Why? 14
› What? 15
› How? 21

Chapter 2 of *Anita and Me*
At a glance 26
› Why? 26
› What? 27
› How? 33

Chapter 3 of *Anita and Me*
At a glance 39
› Why? 39
› What? 40
› How? 45

Chapter 4 of *Anita and Me*
At a glance 49
› Why? 49
› What? 50
› How? 55

Chapter 5 of *Anita and Me*
At a glance 60
› Why? 60
› What? 61
› How? 70

Chapter 6 of *Anita and Me*
At a glance 74
› Why? 74
› What? 75
› How? 82

CONTENTS

Chapter 7 of *Anita and Me*
At a glance 87
› Why? 87
› What? 88
› How? 100

Chapter 8 of *Anita and Me*
At a glance 107
› Why? 107
› What? 108
› How? 118

Chapter 9 of *Anita and Me*
At a glance 124
› Why? 124
› What? 125
› How? 135

Chapter 10 of *Anita and Me*
At a glance 141
› Why? 141
› What? 142
› How? 146

Chapter 11 of *Anita and Me*
At a glance 151
› Why? 151
› What? 152
› How? 158

Chapter 12 of *Anita and Me*
At a glance 163
› Why? 163
› What? 164
› How? 167

Chapter 13 of *Anita and Me*
At a glance 171
› Why? 171
› What? 172
› How? 177

Characters 183
› A note on teaching characters 183
› Scaffolds and worksheets 183
› Character overviews 184

Conclusion 199

Appendix: A contextual timeline 201

References 208

Index 210

ACKNOWLEDGEMENTS

ZARA:

Writing a book is exactly the sort of challenge that makes you appreciate the African philosophy of Ubuntu. The idea that 'I am, because you are'; the belief in universal bonds, the acknowledgement that what we are and what we achieve isn't possible without our support systems, without the wonderful humans in our life who keep us afloat, who show us kindness and who give us words of encouragement when we need it most. This is a thank you from the bottom of my heart to these very special humans – my family, you know who you are. And to my boys, thank you for tolerating my absences. I hope one day you too can say yes to opportunities that come knocking on your door, opportunities that make your hearts beat just a little faster. They are the ones you cherish the most.

And finally, a shout out to my partner in all of this, without whose wisdom, insight and brilliance, and, of course, friendship none of this would have been possible. Thank you, Kerry.

KERRY:

Zara has a habit of inspiring me to push myself. When she first told me about this writing project and asked me to be part of it, I was flattered and energised: already a published educational writer herself, I knew I had the opportunity to learn on the job from a self-taught expert and to gain valuable skills and experiences long the way. This labour of love would not have been possible without her unrivalled powers of organisation, multi-tasking and motivation. She honestly never stops innovating, problem-solving and caring about giving her all to projects that truly matter, and it has been a true pleasure to learn from the best.

My family (human and fur) are everything to me and their love and support throughout the process has made it all the more survivable.

FOREWORD

This line, from Meera Syal's wonderful and astonishing coming-of-age story, *Anita and Me*, is the one that for me, packs a powerful punch; it has lingered in my mind since I first read it, and on occasion will sadly resurface when it has cause to do so, depending on what is happening in the world, in our country, on our doorsteps:

> *'I had seen how in an instant, those you called friends could suddenly become tormentors, sniffing out a weakness or a difference, turning their own fear of ostracism into a weapon with which they could beat the victim away, afraid that being an outsider, and individual even, was somehow infectious.'* (p.142)

This observation, this epiphany, this universal truth, screams its relevance whether we're looking at the text through a historical lens, or for what it says about our society today. For *Anita and Me* is more than merely a tale of cultural collision in the Sixties; it is testament to a universal struggle for self-discovering and acceptance that we have all experienced at some point in our lives. Its exploration of 'difference', of being an 'outsider', of being an 'individual', will always be relevant in a world that immediately feels threatened by something it does not, or will not try to, understand.

Anita and Me is a compelling narrative that invites our students to reflect on their own sense of identity and the diverse world around them, an obvious choice for a GCSE text that can help shape our learners into better human beings. And yet we still find our modern text choices dominated by the likes of *Animal Farm, Lord of the Flies* and *An Inspector Calls*. The question is, why? Is it *Anita and Me*'s unfamiliarity with teachers, who would rather stick with what they know in order to give their students the best chance of success? Is it a concern that some of the themes and ideas contained within the novel are too challenging to tackle in an appropriate and sensitive way? In the *right* way? A quick search online reveals a wealth of support for more popular text choices, yet resources for *Anita and Me* are harder to find.

This is where Zara Shah and Kerry Kurczij's work on *Anita and Me* proves invaluable. The resource you now hold in your hands heralds the arrival of a guide that teachers across the country will find incredibly useful. Containing big questions, commentaries on chapters and key themes, and guidance around areas of Syal's text that needed to handled with care, Shah and Kurczij have created something extremely special. That's before we even get to the essays on the social and historical context, alongside tricky vocabulary that needs to be clarified, teaching ideas and 'S-T-R-E-T-C-H' activities. Everything needed is here, set out clearly and methodically for all to revel in the deep subject knowledge that is provided by these two incredible authors.

Yet when all is said and done, Shah and Kurczij's resource is *more* than just a teacher guide. It is a rallying cry for more teachers to assign *Anita and Me* its rightful place on each individual school's GCSE English Literature curriculum, to get more teachers teaching it and more students experiencing it. It is my hope that, using this superb guide, more teachers take up this call and offer students something different through *Anita and Me,* a story that teaches us all about the dangers of ostracism and the power of individuality.

Stuart Pryke, Assistant Principal and co-author of *Ready to Teach: Macbeth, Ready to Teach: A Christmas Carol* and *100 for 100: Macbeth.*

HOW TO USE THIS BOOK

Why, what and how

This book is designed as a teacher's guide and reference point that can be used at any stage of teaching *Anita and Me* by Meera Syal (unless otherwise specified, bracketed page number references relate to the page numbers of *Anita and Me*, 2004, Harper Perennial). It can be read from start to finish before embarking on a scheme of learning, or dipped into as and when the need arises. It is designed to ease cognitive load and support teaching by guiding you through chapter by chapter of *Anita and Me*, addressing the 'Why', 'What' and 'How' of each section.

There are accompanying PowerPoint materials available for every chapter, which can be used in your classroom with students. The materials include sample answers, scaffolds to support learners, such as key quotations and sentence starters, and models of how learners can plan for and draft responses. A feedback form, an editable contextual timeline (also found in the Appendix) and other materials will also be available to download. You can access these at **bloomsbury.pub/BTG-Anita-and-Me**. Other resources available on this site will be flagged in this book by this icon: 🖱.

Glancing at the 'At a glance' sections

Before the 'Why', 'What' or 'How', each chapter opens with an 'At a glance' section. This section introduces the chapter using six key features.

- **Chapter summary quotation**: Opening with a relevant quotation provides readers with a glimpse at the essence of the upcoming chapter.
- **Big Question**: Engaging the readers with an open, intellectually stimulating question functions as a springboard for ideas and opinions.
- **Significant plot event**: Outlining key moments of the chapter in a summary reminds readers of where they are in the narrative.
- **Character focus**: Identifying key characters for analysis and tracking their development focuses thinking.
- **Key themes**: Outlining the central themes upfront helps orientate readers and encourages critical analysis.
- **Handle with care**: Ensuring that certain language is tackled with knowledge and sensitivity. Taking on the themes of race and social class in a literary text will always result in the inclusion, and therefore teaching, of words and expressions that are partially or completely prohibited from

use in modern social discourse. Peter D'Sena is a historian and Associate Professor of Learning and Teaching at The University of Hertfordshire. His recent work focuses on 'Decoding the Disciplines' and 'Decolonising the Curriculum'. He advises that instead of taking a didactic approach in discussions around the use of taboo language, it is important to position the learners at the head of such conversations and invite them to lead through considered questioning (D'Sena, 2023). The following are examples of such questions:

- Why do you think such language is used so casually by the character in the text?
- How might the usage of such offensive and discriminatory language affect a 21st-century reader?
- How do you think the process of linguistic reclamation affects the usage of such language today? Linguistic reclamation is when a hurtful label is taken by stigmatised group members, reclaimed and turned into a badge of pride. Why is it only acceptable for members of such groups to reclaim these labels?
- To what extent do you think discussions, such as ours, are helpful in challenging the use of racist language?
- How do you think we should address these words when we encounter them in the text?

Considering and discussing the answers to such questions within professional school teams could provide an ideal starting point for this conversation (either at INSET or during CPD time) within the limits of individual school context and policies.

Such positioning can be especially useful to mitigate microaggressions (the subtle gestures of discrimination which can be completely inadvertent, such as the simple turning of heads or sideways glances). Instead, the framed questions serve as both a guide and a catalyst, inviting all learners to lead on these important conversations. Additionally, it can be useful to have a disclaimer slide included at the start of a learning sequence to mentally prepare the learners for the upcoming use of taboo and discriminatory language. This can also acknowledge and support the emotive impact it will undoubtedly have. An example of such a slide is included in our downloadable resources.

Why begin with the 'Why'?

We felt it imperative to position teachers new to this text at the heart of the structural planning of this book. Often, when teaching a new text, prioritising sections based on their contextual or structural significance can be the real challenge, and this is a skill that is honed with experience. It is why our teaching of a text improves each time we revisit and re-teach. Bearing this in mind, we decided to begin with a focus on why each chapter was important, not just within the world of the text, but also when considering authorial intent and messaging.

Each 'Why' section culminates in a Big Question that is intended to be open, intellectually stimulating and function as a springboard for both ideas and opinions, inviting students to consider their existing knowledge base and encouraging the transference of, and connection between, ideas. The Big Question can essentially inform the direction of travel in a lesson or unit of work, be reviewed for formative assessment at the end of a lesson, or serve as a retrieval question to build regular opportunities for knowledge retention.

The writing style within our guide will often mirror dialogic teaching practice through either the structure or the style of questions. This modelled cognitively challenging talk can provide teachers with a road map for structuring high-quality classroom conversation.

What is the 'What' section about?

Each section then moves on to the necessary 'knowledge' to be acquired from each chapter. This ranges from factual knowledge about characters and plot, including tier two and three vocabulary, to more nuanced background knowledge. This nuanced knowledge would fall under the category of 'powerful knowledge' (Young et al., 2014, p. 7), as it is the type of knowledge that has the ability to influence an instrumental shift in the perception of the text.

The 'What' section is sequenced as follows:

- What happens?
- Social, cultural and historical context.
- Vocabulary in context.
- Plot and character development.

What happens?

This section provides a chronological guided summary of events in the chapter structured as questions so that they can be used by teachers for the purposes of:

- dialogic teaching
- assessment for learning
- group work
- retrieval practice.

Social, cultural and historical context

Context illuminates the relevance and meaning of a literary text. Knowledge of context has the power to construct a necessary bridge between authorial intent and reader response, as it frames authorial messaging and enriches the understanding of characters, themes and plots, thereby inviting more personalised engagement from the readers.

In the contextual timeline (page 201 of this guide and available on the Bloomsbury website 🖱), we detail some of the key contextual factors influencing Meena's journey in *Anita and Me* so learners can track key contextual events and begin to explore their significance.

In each subsequent chapter, we signpost and allude to relevant contextual features, marked with this symbol ✺. This is so the 'context lesson', typically delivered at the start of the learning sequence, is not an isolated, tick-box exercise. Instead, the context is indeed contextualised as the teaching of the text progresses. Sequencing the retrieval and re-application of contextual features in this way enriches the processes of reader-response, whilst also supporting the construction of key schematic knowledge.

Vocabulary in context

In recent years, explicit vocabulary instruction has been gradually nudged along from its position as an afterthought to the very front of the planning process, and rightly so. It can often come as a surprise that students need to be able to grasp at least 95 per cent of the vocabulary in an academic text to ensure comprehension (Quigley, 2018). To support and prioritise explicit vocabulary instruction as a necessary pedagogical consideration, the Education Endowment Foundation has dedicated a number of studies and recommendation reports on why and how vocabulary should be taught across the key stages.

> 'By attending to the literacy demands of their subjects, teachers increase their pupils' chance of success in their subjects.'
>
> **Sir Kevan Collins, Chief Executive, Education Endowment Foundation (2021)**

As English teachers, we are always aware of reading gaps and strive to create pathways to make texts accessible for all our learners. In our quest to promote high standards of language and literacy, we wanted to ease the process of decoding and therefore dedicated a section of each chapter to key vocabulary, carefully selected for targeted instruction. In order to scaffold this process and make the vocabulary accessible for all our learners, we have included examples to contextualise its use further. *Bringing Words to Life* (Beck, McKeown and Kucan, 2013) offers evidence-informed advice on teaching vocabulary in context and the benefit of providing multiple exposures to the word, along with giving learners ample opportunities to practise.

This vocabulary can either be pre-taught through the explorations of etymology or set as a challenge for students to explore different contexts of application. It can even be utilised as a flip-lesson learning opportunity where students come prepared for the lesson, secure in their understanding of the selected vocabulary. By looking at the vocabulary in context, students are also provided with scaffolds, not just for elevating expression but a bank of micro-quotations that they can use to enhance their answers and future conversations about the text. The possibilities are endless.

What makes *Anita and Me* distinctive is that, when it comes to vocabulary, it holds the wonderful uniqueness of challenging our learners at more than one level. Firstly, as a text that interrogates complex ideas with complex lexical choices, and secondly, as one that uses a repertoire of words which open windows to rich cultural dimensions as well as the collective politics of racial and social injustice. This in itself presents an invaluable opportunity to nurture our learners' cultural capital by extending their conversations to the plurality of identities, intertwined with social class, religion, cultures and geographical locations. Our 'Vocabulary in context' hence includes references which span across such dimensions: from Meena's Indian heritage to her mining community in the 1970s.

Plot and character development

The final focus of the 'What' section foregrounds key developments in plot and character, carefully outlined for teachers so they can track changes and easily make note of any nuances in the text that need to be signposted to learners. We keep this section simple by organising it as a series of hinge questions that teachers can either use to navigate their own conceptual understanding or plant into their lessons to orchestrate both thought and conversation.

The intention behind the structuring of the 'What' questions is multifaceted. First, it serves as a scaffold to support teachers in 'chunking', a necessary pedagogical tool that makes allowances for working memory capacity restraints whilst also supporting learners with SEND. Breaking the key textual knowledge down through these questions alleviates cognitive load both before and during instruction. Teachers may share questions before reading sections of the chapter to provide learners with a filter and help channel their attention towards key details. The 'What' questions may also be used to set up a method known as 'jigsaw chunking', where groups of learners work on different sections of the text, finding the relevant information before summarising their findings.

Additionally, these questions can be used to set up and scaffold a structured discussion-based comprehension strategy known as reciprocal reading. This is known to improve reading comprehension by two months following targeted intervention (FFT Literacy, 2019). The programme supports learners, particularly those who struggle to decode, to apply four reading strategies in order to scaffold the meaning-making process: questioning, clarifying, summarising and predicting. Our 'What' questions (along with their suggested exemplars) focus on quality as well as depth. They can be used by teachers to model the process of making the implicit comprehension skills of the expert, the teacher, explicit to the novice readers, thereby clarifying any misconceptions. 'Vocabulary in context' can be an additional tool to invite learners to work together to clarify the meaning of tier two vocabulary, and remove one of the barriers to comprehension. Moreover, the 'What' questions can be rephrased to encourage predictions, allowing learners to activate prior knowledge and engage with key plot and character developments, while the process of answering the questions can support learners in summarising key findings. In this way, the process of modelling can be made more effective and lay the foundation for self-regulation and metacognitive practices before the roles of questioner, clarifier, summariser and predictor are handed over to the learners. Finally, this section can also serve as a foundational base for supplementary knowledge quizzes for retrieval practice.

We also use icons to represent key themes (see page 10 of this guide) that are mirrored in our downloadable resources to support pupils with dual coding and allow for the tracking of themes across the text. The intention is to make patterns visible and tracking easier, and provide scaffolds to make the complex task of juggling disciplinary knowledge with core as streamlined as possible.

When approaching the 'What' questions, make sure to:

- Use all-respond methods to assess understanding and engagement with key characters, themes and inferences.
- Use these questions as hinge-points to assess whether you can move on with the learning.
- Use these questions as consolidation/retrieval points when revisiting prior learning.
- Ask learners to generate multiple-choice answers to the questions (engineering distractors and misconceptions) to show their clear understanding of the key aspects of the chapter's narrative and context.

How we approach the 'How' section

This section is where we embark on a literary, linguistic and structural analysis of carefully selected moments from each chapter, interrogating the decisions made by the writer to communicate the underpinning messages in each section. Where relevant, we also track the character arc and draw attention to any significant changes in either plot, characters or themes.

- **Language**: This analysis ranges from the microelements that are more granular, to the macroelements that can be tracked as literary and grammatical patterns.

- **Character focus**: A limited number of characters are identified for closer analysis in this section to help support cognitive load and ensure learners take a directed approach in tracking character development and their contributions to the plot.
- **Structure**: With a predominant focus on how each chapter begins and ends, this section initially invites learners to consider why Syal has chosen to begin and end with the particular focus and what their predictions might be about key characters or plot developments within the chapter. Occasionally, we deviate from this format, as does Syal, to demonstrate to the learners that variation is often intentional, and intended by the author to draw our attention to specific features of the text that are integral to the meaning-making process. The section then moves on to pivotal structural choices made by Syal (where relevant) to introduce, intensify or make links between key plot points, either through the use of dialogue, the manipulation of chronology or the introduction of motifs.
- **Extracts**: This section selects key extracts from the chapter for closer inspection, providing topic sentence scaffolds as well as exemplar materials for closer analysis of methods (necessary skills for both KS3 and KS4).

Pit stops

These features are used as pause points throughout our chapters to provide suggested evidence-informed learning and assessment activities to help you plan and scaffold, and gauge your learners' understanding of the text.

Retrieval points

Throughout the book, you will find a series of 'Retrieval points'. These should be viewed as necessary pit stops to ensure that ample opportunity is built into the scheme of learning for students to revisit prior learning. Mary Myatt's 'high challenge, low threat' model (Myatt, n.d.) was the driving force for our rationale here, which is why the retrieval points are designed to be low effort, but with high impact, taking our learners beyond simple encoding processes to more advanced retention of knowledge in their long-term memory. When we think of scheme building, it is useful to think of retrieval as the cement that secures any multi-store memory models in place. That cement is necessary to lay a solid foundation that our learners can reinforce with each retrieval exercise, and continue to build on.

Retrieval, also known as 'the testing effect' in educational discourse, is described by Kate Jones as going beyond our understanding of formative assessment. It is 'the act of recalling learned information from memory (with little or no support) and every time that information is retrieved, or an answer is generated, it changes that original memory to make it stronger' (Jones, 2019, p. 15). Essentially, it is moving away from the illusion of knowledge to deep knowledge. It is therefore clear that any scheme of learning with long-term goals must not only prioritise, but foster and hone the processes of retrieval.

Direct instruction point

All carefully planned, well-developed lessons will have one thing in common. The core and disciplinary knowledge, essential for unlocking the next stage or establishing a foundation for learning, is not left to chance. Instead, it is handled with precision and intent to ensure necessary engagement from the learners. To help teachers identify such moments, we have earmarked 'Direct instruction points' throughout the text and carefully sequenced them so that the prerequisite skills are delivered before learners are presented with the challenge to apply these within context.

Academic writing point

Essential to disciplinary learning, academic writing is a core component of any secondary English classroom. Introduced too soon without the appropriate tools, there is a risk that it can have a detrimental impact on quality and learner motivation. Writing is undoubtedly hard and a demanding cognitive process, and academic writing is even more so. Learners need explicit preparation to unlock the implicit procedural thinking that goes into academic writing. Therefore, look out for 'Academic writing points' where learners should have developed the cumulative and associative understanding required to tackle some of the implicit ideas within the text.

A 'feedback for progress' sheet is available as part of the downloadable resources. This has been designed for use after an 'Academic writing point' to not only automate the feedback process, but also make it more accessible and effective. The complexity in the language of feedback and the absence of specific models can often be barriers to learners making independent improvements and progress. After all, if learners do not know how to include context, embed quotations and use tentative language the first time they write an essay, merely instructing them to do so the following time is less likely to reap the desired results. Instead, we propose feedback for marginal gains, which focuses on small and incremental improvements.

S-T-R-E-T-C-H

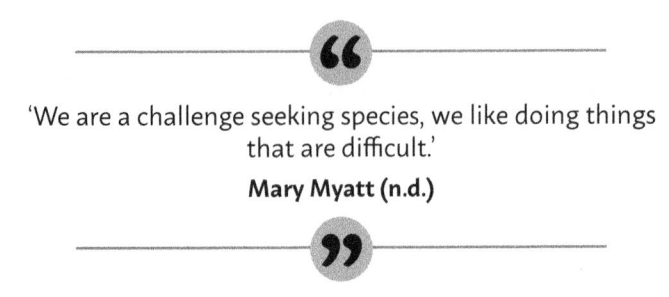

> 'We are a challenge seeking species, we like doing things that are difficult.'
>
> **Mary Myatt (n.d.)**

Professor Daniel Willingham's 'Ask the Cognitive Scientist: How Praise Can Motivate—or Stifle' (2006) draws a strong correlation between two ideas. Firstly, that human beings are naturally curious and secondly, that thinking is hard work. He suggests that we play on our learners' intrinsic motivation by cultivating their curiosity, and then use it as a bridge towards 'hard work'. It is also our moral imperative to design English lessons that are ambitious for all our learners. Lessons should not limit the possibilities of learning, but instead enrich and enhance it. Our 'S-T-R-E-T-C-H' questions are designed to achieve precisely this. They provoke curiosity and provide avenues for ambition, inviting learners to open their minds and consider alternative perspectives and complex associations both within and beyond the text.

Dual coding

A principle put forward by Allan Paivio (1969), and supported by cognitive scientists since, posits that the human brain can process information through separate systems – the verbal and the visual – and that the engagement of both can improve comprehension and facilitate secure grasp of complex concepts. Clark et al. (2004) worked extensively with cognitive scientists to research dual coding. They found that the way visuals align with the learning process can result in six key benefits: direct attention, management of cognitive load, activation of prior knowledge, development of schema, transference to working memory and motivation. It is unsurprising, therefore, just how popular this approach is in pedagogical practice.

Disciplinary literacy

The following is a graphic summary of some of the commonly recurring concepts in disciplinary literacy. These are signposted across the text and our downloadable resources to maximise opportunities for impact.

- Analysis:
- Inference:
- Context:
- Summarise:

- Retrieval:
- Structure:
- Tracking the text:
- Comparison:

Themes

The following is a graphic organiser for some of the key themes (also included in our downloadable resources). Some of these are signposted in the 'At a glance' sections depending on recurrence and significance to the chapter, whilst others can be used by learners as iconic prompts so they can collate their own references during the course of their study and create a personalised knowledge organiser for these key themes.

- Racism:
- Othering:
- Innocence:
- Truth vs lies:
- Neglect, bullying and abuse:
- Family discipline and guidance:
- Conflict and violence:

- Change:
- Cultural identity:
- Belonging:
- Friendship:

INTRODUCTION TO ANITA AND ME

> '...those of us deprived of history sometimes need to turn to mythology to feel complete, to belong.'
>
> **(Syal, 2004, p. 10)**

Born to Indian immigrants in a small mining town in central England, Feroza (Meera) Syal tracks some of her experiences in her critically acclaimed, semi-autobiographical novel, *Anita and Me*. Winning a Betty Trask award and shortlisted for the Guardian Fiction Prize, Syal's novel is set in 1972 Tollington, a fictional mining village on the cusp of change. Syal's protagonist, Meena, tracks the lived experiences of the Indian diaspora. Her daily struggle for individuality and independence runs in parallel to her parents' struggle following partition from the British Raj in 1947 India.

Anita and Me is a typical Bildungsroman with various overt and implicit allusions to Harper Lee's *To Kill a Mockingbird* (1960). The book itself is presented by Meena to her friend Robert, and the 'Big House' in Syal's novel bears a stark resemblance to Harper Lee's depiction of Boo Radley's house. The thematic similarities are also apparent as both protagonists demonstrate a perceptive awareness of racial othering and discrimination, and through their lens of innocence as children, cast a brutally honest light on these issues.

Tracking the text

Considering the structural decisions any writer makes is a crucial way of engaging with and analysing authorial intent and reader positioning. The points below can be used for assessing understanding of the chapter: learners can be asked to place them in the correct order, for example. Discussions can also be had around how things would have been different had the events taken place in a different order.

- The novel begins in Tollington as Meena Kumar (nine years old) is being questioned on why she has a pocket full of sweets. Meena's parents don't like her lying. (Chapter 1.)

INTRODUCTION TO ANITA AND ME

- Announcement of the arrival of Meena's baby brother, Sunil. (Chapter 4.)
- Meena escapes the Diwali celebration to attend a fair while her parents are distracted with Sunil's birth. (Chapter 5.)
- Meena is left to spend unsupervised time with Anita, who is a bad influence on her. They write to the Cathy and Claire problem page. (Chapter 6.)
- Meena and Anita steal a charity box. Meena pins the blame on Baby and Pinky. (Chapter 6.)
- Meena attends a local fete with her papa, where racist tensions arise, driven by Sam Lowbridge. (Chapter 7.)
- Meena's Nanima (grandmother) comes to visit. This visit changes Meena as she connects with her Nanima immediately. Meena starts to develop a bond with Sunil, feel protective towards Nanima and appreciate the sacrifices her parents made. (Chapter 7.)
- Anita's mother, Deirdre, abandons Anita, leaving her to live with the local butcher. This is the first time Meena sees Anita cry. (Chapter 7.)
- Anita is invited round to Meena's for tea. Meena lies and her parents run with it. (Chapter 10.)
- There is a violent race attack in Tollington. (Chapter 11.)
- Meena breaks her leg and ends up in hospital for months. She begins to communicate with another patient, Robert, whilst also studying for the eleven-plus exam. (Chapter 12.)
- Meena gets involved in more mess the night before the eleven-plus. She is discovered in the bushes with Sam Lowbridge. (Chapter 13.)
- Tracey nearly drowns in an accident. Sam and Anita blame each other. (Chapter 13.)
- Meena takes the eleven-plus, passes and moves away from Tollington. (Chapter 13.)

Assessment objectives

Assessment objectives establish the criteria by which pupils will be evaluated. We have aimed to address each objective in every chapter of this guide. It is essential to familiarise yourself with these objectives and also to review past paper questions (available online through respective exam board platforms) to see how these objectives are used in the exam context:

- **AO1** Respond to texts critically and imaginatively; select and evaluate relevant textual detail to illustrate and support interpretations.
- **AO2** Explain how language, structure and form contribute to writers' presentation of ideas, themes and settings.
- **AO3** Relate texts to their social, cultural and historical contexts.
- **AO4** Range of vocabulary and sentence structures for clarity, purpose and effect, with accurate spelling and punctuation.

(Department for Education, 2013)

CHAPTER 1 OF ANITA AND ME

At a glance

> **Chapter summary quotation:** 'a little Indian girl [...] caught telling lies' (p. 15)

> **Big Question:** How does this chapter explore the difficulties associated with living morally?

> **Significant plot event:** Meena is caught lying.

> **Character focus:** Anita, Mr Ormerod

> **Key themes:**
> - Truth vs lies
> - Family discipline and guidance
> - Innocence

> **Handle with care:**
> - Reference to racially offensive and abusive terms in this chapter will need to be handled with sensitivity. Please refer to the 'Handle with care' guidance in the 'How to use this book' section for further support.
>   - 'piccaninny' (p. 20)
>   - 'darkies' (p. 22)
>   - 'peer up girls' dresses' (p. 22).

Why?

'Why' is important not only within the world of the text, but also when considering authorial intent and messaging.

- Why does Meena lie?
- Why does Syal create a protagonist whose first introduction to the reader is to tell lies, even to her own father? Is it so that we, as readers, are immediately hooked? Or perhaps because grappling with 'truth' is a universal experience we all recognise?

Syal has Meena admit the truth, both to the reader and her father, fairly swiftly by the end of Chapter 1: "'I was lying,' I said in a whisper' (p. 23). So, yes, we have a liar on our hands, but a truth-teller too. This is the beauty and appeal of the child narrator: her childish chatter of the mind intertwined with her, at times, searingly insightful moral and social commentary. Will this stay consistent throughout the novel as her age and experience of life and relationships increase? Why is this opening important?

This allows us to consider Chapter 1's Big Question:

> How does this chapter explore the difficulties associated with living morally?

What?

What happens?

Meena, a young girl, is forcibly marched by her father back to the scene of her alleged crime (spending money taken without permission from her mother's purse on sweets at the local corner shop). She recounts details of the local inhabitants and their lives, prompted by landmarks and areas they walk past and through. At first, she protests her innocence, but tells the truth at the end of the chapter.

Social, cultural and historical context

It is important for learners to fully understand, appreciate and be able to realistically envisage life in the fictional village of Tollington in 1972 for nine-year-old Meena. They may require pre-teaching activities on the following features of social, cultural and historical context so they can write about them confidently.

The two main topics to note are immigration to Britain in the second half of the 20th century, particularly partition and colonialism, and the economic and social climate and the divides in 1970s Britain. The following are some useful quotations to consider when discussing this context with learners.

Housing: 'row of terraced houses' (p. 11); 'two-up-two-downs' (p. 11); 'posh, po-faced mansions' (p. 11); 'the Big House' (p. 13).

Gender: 'Working Men's Club' (p. 11); 'the hormonal balance of Tollington was turned upside down' (p. 19); archaic attitudes to early forms of 'upskirting' (p. 22).

Religion: 'Methodist church' and 'Sunday school' (p. 11).

Economic change: 'only one working farm now' (p. 11); 'the old pithead of the mine' (p. 13); 'industrial chimneys' (p. 11); 'new families started moving in' (p. 14).

Social change: corporal punishment; casual racism; 'piccaninny' (p. 20); 'so many darkies' (p. 22).

Vocabulary in context

The following vocabulary from Chapter 1 can be pre-taught to help with reading fluency and reduce cognitive load. What does each of the following words mean in context?

Word	Quotation	Definition
starched (adj.)	'the collar of my starched cotton dress' (p. 11)	stiffened with a cleaning product called starch
jaunty (adj.)	'walking along with that jaunty air' (p. 11)	carefree; hopeful; fun-loving
leonine (adj.)	'the sharp leonine nose' (p. 11)	lion-like
sauntered (v.)	'she had sauntered past' (p. 17)	walked with a confident, almost arrogant, air
cohorts (n., pl.)	'with her two regular cohorts' (p. 17)	people someone associate with
maenads (n., pl.)	'They appeared ensemble as coiffured maenads' (p. 19)	women in a frenzy; showing uncontrolled behaviour
succubus (n.)	'They drew energy from me like a succubus' (p. 20)	powerful female demon

PIT STOP

Retrieval point

Return to this vocabulary in a later lesson, assessing if learners can link each key word to the relevant character(s). For a bonus point, develop each link into an analysis of how the writer's language choice presents that character.

Examples:

- What might 'the starched cotton dress' Meena is made to wear by her mama (perhaps in contrast to her own 'slop-around outfit' (p. 12)) reveal about how much of a struggle it is for her at the beginning of the novel to define her own cultural identity?
- What might 'the starched cotton dress' Meena is made to wear by her mama suggest about how restricted she currently feels, unable to make her own decisions and exercise her own freedoms?
- What first impressions might Syal be trying to give the reader about 12-year-old Anita in choosing 'sauntered' as one of our first descriptors of how she moves?

BLOOMSBURY TEACHER GUIDE: ANITA AND ME

> **PIT STOP**
>
> ### Direct instruction point
>
> Embedding and tailoring quotations to fit our required meaning is an essential skill. Use the 'think-aloud' method (see below) to model how to turn the complete quotation into a summary: 'I realised, sadly, that whoever lived in the Big House would not break their solitude to save a little Indian girl who had been caught telling lies' (p. 15).
>
> The 'think-aloud' method is a live teacher demonstration with metacognitive narrative accompanying writing, meaning the teacher verbalises what they are doing and thinking while completing a task. You might say something like, 'Right, I need to decide which words to focus my attention on when I'm summarising this really important quotation...'

> **PIT STOP**
>
> ### Academic writing point
>
> Learning and rehearsing synonyms for 'lies' could also be a practical, active step to answering the Big Question: **How does this chapter explore the difficulties associated with living morally?** For example: fabrications, untruths and falsehoods.
>
> Discussion point: Why wouldn't 'fibs' or 'porky-pies' serve as well in the context of academic writing?

Plot and character development

For tips on how to approach these 'What' questions, refer to the 'Plot and character development' section of 'How to use this book' on pages 5-6 of this guide.

1. **What is stereotypical about the false family memories Meena fabricates in the opening of the novel?**

    Example responses:
    - Working in a sweatshop.
    - Poor, cramped conditions (including sharing the bed with other immigrants).
    - Out of touch with world affairs.

2. What does the reader learn about Meena's papa and mama in the opening of Chapter 1?

Example responses:

Papa has a strong sense of morals and principles ('public shame' (p. 22) was something he hated). He's not angry initially, but entirely purposeful in returning Meena to the scene of the crime. He is ever-careful and nurturing, checking for traffic along the 'twisting country lane' (p. 11) even though he is set on getting to the shop and the truth. He is courteous to all, exchanging 'pleasantries' (p. 16) with Mr Topsy/Turvey and refusing Mr Ormerod's religious invitations with 'such grace' (p. 21).

Mama fell in love with papa because of his 'jaunty' (p. 11) walk. She sometimes wears 'slop-around outfits' (p. 12). She and her fabrics stand out against the backdrop. She is conservative in that she banned Meena from watching TV for two weeks. She enjoys dressing her daughter in highly embellished feminine wear.

PIT STOP

S-T-R-E-T-C-H

As well as learning about Meena's parents as individuals, what clues can learners identify in Chapter 1 as to their loving, fond relationship, and how it is different, perhaps, to many of the more 'functional' British couples in Tollington?

Example responses:

- 'that jaunty air that my mother said had made her fall in love with him' (p. 11)
- 'my parents for whom every leavetaking was accompanied by squeezes' (p. 20).

3. What does the reader learn about where Meena lives from the opening of Chapter 1?

Example response:

The village of Tollington, formerly a mining community, has a 'single road' and a 'crossroads' (p. 11). The town's 'nerve centre' or hub contains key destinations, including Mr Ormerod's grocery shop, the Wesleyan Methodist church, the Working Men's Club and the school. It has previously been a place of agricultural plenty but now 'only one working farm' (p. 12) remains. Smoking chimneys can be seen in the distance and there is a 'small overgrown park' (p. 12) where the children gather. The Big House, set in its own private grounds, is a mysterious otherly dwelling in Tollington.

4. What does the reader learn about Meena's feelings towards Sunday School?

Example response:

Syal shows us Meena's difficult relationship with the ideas and virtues she has learned at the local Wesleyan Methodist Church Sunday School: when she wishes she did not know about 'sin' and its 'eternal consequences' (p. 12), the reader sees hints of the understanding she has of what she has done wrong and the guilt she is experiencing because of it. When she childishly wishes she had 'never gone to Sunday School' (p. 12), the reader can choose to interpret this either as regret for her actions, or link it to the difficulty Meena is experiencing with living morally – wouldn't her life just be easier if she could follow her instincts?

5. What does the reader learn about 'the Big House' in Chapter 1?

Example response:

The Big House has been a fixture of Tollington for as long as the residents can remember and is set apart from the other dwellings. It is different in its size, how grand it is and in the mystery surrounding its inhabitants. It is introduced at this very early stage deliberately. With its 'private grounds' and 'barbed wire fence' (p. 13), it is bound to be a source of intrigue to the locals. Like Meena and her family, it is otherly.

6. What does the reader learn about how Meena feels about her family's garden in comparison to that of others?

Example response:

Many of the terraced houses in Tollington have well-kept gardens 'crammed full' (p. 15) with decorations. By contrast, Meena's garden, she tells the reader, was 'the odd one out' (p. 15) and it is this otherness which she does not like. Instead of 'shiny horse brasses' and 'copper plates' (p. 15) like the other gardens, Meena's garden has a 'boring rectangle of lumpy grass' (p. 15) and is a place for growing 'various herbs' (p. 15) used in her mama's cooking. The reader learns Meena is desperate for a garden much closer to that of typical British family gardens with 'roses' and 'manicured hedges' (p. 16). She is angry about not fitting in. She seems to want keenly to belong.

7. What does Mr Topsy/Turvey symbolise to Meena?

Example response:

Mr Topsy/Turvey is presented as a source of frustration to Meena in his othering of her: he calls her 'Topsy' having 'christened' her 'thus' not being able to pronounce her name (p. 16) – an action that might be labelled as a microaggression today. She retaliates by referring to him in the narrative as 'Mr Topsy'. The reader might infer from this, therefore, that this character is a symbol of the casual racism endemic in British society at

CHAPTER 1 OF ANITA AND ME

the time and a part of Meena's everyday life and experience. Might living morally be made even more difficult for her under such circumstances with such regular hardships to navigate?

8. What does Anita symbolise to Meena?

Example response:

In Chapter 1, Anita Rutter is presented by Syal as an obvious antagonist: older, confident, arrogant and flanked by her 'regular' cohorts. She is everything Meena is not, and appears to hold the keys and secrets to everything Meena aspires to be and know. Anita is powerful and to Meena, who feels relatively powerless in Chapter 1, this is almost irresistible. She has a physical effect on Meena: her smile causes her 'breath' to catch and her 'throat… to ache' (p. 17). After the brief first exchange with Anita in the first chapter of the novel, Meena is left wondering what she had done to 'deserve' Anita's time and attention. The writer wants us to be fully aware of the power she holds over our young, impressionable protagonist, and how potentially dangerous this could be, setting up possible threat as the narrative develops.

9. What does the reader learn about the women of Tollington in this chapter?

Example response:

The reader learns the women of Tollington are now the workers of the village, and that they exhibit a hive-mind mentality. No longer do they wave 'their men off on doorsteps with lunch boxes' (p. 19). They are now the workforce, almost indistinguishable from one another in the way they merge 'together like mercury' (p. 20). As well as working together and living side-by-side in the terraced houses of the village, they play together, often socialising raucously, and gossiping and back-biting salaciously.

PIT STOP

S-T-R-E-T-C-H

Can learners find an extract or a number of quotations in Chapter 1 where the men of Tollington are shown in a very different light to the women?

Key quotations:

- 'their husbands were incidental' (p. 19)
- 'men in vests and braces' (p. 20)
- 'clutched half-read newspapers' (p. 20)
- 'fiddled absent-mindedly with their testicles' (p. 20)

10. **What does Meena's classroom flashback towards the end of Chapter 1 to her being 'publicly beaten in front of all' her classmates (p. 22) reveal about attitudes to racist and abusive behaviour in early 1970s Britain?**

Example response:

The reader can infer from the classroom flashback that corporal punishment and the use of racist language were commonplace at the time. Peter's comment about 'so many darkies' (p. 22) and Meena's explanation that hers was the only Indian family, or so she thought, ever to have lived in Tollington, reveals the racism born of ignorance. Peter is likely parroting something he has heard angry, uninformed and economically disadvantaged adults say when looking for scapegoats.

11. **What can the reader infer in this chapter that Meena feels about having lied to her father?**

Example response:

The 'fear' which causes Meena to sweat in the opening of Chapter 1 and the associated 'guilt' suggest she regrets having lied to her father, but not necessarily the act of taking the money to buy the sweets from Mr Ormerod's shop. Disappointing her father is mixed with anger: she tells the reader he should have given her the money in the first place. The moral imperative, Meena feels, was on her father to provide for her; he forced her to take the money by denying her it. The reader arguably sees Meena as the young child she really is here – an unreliable narrator trying to justify her actions and grappling somewhat unsuccessfully and unconvincingly with the difficult business of living morally. When, at the end of the chapter, her father 'let go' (p. 23) of her hand that he has held onto so tightly and so constantly throughout the chapter so far, his disappointment is complete, and we imagine this is what Meena feared.

How?

Language

Narrative voice

How does Syal position the audience to view Meena as a narrator, especially when she admits, 'I was lying' (p. 23). Is she reliable or unreliable?

Bird imagery

Key quotations:

- 'I got distracted, noticing a kestrel hovering behind the old pithead of the mine, visible just behind the grey green slates of Big House's roof' (p. 13)

- 'The kestrel gave out a faint cry, sharp and forlorn all at once, and plummeted from view' (p. 15).

As a bird of prey, the writer's choice of a 'kestrel' may be of significance when punctuating Meena's experience on her way to Mr Ormerod's shop with her papa.

Ask learners to consider:

- How Meena herself might feel hunted?
- How the 'kestrel' is used as a motif to keep reminding the reader where Meena is on her way to and the threat she feels?
- How, like the kestrel with its 'sharp and forlorn' cry, Meena herself experiences mixed emotions in this chapter at the thought of whether or not to admit her lie?

Sound imagery

Key quotations:

- 'Somewhere a front door slammed shut. It seemed to reverberate along the terrace, houses nudging each other to wake up and listen in on us, net curtains and scalloped lace drapes all a-flutter now' (p. 22)
- 'Papa pushed open the door of the shop, the brass bell perched on its top rang jauntily. Its clapper looked like a quivering tonsil in a golden throat and it vibrated to the beat of my heart' (p. 23).

Ask learners to identify the way the tension builds here towards the end of the chapter? Syal intends the following images to contribute to a foreboding soundscape for Meena as the time to 'confess' looms and her adrenaline reaches its peak:

- 'slammed shut'
- 'reverberate'
- 'vibrating'.

PIT STOP

S-T-R-E-T-C-H

Ask learners to link these images to the representations of Tollington women (the Ballbearings Committee, in particular) and their unhealthy interest in other people's business.

Example response:

The personification of the terraced houses 'nudging each other' (p. 22) and listening in could be seen to mimic the actions of their inhabitants, always keen to know about and to speculate on the developments in others' lives. The brass bell announcing Meena and her father's arrival at Mr Ormerod's shop could also be seen as a symbol of the need to pay attention and tune in.

Character focus

Anita

Key quotations:

- 'had told me that this sailor was in fact her father' (p. 17)
- 'sauntered past, arm in arm with her two regular cohorts' (p. 17).

Anita is a powerful antagonist. Her first words to Meena are a deliberate lie; she is regularly flanked by two other girls who she has the power to control with just a scowl and she can reduce Meena to an emotional wreck with only a smile. She is created by Syal as the ultimate symbol of desirable danger.

Mr Ormerod

Key quotations:

- 'a chirpy monologue [...] always ending in a hallelujah chorus about the Glory of God' (p. 21)
- 'hyperactive in the local Wesleyan Methodist Church' (p. 21)
- 'continually try and convert us to the ways of Jesus Christ' (p. 21).

He is a paradox: kind and well-meaning in person, but woefully unaware of how condescending and damaging his views and words can be. He is created by Syal as the ideal symbol of ignorance.

Structure

Learners should explore the following examples from the opening and the ending of Chapter 1 and be invited to consider:

- Why Syal has chosen to begin and end with this focus on Meena's 'lie'?
- What their predictions might be about key characters and plot developments within this chapter.

Opening: '"I'm not lying, honest, papa!" I pleaded' (p. 11).

Ending: '"I was lying," I said in a whisper' (p. 23).

Dialogue is crucial to the cyclical nature of the way this chapter's narrative is structured. Meena has already revealed to the reader in the introduction that she views herself as 'really not a liar' (p. 10), but that, even as a young child she began to understand the difficulties and complexities of truth and living morally.

The reader therefore is positioned to view her pleading her innocence in the opening of Chapter 1 as likely to be unrealistic. As the chapter progresses, Meena confides in us more details that leave us certain she was lying originally, that she regrets it certainly, but that she feels it is not entirely her fault and the sense of injustice makes her angry: 'if he had listened to me in the first place and just given me the sodding money, I would not have had to steal anything' (p. 21).

Meena displays attitude and fire here: we like her and recognise those muddled emotions of childhood, indeed even now. Why must it be that doing what is right is so frustrating?

Extracts

1. How does Syal use language to develop a vivid presentation of the women of Tollington in the following extracts from Chapter 1?

'Some of the local women would gather around the van, shaking their heads at the sod-off grandeur of the delivery, muttering at the parade of wines, preserves, spices, monogrammed biscuits and extra soft toilet roll [...] all worked together, lived together and played together, and bounced off the village boundaries like a ballbearing against the sides of a pinball machine' (p. 15-9).

Example response planning, using topic sentence scaffolds: 💡

Syal presents the Tollington women as:

- a powerful collective
- envious of those with wealth
- brazen in their intrusion into the lives of others
- confident and disinclined to listen
- purposeful, busy and full of energy
- concerned with their looks.

Example response, unpacking quotations and language therein to support points: 🔍

Syal presents the Tollington women as a powerful collective: they have a 'communal tone of voice' suggesting a shared way of speaking which unites them, as does their shared way of dressing with their 'belted macs and bright lipsticks' easily identifying them as members of a group. They are presented as gaining shared confidence from this group mentality as they are not afraid to challenge when something displeases them, with verbs such as 'shaking their heads' and 'muttering', showing their public disapproval of the expensive deliveries to Big House, for example. They do not shy away from coarser language themselves in their own speech: 'sod-off grandeur', for example, mirrors their own way of speaking and could perhaps be a sign of their relative power using speech often reserved for more masculine figures traditionally.

2. How does Syal use language to show the differences between Anita and Meena in the following extract from Chapter 1?

'I knew they were all at senior school, I had seen them round the village in their over-large uniforms, customised with badges and cropped-off ties. I was nine but felt three and a half as this particular day, mama had had one of her 'You Always Look Like A Heathen' moods and had forced me into a dinky pleated dress, which despite my efforts at ripping and rolling in mud, still contained enough frills and flowers to give me the appearance of a bad tempered doily' (p. 17).

Example response planning, using topic sentence scaffolds:

Syal presents the difference between Anita and Meena as:

- freedom vs restriction
- age and experience vs youth and innocence
- rebellion vs conformism.

Example response, unpacking quotations and language therein to support points:

Syal presents the difference between Anita and Meena as a contrast between freedom and restriction in this extract: Anita and her friends from the 'senior school' have the freedom to customise their uniforms with 'badges' and rebelliously crop their 'ties'; Meena, however, is still 'forced' to wear outfits chosen by her mother. These outfits, she tells the reader, are restrictive with their pleats and frills, constraining her movements and her freedom to both explore and express herself. As metaphors, the antithetic external appearances of the girls when it comes to their clothing (elements within their control, unlike their race), could perhaps be seen to reflect the different levels of care and influence exercised by their parents as the reader will go on to learn later in the novel.

CHAPTER 2 OF ANITA AND ME

At a glance

> **Chapter summary quotation:** 'this meeting of two worlds, the collision of the epic with the banal' (p. 36)
> **Big Question:** How does this chapter explore the dichotomy of identities?
> **Significant plot event:** Meena reflects on stories from her past.
> **Character focus:** Meena, mama
> **Key themes:**
> - Cultural identity
> - Belonging
> - Racism
> - Family discipline and guidance
> **Handle with care:**
> - Reference to partition stories in this chapter will need to be handled with sensitivity, particularly with students who may have been impacted. Please refer to the 'Handle with care' guidance in the 'How to use this book' section for further support.
>   - 'tear the Punjab in two' (p. 35)
>   - 'partition riots' (p. 36)
>   - a reference to a rickshaw stabbing (p. 36).

Why?

'Why' is important not only within the world of the text, but also when considering authorial intent and messaging.

- Why does Syal explore facades in this chapter? Consider the facade that Meena's mother carefully cultivates to project to the outside world, with her 'tasteful silks', 'sensible' attire and 'English without an accent' (p. 25).

- Why does she position this facade to collide with 'other Indian women' (p. 26)? Perhaps because it speaks to the lived experience of the Indian diaspora, even today. Or perhaps because it resonates with the experience of anyone trying to belong or conform at the expense of who they used to be.

Syal uses Meena's mama to take us back into an important era and unlock the rich histories of another world intrinsically connected with the very fabric of Britain. She also takes us back to another time that marked the end of three hundred years of colonial rule in the Indian subcontinent: partition.

The stories in this chapter are graphic, not for dramatic effect, but because every family that experienced partition has a violent story of heartache and betrayal, hidden behind those carefully cultivated facades. These stories are graphic because they are true.

This allows us to consider Chapter 2's Big Question:

> How does this chapter explore the dichotomy of identities?

What?

What happens?

The chapter begins with Meena reflective, but not enough to forgo the sweets. She eats in defiance; 'it would serve them right if I did choke on a raspberry poppet' (p. 24). This thought takes her back to a memory of her seventh birthday – a moment she chooses to celebrate by going to the theatre instead of hosting a party because she feels she will not have anyone to invite (apart from small children). On the way home, she detects that her mother is upset and remembers her parents talking 'softly' in 'Punjabi', evidence that they were keeping something 'secret' or upsetting from her (p. 24-5). Even nearly choking on a hot dog doesn't get Meena the attention she craves, until the sausage finally falls in her lap and she is reprimanded for ruining her clothes. She is excited by this near-death experience and decides to hold this against her mother in the future. Her thoughts then drift to her mother's personality and the choices she makes to project her identity, before taking us back to the time her parents moved to Britain and the life and world they left behind: the time of partition.

Social, cultural and historical context

It is important for learners to fully understand, appreciate and be able to realistically envisage life in the fictional village of Tollington in 1972 for nine-year-old Meena. They may require pre-teaching activities on the following features of social, cultural and historical context so they can write about them confidently.

CHAPTER 2 OF ANITA AND ME

For Chapter 2, it is necessary to have an understanding of the partition of India. It is no surprise that Meena's parents keep returning to this defining moment of their history, and it becomes a motif throughout the novel. Historian Ayesha Jalal writes, 'a defining moment that is neither beginning nor end, partition continues to influence how the peoples and states of postcolonial South Asia envisage their past, present and future' (2013).

Vocabulary in context

The following vocabulary from Chapter 2 can be pre-taught to help with reading fluency and reduce cognitive load. What does each of the following words mean in context?

Word	Quotation	Definition
rumination (n.)	'I chewed with the pace and rumination of a sulky cow' (p. 24)	deep thought or consideration about something; or the action of chewing partly digested food
incongruous (adj.)	'incongruous with thick woolly socks squeezed into open-toed sandals and men's cardies over their vibrating thin silks' (p. 26)	not in harmony with aspects of something
affronted (adj.)	'My mother never ate out, never, always affronted by paying for some over-boiled, under-seasoned dish of slop' (p. 26)	offended by; insulted by some offence
deferential (adj.)	'with a deferential respect, as if in the company of minor royalty' (p. 28)	showing deference; respectful
epitome (n.)	'she was the epitome of grace, dignity and unthreatening charm' (p. 28)	the perfect example of a particular quality
jamardani (n.)	'Look at you, like a "*jamardani!*"' (p. 30)	a word used in the Indian subcontinent to describe a person employed to sweep homes or offices, and collect garbage (this is the female derivative of the word)
frippery (adj.)	'All this garden frippery, gnomes, wells and the like, was an English thing' (p. 33)	showy or unnecessary ornaments
salwar kameez (n.)	'running in full length *salwar kameez*' (p. 35)	a long tunic and a pair of light, loose, pleated trousers, usually tapering to a tight fit around the ankles, worn by women from South Asia

PIT STOP

Retrieval point ☁

Return to this vocabulary in a later lesson, assessing if learners can link each key word to the relevant character(s). For a bonus point, develop each link into an analysis of how the writer's language choice presents that character.

Examples:

- What impressions might Syal be trying to show the reader about women from the Indian diaspora, such as Meena's mama, who resist eating out and are 'affronted' by 'paying for some over-boiled, under-seasoned dish of slop'?
- How does the language used to describe 'other Indian women' in their 'salwar kameez' and vibrant clothes, 'incongruous with thick woolly socks', reveal that Meena views herself as an outsider and has been conditioned into accepting stereotypes?
- What does the description of Meena's mama as the 'epitome of grace, dignity and unthreatening charm' suggest about the position she holds within Tollington's community?

PIT STOP

Direct instruction point

The dichotomy between social and personal identity. You can extend this to a brief exploration of the five pillars of identity and/or the three stages of social identity: social categorisation, social identification and social comparison. Teach also about the effects of social conditioning and the common literary trope of 'appearance vs reality', which may have crossover with other texts students are studying.

PIT STOP

Academic writing point

The obvious keyword to discuss and unpack for this chapter is 'identity'. In addition, learning and understanding the impact of dichotomies and structural juxtaposition could be a practical, active step to answering the Big Question: **How does this chapter explore the dichotomy of identities?**

- **Internal conflict**: 'finishes the rest of my sweets, feeling the bile rise as I chewed' (p. 24); 'gradually I got [...] jealous of this past that excluded me' (p. 36).

- **Social/personal identity dichotomy**: 'monster beneath the mother' (p. 28).
- **Past/present identity dichotomy**: 'eighteen inch waists' and 'demure demeanours' (p. 32) vs 'milked goats'; 'seen someone stabbed to death'; 'jealous of this past that excluded me' (p. 36).
- **Cultural identity dichotomy**: 'I hadn't completed my homework because of some obscure religious festival about fire eating' (p. 28); 'garden frippery was an English thing' (p. 33); 'pulled sugar-cane from the earth as a mid-morning snack' (p. 36); 'perfectly natural to meet a total stranger and within ten minutes, find him a meal, a home' (p. 31); 'I never think of you as, you know, foreign' (p. 29).
- **The five pillars of identity**: body, social environment, job, material stability and values; 'glamorous in saris' (p. 25); 'English without an accent' (p. 25); 'Don't be so silly! [...] We were introduced by an uncle. It was all done through the proper channels.' (p. 32).
- **Three stages of social identity theory**: social categorization, social identification and social comparison; 'like two rare species' (p. 26).

Discussion point: Why don't Meena and her mother identify with other Indian women?

Possible responses could include the following micro-quotations:

- 'It was her duty to show them' (p. 25)
- 'two rare species' (p. 26)
- 'You're so lovely. You know, I never think of you as, you know, foreign. You're just like one of us' (p. 29).

Plot and character development

For tips on how to approach these 'What' questions, refer to the 'Plot and character development' section of 'How to use this book' on pages 5-6 of this guide.

1. What pressures does Syal allude to in this chapter about maintaining facades?

Example responses:

- Meena's mama conforming to societal expectations through the way she dresses and speaks, 'giving them the illusion that they could control the tides' (p. 28).
- Meena's mama laughing about and reflecting on the facades with the other Indian women as a coping mechanism.

2. What does the reader learn about Meena's papa's and mama's past, before they moved to Britain?

Example response:

Meena's parents came from a world and time that was fractured and fraught with violence and trauma, and coming to Britain came at a cost. Her father arrived with only 'twenty-five pounds in his pocket' (p. 31), forced to reinvent himself and start anew. Her mother came from a 'small Punjabi village' (p. 34), where her childhood was frivolous and joyous, a contrast to her life in Tollington where she conformed in 'sensible' (p. 25) attire. We learn how her mother experienced first-hand how 'partition riots stalked the streets like a ravenous animal' (p. 36), tearing 'Punjab in two' (p. 35). Meena watches her mother recount the story of a stabbing that she witnessed, and how 'it upset her greatly' (p. 36); evident that the trauma she experienced resurfaces occasionally and continues to cause pain. These stories make Meena 'jealous' (p. 36) as she is drawn to the earthiness of their experiences and close encounters with death. Meena's view of her parents' past clearly resonates with the perspective and innocence of the child narrator.

Other responses may include:

- The only picture of her father's departure captures how 'even in such a small photograph her [mother's] longing is palpable' (p. 32).
- Her father arrived, 'sick as a dog from that damned boat', with 'twenty-five pounds' in his pocket, and met Uncle Amman, who initially supported him (p. 31).
- Her mother came from a 'small Punjabi village' (p. 34) where she milked goats, stroked peacocks, and won a race to become 'All Delhi College Champion' (p. 35).
- The time before partition when their Sikh family lived in harmony with their Muslim neighbours before the 'religious differences that would soon tear the Punjab in two' (p. 35) and 'partition riots stalked the streets like a ravenous animal' (p. 36).
- The rickshaw story: her mother witnessed a man in an 'ill-fitting suit' (p. 36) being stabbed, and experiences the trauma every time she revisits the incident.

PIT STOP

S-T-R-E-T-C-H

Ask learners to consider:

- Why they think Syal presents Meena's parents' past as an integral contributor to Meena's identity in the present?
- How her parents' experiences might influence their parental choices, and their subsequent impact on Meena?

3. What does the reader learn about the 'Aunties' in this chapter?

Example response:

In Meena's eyes, 'Auntie and Uncle' is the 'natural respectful term' given to anyone she feels is 'old enough to boss' her around (p. 29). Syal introduces the Aunties in this chapter as an extension of Meena's family, depicting a familial bond that would resonate with the Indian diaspora. The reliance on this support network clearly extends to paternal responsibilities. Meena is aware that the Aunties 'continually interfered' (p. 30) in her upbringing, and were in fact invited to do so. Meena also acknowledges the 'jocular' and 'caring' manner in which these interactions take place and how this 'communal policing' makes her feel 'safe and wanted' (p. 31), secure in her community. She recognises that her parents 'valued' these relations 'intensely' (p. 31), and that they too fulfil their perceived role in order to demonstrate the extent of their love for her parents.

Other responses may include:

- 'Auntie and Uncle were the natural respectful terms given to them, to any Asian person old enough to boss me around' (p. 29).
- 'But I could not imagine existing without them, although they continually interfered in my upbringing' (p. 30).
- '... all done in this jocular caring way, as they showed how much they loved my parents by having a go at me on their behalf' (p. 30).
- '... communal policing [...] made me feel safe and wanted' (p. 31).
- '... gentle malice' (p. 33).
- 'I knew how intensely my parents valued these people' (p. 31).
- 'Individually, the Aunties were a powerful force [...] but together they were a formidable mafia whose collective approval was a blessing, and whose communal contempt was a curse' (p. 33).

4. What does the reader learn about Meena's mother's and Aunties' perception of the 'English'?

Example response:

It is evident in this chapter that, to some extent, both communities believe in and perceive communities through the lens of stereotypes. When Meena confronts her mother about 'the Front Garden dilemma' (p. 33), a discussion ensues where the Aunties launch into their 'collected proverbs on English behaviour', and how even 'gnomes, wells and the like' is an 'English thing' done to 'mark out their territory' (p. 33). There is an implied comparison of the English with 'dogs', followed by a series of communal perceptions that range from dysfunctional family relations and parenting ('Rent from your kid!') to personal hygiene ('Sit in their own dirty water instead of showering') (p. 33). The readers learn that even the smallest differences in cultural behaviours are viewed with prejudice and mistrust.

> **PIT STOP**
>
> ## S-T-R-E-T-C-H
>
> Ask learners if they can find any examples from later on in the text to challenge these preconceived notions, particularly in relation to the relationships within families.
>
> Example response:
>
> Even though Mrs Worrall's dysfunctional relationship with her children is emblematic of Meena's mother's critique, her strength and endurance as she takes care of a severely ill husband is unparalleled and challenges the stereotypical 'English' woman (like the 'barmaid type' (p. 33), running away with other men).

How?

Language

Narrative voice

Key quotations:

- 'I still recognised a few words in between mummy's sobs' (p. 25)
- 'I have heard the excited whispers between the Aunties whenever my parents' marriage was mentioned, odd words from which I concocted a whole scenario' (p. 32)
- 'she looked at me much as I imagine Damien's mother looked' (p. 36)
- 'a shared cigarette and a hidden knife, a too-small suit, probably borrowed from a brother who was expecting it back that evening, and a bloody betrayal' (p. 36).

To what extent does the voice of the child narrator trivialise, dramatise and/or fictionalise these events?

Nature imagery

Key quotations:

- 'the smoke rises like cold-morning breath around his face and he is backlit by a rising sun' (p. 31)
- 'where an old fashioned pump stood under a mango tree' (p. 34)
- 'holding the mug under its nipples, pulling down a foaming jet of milk straight into her father's mug of tea' (p. 35)
- 'cobra who lived in the damp grasses beneath the fallen apples' (p. 35)
- 'rainy monsoon nights' (p. 35)

CHAPTER 2 OF ANITA AND ME

- 'fields and trees, light and space, and a horizon that welcomed the sky' (p. 35).

Ask learners to consider:

- What the 'rising sun' symbolises of Mr Kumar's hopes for his and his family's future in Britain?
- How and why Meena's mother remembers her childhood in Punjab with fondness?
- How and why nature imagery has been used to create a dichotomy between her childhood in Punjab and life in Britain now? How does it emphasise the emotional difficulty of being an immigrant?
- How the 'cobra' might be a symbol to foreshadow how threat was lurking and the previously co-existing communities in Punjab were about to be torn apart?

Hyperbolic language

Key quotations:

- 'I enjoyed her anger, the snapping eyes, the shrieking voice, the glimpse of monster beneath the mother' (p. 28)
- '[Aunties] fulfil the role of Greek chorus to mama's solo role in my life' (p. 29)
- 'My parents in a love story! I kept myself awake imagining them chasing each other around old Indian streets!' (p. 32)
- 'the collision of the epic with the banal' (p. 36)
- 'TOT CHOKES ON UNCOOKED SAUSAGE! BIRTHDAY RUINED, SAY WEEPING PARENTS!' (p. 37).

Ask learners to consider:

- How Meena's enjoyment of her mother's anger might reveal that she associates love with intense and dramatic emotions?
- How Meena's delight in any dramatic events, even when menacing, might establish the basis for her relationship with Anita?
- What do Meena's comedic recounts suggest to the reader about her need for validation? And how might it suggest that she continues to be a character for whom truth is flexible?

Character focus

Meena

Key quotations:

- 'I hadn't completed my homework because of an obscure religious festival about fire eating' (p. 28)

- 'I rarely rebelled openly against this communal policing, firstly because it somehow made me feel safe and wanted ' (p. 31)
- 'The sun was hot now and I felt sick with all the sugar I had consumed; every sweet had tasted only of one thing, Guilt' (p. 34)
- 'But gradually I got bored and then jealous of this past that excluded me' (p. 36).

Whilst Meena chooses to maintain the impression of rebellion and defiance, her moral compass wins eventually. She experiences guilt, recognises consequences and values well-intentioned intervention, even when unsolicited. This capacity is revealing of an underlying emotional maturity. She continues to grapple with her sense of identity, trying to understand her roots and the world her parents have come from. Her acceptance and understanding of cultural traditions and events are still through the lens of someone who feels like an outsider and looking from afar, sometimes tinged with bias, other times with a sense of mysticism.

Mama

Key quotations:

- 'for her, looking glamorous in saris and formal Indian suits was part of the English people's education' (p. 25)
- 'the epitome of grace, dignity and unthreatening charm' (p. 28)
- 'treated her with deferential respect, as if in the company of minor royalty' (p. 28)
- 'Don't be so silly! [...] We were introduced by an uncle. It all was done through the proper channels.' (p. 32)
- came from a 'small Punjabi village' where she 'milked goats, stroked peacocks, pulled sugar-cane from the earth as a mid-morning snack', won a race to become 'All Delhi College Champion' (p. 34–35)
- 'and this memory seemed to upset her greatly' (p. 36).

The duality of Meena's mama's identity is evident throughout this chapter. The juxtaposition of her past life, in sync with nature and free from inhibitions, with her present, where all her decisions are carefully measured as she wears 'sensible' attire and speaks 'English without an accent' (p. 25), shows the conscious burden of representation in her every decision. She recognises being patronised when her white neighbour insists she is 'lovely' and not 'foreign' (p. 29). It is perhaps this exclusion that fuels her own prejudice of the English, revealed when she lets go of her facade and switches to her Indian identity with the Aunties.

Then there is the dichotomous facade in her home life. She masks who she is as a lover and wife in front of Meena, adopting her role as a 'parent' and insisting that her marriage took place through 'proper channels' (p. 32). She denies the rumours about a defiant romance that potentially challenged traditions and societal norms.

Another theme associated with her character that runs through is her sadness and depression, suggested to be linked with the financial pressures of living in Britain (perhaps why she 'never ate out' (p. 26)). She is painfully aware of the absence of her support system back in India. Her moods have begun to 'intrude upon every family outing like a silent guest' (p. 25), foreshadowing that this will be an influencing and integral factor later in her character's development.

Structure

Learners should explore the following examples from the opening and the ending of Chapter 2 and be invited to consider:

- Why Syal has chosen to begin and end with this focus on Meena's 'near-death' experience?
- What the metaphorical significance of being asphyxiated is?
- What their predictions might be about key characters and plot developments within this chapter.

Opening: 'I also knew what it was like to almost choke to death' (p. 24).

Ending: 'I recognised this feeling; it was the same feeling I had when I almost asphyxiated in the back of our car' (p. 37).

Structured as an almost Bildungsroman, the narrative regularly shifts from a linear structure and employs flashbacks (analepsis) to revisit memories and flash-forwards (prolepsis) to hint at events yet to come.

Meena has already suggested to the reader at the beginning of this chapter that the experience she is about to recount is a life-threatening one, even though her style of recount is both dramatic and comedic: 'I was going to die in the back of the car and somewhere inside me, I felt thrilled. It was so dramatic' (p. 27). Whilst the original incident and reference to choking is literal, what's interesting is that as the chapter continues to go back in time, particularly as far back as Meena's mother's childhood and traumatic experience of partition, Meena's revisiting of this feeling of asphyxiation is more metaphorical. Listening to her mother's account of a 'bloody betrayal' and witnessing a 'stabbing' (p. 36) in cold blood, Meena describes her 'centre of gravity' (p. 36) shifting and is taken back to the near-death experience of her seventh birthday. The child narrator still processes this traumatic event with excitement. Meena's fascination with living and leading a life full of drama is realised through this recount. It opens up the possibilities of something 'terrible' (p. 36) and terrifying happening. The chapter therefore ends with this wilful plea, 'When would anything dangerous and cruel ever happen to me?' (p. 37). A plea that is ironically about to be realised as it foreshadows events yet to come, in particular Anita's and Sam's betrayal.

Extracts

1. How does Syal use language to reveal implicit bias and prejudice here?

'...the admiration of the villagers was always tempered with a deferential respect [...] You're so lovely. You know, I never think of you as, you know, foreign. You're just like one of us.' My mother would smile and graciously accept this as a compliment.' (p. 28-29)

Example response planning, using topic sentence scaffolds:

Syal presents the implicit bias in this exchange as:

- yet another way that Meena's mother is viewed as an outsider
- a regular occurrence experienced by ethnic minorities
- the result of frustration and ignorance
- a reinforcement of the power imbalance between communities
- a reinforcement of the expectation of conformity
- reflective of the views held by most of the villagers in Tollington
- reflective of how anyone was capable of harbouring racist ideas
- yet another act of discrimination and othering.

Example response, unpacking quotations and language therein to support points:

Syal presents the idea that even when the villagers express love and acceptance for Meena's mother, they still view and measure her as an outsider. The complimentary adjective 'lovely' is immediately juxtaposed with the elaboration that she doesn't classify as 'foreign'. The connotations of 'foreign' here reveal the underlying prejudice and imply a lack of acceptance of anyone who might behave 'foreign'. Moreover, the fact that this exchange takes place after Meena's mother offers a lift further reinforces how even basic acts of humanity and kindness are measured to prove belonging ('like one of us'), and are disassociated with being 'foreign'. This assumption that kindness and humanity are exclusively British values further reinforces this racial prejudice. It is not only patronising but also reveals a perceived power imbalance, in this case on moral grounds. The casual nature of this exchange is perhaps yet another reminder from Syal of how ignorant comments such as this one would have been a regular occurrence experienced by ethnic minorities, particularly in the 1970s. Moreover, the repetition of 'you know' also generates a self-conscious tone, reiterating that there is certainly an awareness here that what is about to be said is implicit in its bias, and therefore discriminatory.

> **PIT STOP** ▼
>
> ## S-T-R-E-T-C-H
>
> 'And yet afterwards, in front of the Aunties, she would reduce them to tears of laughter by gently poking fun at the habits of her English friends. It was only much later on that I realised in the thirteen years we lived there [...] only once had any of our neighbours been invited in further than the step of our back door' (p. 29).
>
> Ask learners to evaluate the following statement using this extract:
>
> To what extent would you agree that Meena's mother's response can be explained in light of the prejudice that she experiences?

CHAPTER 3 OF ANITA AND ME

At a glance

- **Chapter summary quotation:** 'I shook with how powerful I suddenly felt' (p. 60)
- **Big Question:** How does this chapter explore different types of power and strength?
- **Significant plot event:** Meena interacts with her neighbours and begins to be influenced by Anita.
- **Character focus:** Tracey, Deirdre
- **Key themes:**
  - Cultural identity
  - Belonging
  - Friendship
- **Handle with care:**
  - Reference to adult content and health issues in this chapter will need to be handled with sensitivity. Please refer to the 'Handle with care' guidance in the 'How to use this book' section for further support.
    - 'cancer' (p. 40)
    - 'kamasutra' (p. 49).

Why?

'Why' is important not only within the world of the text, but also when considering authorial intent and messaging.

- Why does Meena 'physically ache' to be one of Anita's 'constant cohorts' (p. 39)?
- Why does Syal create a narrator-protagonist who provides us with such a candid view of human power dynamics and abuses thereof? Are there, perhaps, unexpected power dynamics revealed: a child being more powerful than an adult and/or an 'outsider' considering themselves superior?

CHAPTER 3 OF ANITA AND ME

- Why is this chapter important with its multiple perspectives in developing the narrative?

This allows us to consider Chapter 3's Big Question:

> How does this chapter explore different types of power and strength?

What?
What happens?

As if in answer to the question posed at the end of the previous chapter, Chapter 3 opens with Meena meeting and being invited to join the 'undisputed 'cock'' of the yard (p. 38), Anita Rutter, for the 'best day' of her life (p. 60). Her power over our narrator is clear. We also meet various other characters both in Meena's present and past through related flashbacks:

- Mrs Christmas and Mr Worrall, who are both seriously ill, and their spouses
- Anita's sister, Tracey
- Anita's mother, Deidre
- Hairy Neddy and Sandy
- the Yard's 'Bad Boy', Sam Lowbridge
- the Yard's Methodist volunteer youth worker and 'sex symbol', Uncle Alan.

We learn of Meena's fear of the characteristic passageways or 'entries' between the houses in the area, burgeoning desire for British cuisine over traditional Indian fare, love of the popular TV show *Opportunity Knocks*, and realisation of her own power, even as a child, when it comes to manipulating those who love her by telling a lie or the truth.

Social, cultural and historical context

It is important for learners to fully understand, appreciate and be able to realistically envisage life in the fictional village of Tollington in 1972 for nine-year-old Meena. They may require pre-teaching activities on the following features of social, cultural and historical context so they can write about them confidently.

Opportunity Knocks was one of the most popular TV shows of the 1960s and 1970s. This was the original TV talent show and regularly had viewing figures of 20 million viewers. Also, the Betting and Gambling Act of 1960 allowed commercial bingo to take off and it became played regularly by hundreds of thousands of people in Britain.

BLOOMSBURY TEACHER GUIDE: ANITA AND ME

Vocabulary in context

The following vocabulary from Chapter 3 can be pre-taught to help with reading fluency and reduce cognitive load. What does each of the following words mean in context?

Word	Quotation	Definition
kamasutra (n.)	'whilst they tried various kamasutra positions for his organ' (p. 49)	an ancient Sanskrit text on the principles of attaining emotional, connective and sexual fulfilment
fecund (adj.)	'Mrs K (the fecund divorcee)' (p. 52)	highly fertile
tinnitus (n.)	'this tinnitus of conscience forever buzzing in my ears' (p. 53)	ringing sound in one's ears
piece (n.)	a 'piece' being a peculiar Tollington word for a sandwich which my mother had banned me from saying' (p. 53)	dialect word for sandwich
euphemism (n.)	'our family Punjabi euphemism for shit' (p. 56)	a more polite or less direct way of expressing something

PIT STOP

Retrieval point

Return to this vocabulary in a later lesson, assessing if learners can link each key word to the relevant character(s). For a bonus point, develop each link into an analysis of how the writer's language choice presents that character.

Examples:

- How might the mention of the kamasutra provide a cultural bridge in the novel? Consider what is being described: the playful, sexualised dancing as the 'Bontempi organ' (p. 48) plays its music in the Yard, having fallen out of Hairy Neddy's car. Also, consider Meena's description of him as a man 'who lived for giving people the kind of pleasure and release he'd just given' them (p. 50).
- What might Syal be trying to show the reader about how people view, categorise and label one another (especially women) when she uses the term 'the fecund divorcee' (p. 52) to describe Mrs K?
- In what way are the terms 'poorly' and 'down there' (in reference to Mrs Christmas in this chapter) euphemisms (p. 40)?
- Who does Syal present as a true caretaker in the community by offering Tracey a 'piece' when she expresses hunger in the absence of her mother (p. 53)?

CHAPTER 3 OF ANITA AND ME

> **PIT STOP** ▼
>
> ## Direct instruction point
>
> Learners need to be able to use juxtaposition to make a line of argument convincing and compelling. They should use scaffolds to complete the following guided writing:
>
> Meena's main attraction to Anita is her power and her apparent ability not to care. Up until this point in the chapter, Meena has been presented as relatively weak and a follower. Ask learners to complete the table below to evidence this theory, using quotations and analysis.
>
> | Examples/events from chapter | Quotations and analysis |
> | --- | --- |
> | Inferior to Anita | |
> | 'The entry' | |
> | Being scolded by Mr Christmas | |
> | Deidre | |
> | Misty | |
> | Mr Worrall | |
>
> Then, use the 'think-aloud' method (see below) to model how to incorporate the method in a line of argument. For example:
>
> At home, however, Meena revels in exercising her newfound command of her mother: she shakes 'with how powerful' she 'suddenly felt' (p. 60). This important contrast and shift in our narrator positions the reader to consider the novel's title *Anita and Me*.
>
> The 'think-aloud' method is a live teacher demonstration with metacognitive narrative accompanying writing, meaning the teacher verbalises what they are doing and thinking while completing a task. You might say something like, 'Right, I need to decide which words to focus my attention on when I'm exploring the impact of juxtaposition...'

> **PIT STOP** ▼
>
> ## S-T-R-E-T-C-H
>
> 'I shook with how powerful I suddenly felt' (p. 60).
>
> What could an alternative reading of the verb 'shook' be? Which other verbs is it similar to in suggesting fear or nerves, rather than excitement and anticipation?

BLOOMSBURY TEACHER GUIDE: ANITA AND ME

Plot and character development

For tips on how to approach these 'What' questions, refer to the 'Plot and character development' section of 'How to use this book' on pages 5-6 of this guide.

1. **What adds to the sense of foreboding in terms of how Anita is introduced to the reader in the opening of Chapter 3?**

    Example responses:

    - she is referred to at first as 'a shadow' (p. 38)
    - her first act is to destroy life: 'butterflies' eggs' (p. 38)
    - she hurts Meena
    - she snatches Meena's sweets
    - Meena walks behind her
    - she is 'cock' (rather than 'hen') of the yard, suggesting more violent, combative tendencies (p. 38)
    - she litters.

2. **What does the reader learn about the 'entry' passages, characteristic of the local area, running between the terraced homes?**

    Example response:

    They evoke typical childhood fear with their gothic 'slimy walls' (p. 44) and cavernous echoes. They are a place for 'screams' (p. 44) and run for the safety of 'daylight' (p. 39). They combine something frightening and exciting – the perfect mix for thrilling mischief-making.

3. **What does the reader learn about the differences between English and Indian fabrics, and the differences in the way English and Indian women express hurt and upset?**

    Example response:

    The fabrics contrast significantly: the patterns on Mrs Christmas's clothes are 'delicate' florals in 'English drawing room colours' and Meena feels 'as if a meadow had landed' in her lap (p. 43). In comparison, the clothes her mother wears are made of fabric 'deep' in colour and rich with wildlife such as 'dancing elephants' and 'strutting peacocks' (p. 43). A similar stark contrast is illustrated in the way the women express emotions linked to sadness: Meena's mother sobs and wails openly, while the Tollington women channel violent anger into silent, seething hatred. They recognise the need to be tough.

CHAPTER 3 OF ANITA AND ME

> **PIT STOP**
>
> ## S-T-R-E-T-C-H
>
> - What might Syal be trying to suggest with these two key contrasts in question 3? How is this difference perhaps offset by the paragraph towards the end of the chapter which begins, 'Not all the English were selfish' (p. 67)?

4. What does the reader learn about the types of activities local children engage in with Uncle Alan, the Methodist youth leader?

Example responses:

- collecting donations for the bring and buy sale
- litter picking
- fruit picking
- cleaning play equipment at the park
- Sunday 'Youth Chats'.

5. What does the reader learn about how the Tollington women view Uncle Alan?

Example response:

Humorously billed as 'the nearest thing' Tollington had to a 'sex symbol in a ten-mile radius' (p. 41), Uncle Alan is begrudgingly tolerated by the children who have nothing better to do, and lusted after by the Tollington women who openly discuss him in lewd terms. This appears normalised amongst the sexes in the community, as we also witness Hairy Neddy giving and receiving the same sort of verbal vulgarity.

6. What does the reader learn about how Meena feels about being 'told off by a white person' (p. 45)?

Example response:

Meena has been raised to view being chastised by a white person as an entirely reprehensible act: enough to let down 'the whole Indian nation' no less (p. 45). Where Anita is emboldened by the adult challenge, Meena is conditioned to apologise and beg that Mr Christmas not inform her parents of her misdeeds. She immediately chastises herself, however, for not being more like Anita, which suggests the power her new 'friend' is beginning to have over her, and how powerful the draw to imitate her is becoming.

7. What does Anita symbolise to Meena?

Example response:

It is possible that, by the end of this chapter, Syal wishes for Anita to symbolise two things for Meena: a powerful role model and a potential source of conflict. It is very clear to the reader that Meena wants to be like and be liked by Anita. When Meena is comforted slightly by the fact that Tracey (Anita's sister) is a 'bigger coward' (p. 53) than her, she shows a darker side to her personality which is troublesome for us as readers, who have been rooting for her. The potential for her to move closer to Anita and emulate some of her unkind characteristics is brought closer. When Deidre (Anita's mum) looks Meena 'up and down as if making a decision' (p. 55) and no tea invitation is forthcoming, we sense a complication. Why was she not asked in and why did Anita whisper 'See you tomorrow' (p. 55)? Here, Anita could be seen to symbolise a temptation which is, for now at least, just out of reach.

8. What does Meena's mother symbolise to Meena?

Example response:

By not being a 'Yard Mama' (p. 53), Meena's mother is something of a disappointment to her, made clear from the fact that she will not be rushing 'into the yard in curlers and a pinny' to 'beat the crap out of' her 'tormentors' (p. 53). Meena's mother also refuses to conform to the English 'beige food' stereotype Meena so desires: no fish fingers or 'pieces' for her. Whilst Meena is not openly critical of her mother's 'fresh vegetable *sabzi*' (p. 54) or her fabric 'colours that made [one's] pupils dilate' (p. 43), the reader is positioned to feel it is her otherness that Meena resents. Her need to fit in and do the same as her peers is fierce, and her mother represents barrier after barrier to achieving that.

9. What does Mrs Worrall symbolise to Meena?

Example response:

Mrs Worrall is a reminder to Meena of the power and strength of the human spirit. Her 'three grown-up sons' (p. 54) rarely visit and she copes alone. Much like other strong women in Meena's life, such as her Aunties, Mrs Worrall displayed a 'stoic muscular resistance' (p. 67) – a constancy, solidity and immovability.

How?

Language

Music/dance imagery

Key quotations:

- 'whilst this strange one-sided tango was going on' (p. 51)

- 'her pointy boobs doing a jive under a very tight white polo neck sweater' (p. 54).

Following the comical scene where Hairy Neddy's organ slides out of his car and the whole Yard ends up dancing with abandon to the 'pulsing electronic rhythm of a bossa nova' (p. 49), Syal uses other music/dance-related descriptions as the chapter develops.

Ask learners to consider:

- How the two further references are also related to intimacy and relationships?
- How the images may be used as a motif/extended metaphor to keep reminding the reader of the 'grown-up' world Meena inhabits when she is not at home?
- How performance for an audience appears as a key idea elsewhere in the chapter (i.e. what is on the television at the Worrall's house)?

Juxtaposition

Syal wants the reader to view Anita and her sister as polar opposites, both physically and in their characters.

Challenge learners to prove this statement by collecting examples from the text in two columns (one per sister). For example:

Anita	Tracey
Rottweiler	Whippet
Blonde and pale	Dark and pinched
Cheerful, flirty	Drag queen with a migraine

Character focus

Tracey

Key quotation:

- 'Where's me mum? I'm hungry' (p. 53).

Tracey is a victim, even for Meena. She is created by Syal as an important symbol of an easy target.

Deirdre

Key quotation:

- 'she pushed her off, irritated' (p. 54).

Deirdre is created by Syal as the ultimate symbol of threat.

Structure

Learners should explore the following examples from the opening and the ending of Chapter 3 and be invited to consider:

- Why Syal has chosen to begin and end with a focus on Meena's very different experiences?
- What the focus on powerful interactions with strong female characters might suggest?
- What their predictions might be about key characters and plot developments within this chapter?

Opening: 'A shadow fell over my T-bar sandals and I looked up to see Anita Rutter through squinted eyes ringed in bright blue eye shadow' (p. 38).

Ending: 'I felt Mrs Worrall's eyes gently guide me to my back door' (p. 68).

Learners should be able to identify the antithesis between Meena's 'T-bar sandals' (which betray her childhood innocence) and Anita's pre-teen 'bright blue eyeshadow'. This should confirm for the reader that Anita will most certainly be a source of danger and aspiration for our protagonist, as she represents everything that Meena is not. Describing her as a 'shadow' towering above Meena and the way she 'looked up' at her suggests a dark power and controlling nature, perhaps learned from the adults in her life. By contrast, Mrs Worrall shows Meena how to be 'gently' strong through compassion and care: both for her own husband and for Meena, her neighbour. Structurally, the reader is taken on a journey in this chapter through a series of meetings and interactions: Syal uses Meena's internal perspective to show us how prejudice and suffering are universal.

Extracts

1. How does Syal use language to position the reader to view Deidre in this extract?

'Deidre looked at me for the first time. I had forgotten how scary the bottom half of her face was [...] Deidre looked me up and down as if making a decision, then turned on her heel and tip-tapped into her yard' (p. 55).

Example response planning, using topic sentence scaffolds:

Syal uses language to position the reader to view Deidre as:

- judgemental/prejudiced
- dangerous
- damaged
- not like other mothers.

Example response, unpacking quotations and language therein to support points:

Syal shifts the focus in her description of Deidre to her mouth using the conjunction 'But'. This changes the tone to a more sinister one. Additionally, she presents her lips as 'bee-stung' (evoking sensory images of pain and suffering) and 'always on the edge of a sneer' ('always' suggesting the fixed, unrelenting nature of her expression). This positions the reader to view her with apprehension and foreboding. They perhaps fear Meena will be hurt by this woman, just as likely her own daughters already have been hurt. Indeed, perhaps she has already been hurt by others in a perpetual painful cycle of abuse and suffering.

2. **How does Syal use language to show the differences between Anita and her sister, Tracey, in the following extract from Chapter 3?**

'Tracey threw herself at Deidre's legs but she pushed her off, irritated, pausing only to cuff Anita on the side of the head. Anita laughed [...] 'Yeah!' yelled Tracey, happy again, all those hours of anguish and abandonment instantly forgotten' (p. 54).

Example response planning, using topic sentence scaffolds:

Syal presents the stark difference between Anita and her sister as though they were:

- polar opposites
- foil characters.

Example response, unpacking quotations and language therein to support points:

Tracey's happiness is represented as entirely contingent upon her mother's presence – she is anxious and depressed when Deidre is not present. By contrast, Anita appears far more self-sufficient and independent. Anita's 'laugh' when her mother 'cuff[s]' her suggests a lack of any concern for her mother's presence, absence or actions (although the reader might question how genuine Anita is being, and whether she puts on a brave public face to preserve her reputation).

Tracey is presented by Syal as the polar opposite, not caring at all about how she is perceived by others. She 'throws' herself at her mother's legs in relief and desperation, which is arguably the behaviour of a much younger child. She also feels intense 'abandonment' each time Deidre is away from them for any amount of time. This appears to be amplified by her mother's unkindness.

It is quite hard to read of a mother 'irritated' with their own child for showing affection and 'pushing' them away as a result. Syal expertly positions the reader to judge Deidre for her parenting choices and the contrasting consequences they appear to be having on her two daughters.

CHAPTER 4 OF ANITA AND ME

At a glance

- **Chapter summary quotation:** 'all the old wounds being reopened' (p. 73)
- **Big Question:** How does this chapter present different experiences of trauma and guilt?
- **Significant plot event:** Mrs Christmas's dead body is discovered and Meena learns that mama is pregnant.
- **Character focus:** Papa, Anita, Meena
- **Key themes:**
  - Truth vs lies
  - Conflict and violence
  - Cultural identity
- **Handle with care:**
  - Reference to racially offensive terms in this chapter will need to be handled with sensitivity. Please refer to the 'Handle with care' guidance in the 'How to use this book' section for further support.
    - 'gores' (p. 73).

Why?

'Why' is important not only within the world of the text, but also when considering authorial intent and messaging.

- Why do Meena's thoughts turn to 'lime hot pants and blond hair' (p. 70) when she is meant to be listening to her father's story of the boy and the tiger?
- Why does Meena flashback to her papa's 'legendary' mehfils? (p. 71)
- Why does Meena's father tell her the story of how he inadvertently planted a bomb?
- Why does Meena's mother make her fish fingers for dinner?
- Why does Meena quickly change her story about when she last saw Mrs Christmas?

CHAPTER 4 OF ANITA AND ME

- Why does Meena's mother agonise about what to wear for the funeral?
- Why does Meena stop 'hanging around the adults' (p. 83) to see her father perform once she learns he had to turn down a contract in his youth?
- Why are Meena's parents and their relationship seemingly different from the other adults she observes, both Indian and British?
- Why does Meena react to the news with such hostility at the end of the chapter?

This allows us to consider Chapter 4's Big Question:

> How does this chapter present different experiences of trauma and guilt?

What?
What happens? ☁

Meena returns home from the Worralls proud of, and desperate to eat, her jam tarts. Aware her parents have been discussing her and the events at Mr Omerod's shop in her absence, her mother swiftly departs and her father proceeds to counsel her through a moral story on the ills of lying. Keen to steer the conversation to stories from her father she truly wants to hear, Meena enquires about whether her father was 'in the war' (p. 70). At the mention of 'partition' (p. 71), what follows is a flashback to a traditional family gathering, a mehfil, at which Meena's father would begin the magical musical performance. Meena remembers one particular mehfil which was different: she recalls overhearing raised voices and harrowing snippets of what the adults saw, endured and experienced, in stark, graphic detail. That night her dreams were haunted by images of what she had heard.

As we return to the present, Meena is thrilled that her father is sharing precious 'grown-up' facts and memories with her from the time of partition. He reveals how he was inadvertently involved in delivering a bomb to a house as a young man.

The family wake the next day to ambulance sirens and it is revealed that Mrs Christmas has been found dead (apparently for quite some time) at home, by Deidre. Meena almost gives away her passageway antics with Anita. Meena's mama attends the funeral and, when Mr Christmas passes away too, a deep sadness descends over her papa as he worries about his own parents and being so far away from them. Reflection on his parents leads to the revelation that he was offered a film contract in his youth, such was his performance talent, but his father refused. Meena at first mourns the life she could have had as the daughter of a famous star and then reflects on the opportunity her dear papa lost out on. She feels it is in some way her fault.

Meena then moves to reviewing her parents' relationship and remarking on its uniqueness: in comparison to the other models she has observed (the youngsters in the local park, the Indian aunties and uncles, the married English neighbours and the Yard couples), they were truly special and different in their commitment and connection. This leads to the news that Meena is to become a sister.

Social, cultural and historical context

It is important for learners to fully understand, appreciate and be able to realistically envisage life in the fictional village of Tollington in 1972 for Meena. They may require pre-teaching activities on the following features of social, cultural and historical context so they can write about them confidently.

The following are some useful topics or terms to consider when discussing the context of this chapter with learners.

- **The Boy Who Cried Wolf**: a moral tale (fable) intended to teach children not to tell lies for fear when they most need help they will not be believed.
- **Mehfil**: A social gathering, often in intimate settings and common in some parts of South Asia, where recreational activities such as poetry ('mushaira'), classical Indian singing and music are enjoyed. The seating is often on the floor.
- **Partition**: refer to the contextual timeline (page 201 of this guide).
- **Ghazals**: a lyric poem from Middle Eastern or Indian literature with a fixed number of verses, typically on the theme of love and often set to music. Pronounced 'guzzle'.
- **Pre-booked single grave**: couples who have thought about and planned for their deaths and funerals can purchase a single grave plot in advance so they can be interred together when the time comes. This was common practice for married couples in the 1960s and 70s.
- **Troy Tempest**: a fictional character in the popular 1960s puppet TV show *Stingray*, the first to be made entirely in colour; Troy was Captain of the submarine Stingray.

Vocabulary in context

The following vocabulary from Chapter 4 can be pre-taught to help with reading fluency and reduce cognitive load. What does each of the following words mean in context?

CHAPTER 4 OF ANITA AND ME

Words	Quotation	Definition
corpulent (adj.)	'seeing corpulent uncles parp their way through their starters' (p. 69)	fat; overweight
timbre (n.)	'I loved the timbre of his voice' (p. 70)	sound quality
leonine (adj.)	'there was something leonine in his expression' (p. 70)	resembling a lion
innuendoes (n., pl.)	'their husbands' smiling innuendoes' (p. 72)	suggestive remarks; often about sex or unkind
berating (v.)	'the sound of a man's voice berating someone' (p. 72)	scolding or telling-off
bovine (adj.)	'she seemed swollen and bovine' (p. 80)	like a cow
nonchalantly (adv.)	'these men, nonchalantly chewing or smoking' (p. 80)	without care or worry
discordant (adj.)	'played a discordant fanfare' (p. 82)	harsh-sounding; melodically mismatched
abated (v.)	'the tension had now somehow abated' (p. 83)	lessened; eased away
brazenness (n.)	'the brazenness of their behaviour' (p. 86)	lack of shame or embarrassment

PIT STOP

Retrieval point

Return to this vocabulary in a later lesson, assessing if learners can link each key word to the relevant character(s). For a bonus point, develop each link into an analysis of how the writer's language choice presents that character.

Examples:

- Who does Syal describe as 'leonine' on two occasions and how might this suggest the mixed emotions Meena feels towards this key figure in her life?

- Which group's choice of physical presentation and behaviour fits with the term 'brazenness' and what could this be masking?

- How does the adverb 'nonchalantly' present the men in the novel and their position and behaviour socially relative to the women presented in the text?

BLOOMSBURY TEACHER GUIDE: ANITA AND ME

> **PIT STOP**
>
> ### S-T-R-E-T-C-H
>
> Compare the adjectives 'leonine' and 'bovine' after reading the chapter pointing out their similar suffixes and animalistic semantics. In terms of their meanings and the characters to whom they refer (Meena's father and mother respectively), ask learners to consider:
>
> - What this might reveal about Meena's feelings about her parents?
> - How the second foreshadows the reveal at the end of the chapter structurally?

Plot and character development

For tips on how to approach these 'What' questions, refer to the 'Plot and character development' section of 'How to use this book' on pages 5-6 of this guide.

1. What does the reader learn about how families like Meena's typically welcomed and entertained guests in the opening paragraph of Chapter 4?

Example response:

They were received in a more formal 'front' room where more prized possessions and grander furniture were kept, rather than the more informal family 'lounge', described as the 'telly and flop room' (p. 69).

2. What details on pages 69, 70 and 71 might present Meena's mother as more authoritarian than her father?

Example responses:

- 'Mama got up slowly and brushed past me' (p. 69)
- 'I remembered mama's expression' (p. 70)
- 'He checked the kitchen quickly, making sure mama was still occupied' (p. 71).

3. What sorts of acts of violence does Meena overhear at the particular mehfil she recalls in this chapter and what effect does it have on her?

Example response:

Syal presents Meena eavesdropping on the adults' conversation from the staircase into the front room, their raised voices having woken her. She overhears recounts of beheadings, kidnaps and mass murder. That night she suffered from nightmares combining graphic details of 'severed limbs' and 'beautiful sisters' (p. 75) and she was left with a thirst to discover more.

4. **What does Meena mean when she says her papa speaking to her about partition was 'a gift' to her (p. 76)?**

   Example response:

   Stories are very important to Meena. Her desires to be treated like an adult and to learn more about her heritage and her father's past are both satisfied by his opening up to her about his experiences as an aspiring 'freedom fighter' (p. 76). His confiding in her and trusting her with the story means he has forgiven her for her childish behaviour in Mr Omerod's shop and that she is his 'beti' once more (p. 86).

5. **What reaction does the discovery of Mrs Christmas's death provoke in different characters?**

   Example responses:

   - Meena: horror; guilt
   - Mama: intrigue; suspicion; respect
   - Papa: depression
   - Deirdre: hysterical; attention-seeking
   - Anita: perversely happy
   - Mr Omerod: pious
   - Hairy Neddy: upset; regretful.

6. **What does Meena think 'love meant' (p. 82) and to what extent do you agree?**

   Example response:

   Meena shares with the reader how both of her parents have at one time told her that they feel lucky the other 'picked' them as their love; that they can't really understand what the other saw in them. From this Meena presumes this is what love means: counting oneself as fortunate and blessed that the person they love loves them – 'both people thinking they were the lucky one' (p. 82).

7. **What different types of 'Sin' are mentioned in this chapter? Focus your answer from Meena's perspective on pages 79 and 85.**

   Example response:

   On learning of Mrs Christmas's death, Meena worries her prank with Anita in the passageway might have contributed and that they might be guilty of murder and thus be 'joined in Sin' (p. 79). Later in the chapter when Meena is reviewing the different types of adult relationships she is surrounded by and how they contrast with her parents' relationship, she reflects on the antics of the Ballbearings Committee whilst under the influence of alcohol and their 'sinful' discussions of their husbands' sexual prowess (p. 85).

8. **At the end of the chapter, what prepares the reader for the fact that Meena will not react well to the announcement of the new baby?**

Example responses:

- 'accusingly' (p. 86)
- 'another secret' (p. 86)
- 'added to the list' (p. 86)
- 'kept from me' (p. 86).

How?
Language

Exclamatives

How does Syal use exclamatives to convey Meena's reaction to learning her papa was offered a film contract in his youth?

Meena's immediate reaction on learning her father was denied the chance to become a film star is one of utter disbelief: the parallel exclamatives 'Oh but in that pause what possibilities hovered!' (p. 82) and 'Papa could have been a film star!' (p. 82) communicate an emotional response to her beloved father's lost opportunity. Syal couples the exclamatives with the word 'Oh' to amplify Meena's shock and awe.

> **PIT STOP**
>
> **S-T-R-E-T-C-H**
>
> What synonym can learners find for 'disbelief'? Can they use them to vary their vocabulary and give more precise, nuanced analysis?

Anaphora

How is Meena's love for her papa presented through anaphora on page 83 when she has the epiphany about his true calling?

Syal has Meena describe her father adoringly as: 'My tender papa, my flying papa, the papa with hope and infinite variety' (p. 83). This beautiful, image-rich, heartfelt tricolon communicates her deep love and reverence for him.

Dialogue

How is dialogue used to reveal the details surrounding Mrs Christmas's death?

Characteristically, the whole Yard is out on the street at the sound of the sirens and raised voices so it is entirely fitting that rapid dialogue shared between multiple speakers is used by the writer to immerse the reader in the

CHAPTER 4 OF ANITA AND ME

events as they unfold. Meena, too, is learning as we read, as she eavesdrops (something she is very skilled at!) from her bedroom window with mama, making for an interesting narrative perspective. Ever powerful, Deidre speaks first and for the longest, revealing gruesome details of how she had found Mrs Christmas with 'no face left. Gone. Eaten away' (p. 77). Reported speech is then used when Sandy informs those gathered that the 'ambulance blokes said she's been dead for weeks' (p. 78). Various other contributions ensue, each giving a personal take and revealing more about the character speaking than the events themselves.

Antithesis

How is antithesis used to highlight the unique and special nature of Meena's parents' relationship in comparison to that of others?

Others:

- 'contacted each other through their children' (p. 85)
- 'nocturnal dramas [...] fun was infectious and laced with Sin' (p. 85).

Meena's parents:

- 'volunteer hugs and kisses' (p. 85)
- 'almost claustrophobic connection' (p. 86).

Character focus

Papa

Key quotations:

- 'My father had planted a real live bomb!' (p. 76)
- 'Papa could have been a film star!' (p. 82).

Syal reveals much about Meena's papa in this chapter which is crucial to shaping our reading of him and how we see him as the novel develops. He is presented as a man who has experienced but also sacrificed much in his life. We are positioned to revere but also pity him through Meena's eyes.

Anita

Key quotations:

- 'Maybe me and Anita Rutter were murderers' (p. 78)
- 'I could have sworn that she winked' (p. 79).

Anita is further vilified in this chapter when we are shown her possibly heartless reaction to the death of Mrs Christmas. Whilst Meena is presented as horrified in her hyperbolic presupposition that she may be partly responsible for the elderly woman's death, Anita's 'wink' could be interpreted as a cruel gesture in the face of such a sad scene.

Meena

Key quotations:

- 'if my singing papa was the real man, how did he feel the rest of the time?' (p. 83)
- 'Their intimacies unsettled me' (p. 83)
- 'I could not imagine one day how I could be capable of such sweetness' (p. 86).

Meena's knowledge of the world and its realities develops further in this chapter. Whilst the draw of typical English relationships with their glamour and 'fun' is clear for her, and the mysticism of her parents' special relationship even within their own community is emphasised, there is a romanticism around her father in particular and the hero figure he represents for her. Will anyone ever match up to him in Meena's eyes?

Structure

N.B. The format of this section deviates from that ordinarily used to foreground the importance of the link to the previous chapter and the other key structural methods recommended for focus in teaching.

1. How is the opening paragraph of the chapter comedic and how does it provide a link to the previous chapter?

The 'mock leather yellow settee' (p. 69) and the sounds it emits when people sit and move on it provide the comedy to open Chapter 4. This is where Meena's parents are sitting when she returns from the Worralls so provides momentary light relief (with the delightful description of 'leathery farts and squeaks') as the readers anticipate more conflict following the events at Mr Omerod's shop (p. 69).

2. How are the revelation of papa's bomb story and the revelation of Mrs Christmas's death structured in the chapter, and what is the effect of this?

The two events are revealed concurrently in short succession creating a deliberate parallel. Syal presents Meena as entirely sympathetic to her father: she says, 'I'm sorry' (p. 77) hinting she understands the guilt and shame he might feel at having been involved in the bombing. Interestingly, rather than seeing her father as a result of this as someone she can confide in, when she suspects she may have been, in part, responsible for Mrs Christmas's death, she quickly reverts to a more childlike position and decrees that she will 'carry around' the 'guilty secret' until she dies (p. 78). Arguably the effect of this is to remind the reader of Meena's young age and naivety.

3. How are the mehfils used structurally in the chapter?

They are used as flashback sequences which reveal key details about what Meena has learned about her heritage and her family (either indirectly or directly). They punctuate the present narrative to help explain to the reader what 'secrets' Meena already feels have been kept from her and what her father was denied and sacrificed which makes him even more dear to her.

4. How does the end of the chapter hint at Meena becoming more like Anita?

Earlier in the chapter the reader is positioned to react unfavourably to Anita as she is seen grinning, possibly even winking, at Meena in the aftermath of the sirens and the drama following the discovery of Mrs Christmas's body, a most perverse reaction. At the end of the chapter, rather than expressing the expected happiness or excitement at the news that she is to become a big sister, Meena reacts in a similarly unorthodox way, offering her parents a halting singular 'No' when asked (p. 87). The reader may connect the two incidents, wondering if nine-year-old Meena is moving closer to the behaviour of her new 'friend' (p. 60).

Extracts

1. How does Syal use language to convey Meena's feelings of distress on hearing the adults' partition stories?

'My heart was trying to break [...] How could they have kept this from me for so long?' (p. 74).

Example response planning, using topic sentence scaffolds:

Syal presents Meena's feelings of distress as:

- powerful and urgent
- coupled with a strange excitement to be finally learning about 'grown-up' secrets
- amplified by disbelief.

Example response, unpacking quotations and language therein to support points:

Syal presents Meena's feelings of distress as powerful and urgent on hearing the adults' partition stories: the way her heart was 'trying to break out' of her chest suggests a strong physical reaction to what she is secretly discovering and an urgent desire to learn more about her heritage. That she is 'terrified' she will be discovered and depicted holding on to the 'bannister' to steady herself is not perceived as hyperbole by the reader: the stories are shocking, not least for a child to overhear.

2. How does Syal use language to present Meena's emotional reaction to the realisation that she may have played a part in Mrs Christmas's death?

'I imagined having to retell the whole story [...] we would have to carry around our guilty secret until we died.' (p. 79)

Example response planning, using topic sentence scaffolds: 💡

Syal presents Meena as:

- feeling guilty
- experiencing intense and sudden anxiety
- catastrophising.

Unpacking quotations and the language therein to support points like this might look like: 🔍

Syal presents Meena as experiencing intense and sudden anxiety at the realisation that she may have played a part in Mrs Christmas's death alongside the far more powerful Anita: she describes the feeling hitting her 'in the solar plexus' – an image full of violent force and aggression. There is an irony not lost on the reader here that, up until this point, Meena has been presented by the writer as longing to be accepted and liked by the older girl, but now that possibility brings her only dread and thoughts of 'Sin' and guilt. Syal is perhaps commenting here on the vulnerability and naivety of youth, drawing parallels between Meena's actions and those of her father with the bomb.

CHAPTER 5 OF ANITA AND ME

At a glance

- **Chapter summary quotation:** 'But no one seemed to care that today was our Christmas' (p. 91)
- **Big Questions:** How does the process of othering take place in this chapter? How does Meena feel torn between two worlds?
- **Significant plot event:** Meena breaks into the Big House estate, discovers a statue of Ganesha and misplaces mama's diamond necklace.
- **Character focus:** Papa, Meena
- **Key themes:**
  - Racism
  - Family discipline and guidance
  - Friendship
- **Handle with care:**
  - Reference to a range of racially offensive terms in this chapter will need to be handled with sensitivity. Please refer to the 'Handle with care' guidance in the 'How to use this book' section for further support.
    - 'Nigger' (p. 90) – the name of the Rutters' dog
    - 'wog' (p. 97)
    - 'gippos' (p. 102)
    - 'tinkers' (p. 102).

Why?

'Why' is important not only within the world of the text, but also when considering authorial intent and messaging.

- Why does Meena not have the 'courage' to take 'sides against Anita', even when she recognises that she 'played off one girlfriend against another' and is regularly made to feel 'invisible' (p. 88)?

- Meena will 'stand open-mouthed in admiration' (p. 104), trying to conform, with her changed language, intentional use of makeup, acts of rebellion and decision to stand by Anita's side. Why does she do this when Anita shows disinterest in her cultural celebration, is repeatedly dismissive of her, scares her with fanciful tales about witches peering into her bedroom and does not even introduce her to Dave, the Poet?
- Why also does Syal explore incidents of racism, both intentional and casual, through the lens of both cultures, and what effect does this have on Meena's sense of belonging?
- Why does Meena choose not to share the burden of the 'othering' that she experiences with her father?
- Why does she choose to move away from Auntie Shaila and stand with Cara instead towards the end of the chapter?
- The Big House is depicted with the 'sense of menace surrounding the place' and no sign of 'visitors' (p. 100). How significant is the intertextuality and connection with Boo Radley's house in *To Kill a Mockingbird* here? Does Syal do this to emphasise the impact that collective ostracisation can have on sensibilities? Is this, perhaps, to make us consider the relentless process of 'othering' and its continued ability to fracture societies?
- Why is this chapter important, therefore, with its consistent references to the juxtaposing worlds that pull Meena in different directions, and the epiphanic incidents that begin to awaken her sense of identity and maturity?

This allows us to consider Chapter 5's Big Questions:

> How does the process of othering take place in this chapter? How does Meena feel torn between two worlds?

What?
What happens?

This chapter is about confronting societal pressures, ranging from racial prejudice to gendered expectations, and how Meena's two worlds collide in the process. We learn that the Rutter family acquires a 'stringy black poodle' (p. 89) that Deidre starts to refer to using a racially offensive slur. From this moment onwards, Meena's mother decidedly treats Deidre with a pretence of politeness, yet detachment.

Anita and Meena, who have been avoiding each other through 'unspoken mutual understanding' finally meet in 'late October' when Anita knocks on her door on the day of Diwali, 'the Hindu festival of light' (p. 91). Meena is 'stunned' by everyone's 'indifference' to the celebration (p. 92), beginning to appreciate her parents' concerted efforts to celebrate Christmas for Meena to experience a sense of belonging. We learn in this chapter the nuances around Meena's religious identity as we revisit a transformative trip in the past to the nearest gurudwara in an attempt to connect Meena with her religious values and roots (p. 94). What follows is an unfortunate incident where Meena experiences microaggressions, feeling othered through the way they are observed, 'coping with the complexities of the modern world' (p. 87). This is followed by a blunt and brutal racist incident that serves as an epiphanic moment for Meena, a moment she tries, but fails, to share with her father, suddenly aware of the years of marginalisation he would have endured. Instead, she ends up feeling 'hurt, angry, confused, and horribly powerless because this kind of racism could not be explained' (p. 98).

As the Diwali celebrations and the local fair take place simultaneously, significant parallels are brought to light. Meena visits the fair with Anita twice, initially with permission, and later on in the evening as an act of rebellion. On the way to the fair, Anita scares Meena with a story about a witch at The Big House, dismissing the 'loads of prayers' Meena proposes to use as protection (p. 101). Joining Sherrie and Fat Sally, they draw the attention of three 'young blokes', potentially adults, who stop work to observe them, 'pouted to attention, flicking their hair' with their heavily made-up faces (p. 103). Meena is fascinated at Anita's ability to make the men laugh and marvels at Anita's lack of conscience as she announces, 'I'm having the tall one', referring to 'Dave, the Poet' (p. 103). Increasingly uncomfortable with the sexual innuendos that she fails to understand, and the over-familiar interaction as Anita starts to share a cigarette with Dave, Meena runs back home to the Diwali festivities where her mother, fairly early on in her pregnancy, is showing signs of exhaustion.

At the Diwali mehfil, a traditional music celebration, Meena stuns the room into 'complete silence' (p. 113) for parroting a vulgar expression that she has picked up from Anita ('I could shag the arse off it'), and subsequently sneaks out, taking her mother's diamond necklace with her. At the fair, she sees Deidre pull the Poet 'into the caravan' and recognises this as a moment she 'could not leave Anita alone' (p. 122). On the way home, Anita insists on a detour and breaks into the grounds of the Big House, against Meena's feeble protests, who complies, obeying Anita against her own sense of prudence. On the grounds, Meena is drawn to a 'bust of some kind', 'mounted on a plinth' (p. 126), and surprisingly discovers it to be the statue of the Indian 'elephant god, Ganesha' (p. 127). Hearing 'mad, ragged barking' in the distance (p. 127), both escape in panic and Meena loses her mother's necklace in the process. She returns home to find her mother 'lying on a stretcher' being taken away in an ambulance as both communities gather in solidarity (p. 129). Her parting words to Meena, 'Meena, look after papa' (p. 129), as Meena 'pulls away' from Auntie Shaila and chooses to stand next to Cara instead (p. 130).

Social, cultural and historical context

It is important for learners to fully understand, appreciate and be able to realistically envisage life in the fictional village of Tollington in 1972 for Meena. They may require pre-teaching activities on the following features of social, cultural and historical context so they can write about them confidently.

The following are some useful topics or terms to consider when discussing the context of this chapter with learners:

- **Partition of Punjab and the religious communities in India**: refer to contextual timeline, page 201 of this guide.
- **Celebration of Diwali, the festival of new beginnings and the triumph of light over darkness**: an important religious and cultural celebration for Meena and her family.
- **1970s working class miners' village, including reference to Hollow Ponds**: 'the deep water-filled old mine shafts', and the threat it poses, resulting in the death of four-year-old Jodie Bagshot and 'a dumb sense of shame that Tollington had finally been put on the map in this tainted way.' (p. 100).

Vocabulary in context

The following vocabulary from Chapter 5 can be pre-taught to help with reading fluency and reduce cognitive load. What does each of the following words mean in context?

Word	Quotation	Definition
aarti (n.)	'I never saw mama or papa bow their heads in prayer or sing one of the minor key aartis' (p. 93)	a Hindu religious ritual where a song is sung in praise of a deity
beatific (adj.)	'Aartis that Auntie Shaila would regularly perform with closed eyes and a long suffering, beatific look' (p. 93)	expressing holy bliss
gurudwara (n.)	'declared that she was taking me to the gurudwara in Birmingham the very next day' (p. 94)	Sikh place of worship, literally meaning home of the guru (teacher and founder of Sikh religion, Guru Nanak)
caste system (n.)	'We Sikhs do not believe in the caste system at all' (p. 94)	developed in Hindu societies in India, it is a rigid social structure in which social class is determined by heredity
mehfil (n.)	'My parents were celebrating it, as they celebrated nearly everything else, with a mehfil.' (p. 98)	a social gathering, often in intimate settings and common in some parts of South Asia, where recreational activities such as poetry ('mushaira'), classical Indian singing and music are enjoyed

cosseted (v.)	'I felt babyish and cosseted, wrapped up in my hooded anorak and thick socks' (p. 99)	protected and cared for in an overindulgent way
cache (n.)	'I spotted mama's hidden cache of makeup' (p. 107)	a collection of items of the same type stored in a hidden or inaccessible place
renegades (n., pl.)	'This crocodile of renegades moved slowly' (p. 109)	a person who deserts and betrays an organisation, country, or set of principles
vermillion (adj.)	'A streak of vermillion silk exposed by a winter coat' (p. 109)	a vivid reddish-orange pigment
ghazal (n.)	'Papa leafed through his tattered notebook containing ghazal lyrics' (p. 109)	a lyric poem from Middle Eastern or Indian literature with a fixed number of verses, typically on the theme of love and often set to music (pronounced 'guzzle')
harmonium (n.)	'my papa began tuning up the harmonium in the room below' (p. 113)	one of the most used percussion instruments in South Asia – it is a keyboard instrument that is a lot like an organ, with notes produced by air driven through metal reeds (thin pieces of metal)
diyas (n., pl)	'Ganesha [...] surrounded by incense sticks, diyas' (p. 127)	a small cup-shaped oil lamp made of baked clay

PIT STOP

Retrieval point

Return to this vocabulary in a later lesson, assessing if learners can link each key word to the relevant character(s). For a bonus point, develop each link into an analysis of how the writer's language choice presents that character.

Examples:

- How might the mention of the mehfil provide a cultural bridge in the novel? Consider the description of the atmosphere and the interactions juxtaposed against the interactions and entertainment at the fair. What is the appeal for Meena and is she able to truly enjoy both?

- What might Syal's depiction of Auntie Shaila's regular performance of aartis, 'with closed eyes and a long suffering, beatific look' reveal? Is this depiction reflective of her sincerity of worship or representative instead of Meena's perception of feigned sincerity?

- What do we learn about how Meena views and feels about their guests, moving through the 'couples' at the fair, when she uses the phrase 'crocodile of renegades' to describe them?

> **PIT STOP**
>
> ## Direct instruction point
>
> Introduce the process of racial othering with a brief reference to literary theory: the idea of the creation of the 'self' or 'in-group', and its impact on Meena's developing identity. Meena begins the chapter, frustrated that no one seems to care about Diwali, and ends it physically distancing herself from her community. In order for learners to understand this, discuss with them the use of racial slurs and their impact on Meena. Refer back to the 'Handle with care' advice in 'How to use this book' to discuss the impact of the following incidents:
>
> - Deidre's naming of the family dog and the resonance with the film, *The Dam Busters*.
> - The name of the colour in the paint shop.
> - 'You ask any man on the street to tell the difference between us and a Jamaican fellow, he will still see us as the same colour' (p. 90).
> - Marginalisation across communities and social groups – a reference to the caste system, description of Cara, Meena's reference to the 'day-to-day bullying' of 'the fatties, spotties, the swots and naturally, the [...] non-white children' (p. 118).
> - Meena's experience of racial othering when the seemingly charitable attitude of the drivers creates a power imbalance as she is made to feel inferior and less capable, followed by her first experience of blunt hostility and direct racism: 'None of them looked like they wanted to be related to me' (p. 96); 'Bloody stupid wog. Stupid woggy wog. Stupid' (p. 97).
> - Anita's overtly racist references to the nomadic workers, the 'travelling people' (p. 102): 'Them's gippos, them is. Tinkers. Yow'll catch summat' (p. 102) in contrast to Meena's open-minded interest.
> - Gary's superficial judgement as he shows a preference for Fat Sally, suggesting that Meena is so unattractive that Fat Sally appeals by contrast.
> - Ostracization of the Big House, later revealed to house a statue of Ganesha: 'sense of menace surrounding the place'; 'no one ever saw visitors' (p. 100).
> - The impact of 'othering' as Meena begins to see her guests as 'crocodile of renegades' juxtaposed against 'couples' at the fair (p. 109).

> **PIT STOP**
>
> ### Academic writing point
>
> Introduce the concept of 'marginalisation' and the process of 'othering', building on the impact of dichotomies from the previous chapter before exploring the structural juxtaposition of the community celebrating Diwali and the communities enjoying the fair. This will allow learners to take a critical approach to answering the Big Questions: **How does the process of othering take place in this chapter? How does Meena feel torn between two worlds?**

> **PIT STOP**
>
> ### S-T-R-E-T-C-H
>
> What could an alternative reading of Meena's growing disconnect with her community be? Could this be more about 'coming-of-age' and her desperation to conform to the gendered behaviours she witnesses in the interactions of her peers?

Plot and character development

For tips on how to approach these 'What' questions, refer to the 'Plot and character development' section of 'How to use this book' on pages 5-6 of this guide.

1. **What does the reader learn about the way Anita treats her friends in this chapter?**

   Example responses:
   - often 'play(s) off one girlfriend against another' (p. 88) – her obsession with having power over others is evident from the outset
   - shifts focus to self, boasting about her mother supposedly buying her a pony for Christmas and her plans to share an apartment with Sherrie in London, as soon as Meena informs her about Diwali
   - scares Meena, telling her the witch from the Big House can see into her bedroom
   - abruptly points at Fat Sally's lips as soon as she meets her, asks for her 'Minner's Lip Gloss', 'Giz sum', grabs it and starts 'smearing over her lips' (p. 103)
   - declares to everyone who she is 'having' to herself: 'I'm having the tall one, right?' (p. 103)

- asserts her authority and power: 'This is the captain of your ship, your soul speaking' (p. 103)
- huddles in a group, ignoring Meena: 'I might as well have been invisible' (p. 105)
- does not even introduce Meena to Dave
- impressed when Meena puts on a Yard accent
- kisses Dave in front of Meena for her benefit
- intimidates Meena into compliance so they can trespass: 'Yow don't know the way I know so shurrup' (p. 123); 'I thought yow said yow wanted to hand around with uz?' (p. 124).

2. What does the reader learn about the religious history in India and how does it impact the Kumars?

Example response:

The Kumars celebrate Christmas so that Meena would not feel 'left out' (p. 92). They consider their openness to 'mark Jesus' birthday' a result of their core values, and the reason 'so many religions happily coexisted in India – Buddhism, Christianity, Judaism, Sikhism and especially Islam' (p. 92). They focus on instilling the message that 'Every path leads to the same god' (p. 92), although it seems that not everyone they know seems to agree; the Aunties and Uncles clearly pass remarks suggesting that they might not share the sentiments. Auntie Shaila is especially concerned when she learns that Meena is a 'regular visitor to Uncle Alan's Sunday school' (p. 92) and her comments seem to juxtapose the 'Hindu tolerance' (p. 92) that Meena's parents believe to be universal: 'All that boring sitting around and amen this and that, no joy and those damn hard seats and that awful organ music, like a donkey in pain' (p. 92). It's clear that Meena's father's upbringing isn't as religious as Auntie Shaila's, partly due to his father's communist beliefs and there seems to be an underlying distrust for what people can do 'in the name of religion' (p. 92). Meena on the other hand longs for that connection and 'continually' mourns the 'fact' that they did not 'have a shrine' (p. 93).

PIT STOP

S-T-R-E-T-C-H

To what extent do you think Auntie Shaila's emotions are motivated by fear, rather than intolerance? Is she more concerned about how it might 'confuse' the children's religious identity, something she is desperate to cultivate as a first-generation migrant?

CHAPTER 5 OF ANITA AND ME

3. What does the reader learn in the chapter about Deidre's relationship with Anita?

Example response:

Although Meena is 'impressed' that 'Anita's mother has brought her to the fair' (p. 121), we learn very quickly that Deidre, seen patting her perm and looking bored, is actually there for her own gratification. She behaves as her daughter's romantic rival, in a shockingly reckless and self-centred manner. Distracting Anita with 'some money', which Anita takes with 'grateful amazement' (p. 121), she disappears with the Poet, despite bearing witness to her daughter giving him a 'light kiss on the face' (p. 121). By the time Anita walks back, asking for her mother, Deidre has already 'pulled the Poet into the caravan' (p. 122).

4. What does the reader learn about the differences between the Diwali celebrations and the festivity at the fair?

Use this table as a scaffold to start a discussion by collaboratively filling in the gaps.

Focus of comparison	Diwali	The Fair
Entertainment	• Diwali is celebrated with a 'mehfil' (p. 71)	• a range of fairground rides • 'side show stalls offering such delights as a free goldfish with every fallen coconut' (p. 102)
Music	• Uncle Tendon playing '*tabla*' (p. 110) • 'tattered notebook containing ghazal lyrics' (p. 109) • 'as papa started singing [a romantic song], his rich vibrato climbed slowly up my spine' (p. 111)	• 'thumping soundtrack of a pop song, *One Two Three, Oh it's So Easy, Ba-by!* as my papa began tuning up his harmonium' (p. 109) • 'ear-splitting soundtrack of The Kinks' (p. 123)
Description of people	• 'crocodile of renegades' (p. 109) • 'my elders [...] so shiny and joyous' (p. 112) • 'The men [...] divided up into two distinct groups [...] smoked and joked and retired to women-free corners' (p. 110)	• 'couples drawn by the music and lights' (p. 109)
Description of clothes	• 'I felt I was drowning in a sea of rustling saris, clinking gold jewellery and warm, brown, overpowering flesh' (p. 110) • 'witty men in crisp suits' (p. 110)	
Description of food		• 'toffee apples' (p. 122) • 'bags of chips' (p. 122)

> **PIT STOP**
>
> **S-T-R-E-T-C-H**
>
> What might Syal be trying to suggest with the juxtaposition of these two celebrations in the chapter and their impact on Meena? To what extent are these descriptions a reflection of how Meena feels in the moment and how does that influence her reliability as a narrator?

5. What does the reader learn about Auntie Shaila, and why does Meena distance herself from her towards the end?

Example response:

- Meena describes Auntie Shaila as the 'fattest, noisiest, and most fun of all the Aunties' (p. 74), yet we see in this chapter that her relationship with Auntie Shaila begins to evolve.
- Auntie Shaila releases a 'shriek of alarm' on seeing Meena open the door with makeup on; 'What is this? Looking like a rumpty tumpty dancing girl already' (p. 108).
- 'Auntie Shaila spoke carefully, as if addressing an idiot [...] Tonight is for grown-ups. Please no naughtiness' (p. 109).
- Although not intended to be hurtful, she comments on how Meena sings in Punjabi with a Birmingham accent when Meena is already insecure about her Indian identity.
- Meena's mother chooses to confide in Auntie Shaila about the frequency of her 'misdemeanours' (p. 117) and Auntie Shaila pronounces it as attention-seeking behaviour.
- She 'wordlessly' grabs Meena's arm and pulls her towards the kitchen to protect her from seeing her mama in distress (p. 129).
- She refuses Mrs Worrall's offer to help: 'Drew herself up, her triple chins wobbling in indignation' (p. 130), and blames the situation on 'this bloody country' (p. 130), upon which Meena pulls away and goes to stand next to Cara instead.

> **PIT STOP**
>
> **S-T-R-E-T-C-H**
>
> What role does Auntie Shaila play in the Kumar's lives and to what extent is her depiction unreliable through the lens of Meena, the child narrator?

6. What does the Big House symbolise to Meena?

Example response:

Meena recognises the symbolism of the Big House in this chapter: 'which from my bedroom window looked distant and symbolic' (p. 123), playing on her fantastical imagination, almost gothic-like with its sense of mystery and intrigue. Anita's stories about the witch at the house peering into Meena's window further elevate the fear and paranoia she experiences, and her resistance to trespass is therefore unsurprising. However, as she draws closer and sees the 'chandelier out of a fairy story' (p. 125), she is hit by its extravagance and sees it as a temptation, a sneak preview of a world that promises a life of liberation and power, leaving her with a 'sharp aftertaste' that makes her 'hungry and resentful all at once' (p. 126).

> **PIT STOP**
>
> ### S-T-R-E-T-C-H
>
> Can learners research and compare this to the depiction and significance of Boo Radley's house in *To Kill a Mockingbird*?

How?

Language

Narrative voice

Explore the unreliability of the narrative voice by analysing the following:

- The variations in Meena's description of the mehfil and musical entertainment at different stages in the day.
- The variations in Meena's description of the guests at different stages in the celebration.

Music/dance imagery

Key quotations:

- 'As papa began singing, his rich vibrato climbed slowly up my spine. I knew this song, a romantic song, naturally, of a lover singing to his beloved' (p. 111)
- 'Uncle Tendon joined in with a soft heartbeat accompaniment and a collective sigh of longing swelled the air' (p. 111)
- 'These were my versions of their stories and I set them free during papa's songs' (p. 112)

- 'Papa's singing always unleashed these emotions which were unfamiliar and instinctive [...] in a language I could not recognise but felt I could speak in my sleep, in my dreams, evocative of a country I have never visited but which sounded like the only home I had known...' (p. 112).

Syal continues to use the motif of music to symbolise not only the sanctity of artistic expression, but also to showcase how the Kumars keep alive the folk tradition of songs and ghazals from their Indian heritage. It is fascinating to see the almost trance-like state of communal enjoyment, emphasised through the sensory explosion, described to resonate with beating hearts as Uncle Tendon joins in with his tabla, and Meena, illustrated through the asyndetic listing, begins to re-imagine the stories of those around her. The music serves not only to connect her to her sense of culture and roots, as what she imagines is almost akin to the rich imagery and story-telling of Bollywood films, but also reveals her freedom of spirit and the vivaciousness of her imagination. The music allows Meena to create existential meaning for herself, and we begin to notice how she relaxes into the evening, no longer drawing comparisons with the fair, but instead feeling at one with emotions 'unfamiliar', yet 'instinctive' (p. 112).

Ask learners to consider:

- How Meena's decision to sing the songs reveal her search for both self-expression and connection?
- How important the element of performance is to Meena as a form of self-expression, and where else in the novel we see her rising to the occasion and putting on a show?

Literary allusions (intertextuality)

Consider the symbolic significance of the following allusions:

- parallels drawn between Boo Radley's house and the Big House
- allusions to Bollywood tropes: 'My beaming admirers had become parodies of Hindi film villains' (p. 115).

Character focus

Papa

Key quotations:

- 'I have seen what we do in the name of religion [...] What I do and how I behave, will be in the name of humanity' (p. 93)
- 'a million of these encounters written in the lines around his warm, hopeful eyes, lurking in the furrows of his brow, shadowing the soft curves of his mouth. I suddenly realised that what had happened to me must have happened to papa countless times' (p. 98)
- 'not once had he ever shared his upset with me' (p. 98)
- 'Papa laughed, 'Leave her! It was very groovy, Meena!' (p. 115)

CHAPTER 5 OF ANITA AND ME

- 'It was papa, in a tone of voice I had not heard before, which shot right off the Outraged Parent clapometer' (p. 116).

Papa displays stoicism in the face of adversity. He champions Meena, and celebrates her experiments with self-expression. He takes a strong stance on discipline and instilling his moral values.

> **PIT STOP** ▼
>
> ### S-T-R-E-T-C-H
> Ask learners to explore how papa's outrage at Meena's use of language offsets his previous allowances, and what the extremity of his reaction might suggest about his own identity.

Meena

Key quotations:

- 'I had been born to the wrong type of Indian woman. If I had been given a mother like Auntie Shaila, the fat loud type who didn't mind the patches of sweat forming under their sari blouses [...] I would not have to feel so angry at my body [...] it was never meant to behave like the body of a lady' (p. 110)
- 'I wondered how many girls he had kissed and why he ever bothered to talk to me' (p. 120)
- 'wondering if this abuse was part and parcel of hanging around boys' (p. 120).

Meena has a growing intrigue and understanding of physical intimacy and relationships. She is also questioning her relationship with her mother and her body.

Structure

Learners should explore the following examples from the opening and the ending of Chapter 5 and be invited to consider:

- Why Syal has chosen to begin and end with this focus on the symbolism of the colour red?
- What the literal and metaphorical significance might be of the colour red?
- What their predictions might be about key characters and plot developments within this chapter?

Opening: 'Huge fat leaves of blood red and burnt gold covered every available surface' (p. 88).

Ending: 'A small pool of red lay like fallen poppies in the middle of the white groundsheet' (p. 129).

Extracts

1. How does Syal use language to develop a vivid presentation of the different types of 'Aunties' and 'Uncles' and why does Syal highlight this variation?

'The men, as usual, had divided up into two distinct groups [...] Mama was in the minority group of Auntie types' (p. 110).

Example response planning, using topic sentence scaffolds:

Syal presents the uncles and aunties as:

- a powerful collective
- secure in their almost familial and unfiltered relationships
- accomplished and self-assured
- 'self-effacing' and defined by their relationship with their spouses
- brazen in their intrusion into the lives of others
- confident and disinclined to listen
- purposeful, busy and full of energy
- loud and boisterous, 'bursting [...] with unsolicited advice'
- the epitome of grace and elegance
- carefully cultivated facades of stoicism.

Example response, unpacking quotations and language therein to support points:

Syal presents juxtaposing versions of the Aunties, both conforming to, and defying existing stereotypes. The women are generally presented as a powerful collective 'bursting with optimism and unsolicited advice'. The metaphorical references to the social role they play, both through their intrusion, as well as infectious displays of zealous energy, is a testament to the power and self-assurance they have. What's more, the security with which they operate, confident and accepting of their 'plump, bosomy' bodies, enhanced unapologetically in 'bright tight outfits' suggests an assuredness that is unparalleled. In contrast, the cultural allusion to 'Mughal miniature paintings' to describe Meena's mama and the 'minority group' she belongs to not only elucidates Syal's intentional dismantling of the stereotype of the 'Auntie', but also emphasises the extent of their strength, composure and stoicism, likened to 'Gandhiji himself'. Perhaps Syal adopts this unfiltered depiction to both challenge, and present a refreshing alternative, inviting the reader to interrogate any social conditioning and unconscious biases.

CHAPTER 6 OF ANITA AND ME

At a glance

- **Chapter summary quotation:** 'We will always have the children, the village mothers said, our only investment for the future, and then they sounded exactly like my Aunties' (p. 135)
- **Big Question:** How do relationships change after Sunil's birth?
- **Significant plot event:** Sunil is born and Meena starts to spend more time with Anita.
- **Character focus:** Meena, Meena and Anita's relationship, Meena and papa's relationship
- **Key themes:**
  - Change
  - Belonging
  - Friendship
- **Handle with care:**
  - Reference to suicide, disordered eating, sexual abuse and neglect in this chapter will need to be handled with sensitivity. Please refer to the 'Handle with care' guidance in the 'How to use this book' section for further support.
    - 'having spots was not a valid reason for suicide' (p. 137)
    - 'all of them featuring a limpid-eyed, anorexic blonde, heroine' (p. 137-8)
    - sexual abuse and neglect in reference to Tracey.

Why?

'Why' is important not only within the world of the text, but also when considering authorial intent and messaging.

BLOOMSBURY TEACHER GUIDE: ANITA AND ME

- Why does Syal allow Meena to finally develop the unrestrained relationship she's been longing for with Anita? Why use this moment, the pivotal moment of her brother's birth, 'tilting' her 'world slightly off its axis' (p. 138) and allow her to journey on this incremental shift in both her sense of identity and maturity? Is it to play with the age-old narrative of adolescent rebellion and pressures around sexual conformity? Is it to expose yet again how Meena, despite her best efforts, will always have to juggle conflicting value systems?
- Why does Syal use the children as the focal point for these narratives? Perhaps it is to remind us that it is the children who eventually suffer, torn between economic pressures, paternal expectations, raging hormones and changing landscapes.
- Why is this chapter important, therefore, for the readers to see Meena's slow but assured transition, from one realm of identity to another, all the while navigating her way through the murky back alleys of experience, leaving her innocence behind?

This allows us to consider Chapter 6's Big Question:

> How do relationships change after Sunil's birth?

What?
What happens? ☁

Sunil arrives with a dramatic birth story, having 'nearly ripped' his mother apart (p. 131), but heralded nonetheless for being the 'boy' who has finally made the 'family complete' (p. 131). As expected, Meena's centre of gravity shifts and the family adjusts, like all families do, to the arrival of a new member into their dynamic. Relationships change too, some welcome: 'Papa and I spent a few glorious mad weeks together' (p. 132). While others are less so: 'the mutual decision we made, mama and I, to forget each other temporarily and move on to other loves' (p. 135).

Sunil's arrival moves the Kumars into the limelight, as Tollington 'loved new babies' (p. 134) and the 'mothers in the village' start pouring in, 'bearing gifts or full of advice' (p. 135). Amidst this surge of community support, Meena begins to slip away, unnoticed. She spends more and more time with Anita, away from her protected world, and towards the 'gangs of no-hope teenagers' (p. 135), forming a gang of their own: the Wenches Brigade. The unrestrained time spent with Anita initiates Meena's metamorphosis: her awe and admiration that 'flowed from every pore' continues to intensify as Anita gives 'voice' to all the 'wicked things' she's often considered, but kept 'zipped up' (p. 138). We see Meena start to provoke boundaries, swapping *Twinkle* for *Jackie* magazine, accepting Anita's ridicule of Mrs Todd, someone who had never passed her 'without a radiant smile', and joining in with Anita's 'peeing competition' (p. 139). Even though Meena notices how 'those

CHAPTER 6 OF ANITA AND ME

you called friends suddenly become tormentors', she doesn't yet have the agency or conviction to stand up to this 'group hostility' (p. 142). She instead conforms, exacting it eventually on the unsuspecting Pinky and Baby, who she starts to see through Anita's lens as 'too easy a target' and 'mere hors d'oeuvres' (p. 151). She pins the blame on them for one of her most serious transgressions to date – the stealing of a charity tin.

Social, cultural and historical context

It is important for learners to fully understand, appreciate and be able to realistically envisage life in the fictional village of Tollington in 1972 for Meena. They may require pre-teaching activities on the following features of social, cultural and historical context so they can write about them confidently.

The following are some useful quotations to consider when discussing this context with learners.

- **Influence of industrialisation**: 'This new road linking up the industrial estate some twenty miles away and the motorway to Wolverhampton had been discussed for years' (p. 143); 'Protest march […] christened, Tollington in Turmoil!' (p. 143); 'Birmingham was about to explore with richness and vitality […] wouldn't everyone in Tollington want to be part of this Black Country Renaissance?' (p. 143).

- **Pop culture influences in the 1970s**: 'Turned to my oracle […] *Jackie* magazine' (p. 137); '*Jackie* was all about Boys; how to attract them, keep them, get rid of them […] where the highlighter actually goes, what Donny Osmond's favourite colour was' (p. 137).

- **Discrimination in maternal health**: 'When she cried out that she could feel every stitch when they were sewing her up, a sour-faced nurse told her to be grateful she was still alive and to shut it' (p. 132); 'They were the same when I had you, Meena. They left me in a room with a dirty blanket for ten hours. When I asked for drugs, the nurse said, 'Oh, you Asian ladies have a very low pain threshold."' (p. 132).

Vocabulary in context

The following vocabulary from Chapter 6 can be pre-taught to help with reading fluency and reduce cognitive load. What does each of the following words mean in context?

Word	Quotation	Definition
prodigal (n.)	'he had the face of a travel-weary prodigal' (p. 131)	someone who spends money in a reckless and extravagant manner
amorphous (adj.)	'a forgotten village in no man's land between a ten-shop town and an amorphous industrial sprawl' (p. 135)	without a clearly defined structure or form

BLOOMSBURY TEACHER GUIDE: ANITA AND ME

incongruous (adj.)	'Their sober respectability completely incongruous with their shocking carrot-coloured hair' (p. 136)	out of place; not in harmony with surroundings or other aspects of something
irreverence (n.)	'Her irreverence was high summer for me' (p. 138)	disrespect for people or things generally taken seriously
halcyon (adj.)	'the old mine would remain exactly what it was, a crumbling monument to a halcyon past' (p. 143)	denoting a period of time in the past that is idyllically remembered to be happy or prosperous

PIT STOP

Retrieval point

Return to this vocabulary in a later lesson, assessing if learners can link each key word to the relevant character(s). For a bonus point, develop each link into an analysis of how the writer's language choice presents that character.

Examples:

- How might Meena's rejection of Auntie Shaila's 'interminable five-course breakfast' (p. 133) convey emerging egocentrism? And what does it reveal about Auntie Shaila herself? Is she merely the interfering character that Meena portrays her to be?
- Why is Meena's fascination with Anita's 'irreverence' significant? What is the appeal to her of the rejection of societal norms and customs?
- What might Syal's depiction of the relished 'halcyon' past suggest about the significance of Tollington's mining history? How has it influenced its identity in the present?

PIT STOP

Direct instruction point

Understanding common features of regional variations in accent and dialect of the Black Country.

Learners use the following scaffold and the quotations included to discuss their thoughts on non-standard grammatical forms in English, and what the use of these variations indicate about the characters' sense of identity:

- h-dropping at the beginning of words
- non-rhotic pronunciation: 'r' sound isn't pronounced at the end of words and syllables
- vowel shifts

- consonant changes
- vocabulary and expressions
- 'th' sounds: might be pronounced 'f' or 'v'.

	Regional variation	Meaning
Expression	dead saucy	behaving in a very suggestive or cheeky manner
Vowel shift	gorra	got a
Expression	bostin	excellent/great
H-dropping	see er	see her

References to the history of the Black Country Renaissance and the subsequent changes in the landscape of the West Midlands in the 1960s:

- 'Wouldn't everyone in Tollington want to be part of the Black Country Renaissance?' (p. 143)
- 'Once there had been rumours that the old mine would be turned into variously a supermarket, a leisure centre, a baby clinic and a builder's yard' (p. 143)
- 'The promised Renaissance had taken a diversion somewhere round Wolverhampton and missed us out completely' (p. 143).

PIT STOP

Academic writing point

Revisit the concepts of 'belonging' and 'social identity' to allow learners to take a critical approach to answering the Big Question: **How do relationships change after Sunil's birth?**

PIT STOP

S-T-R-E-T-C-H

Ask learners to analyse the extent to which Sunil's birth might act as a catalyst in changing the Kumar's relationship with the Tollington community. Do they think this change in dynamics would have happened in due course, or was the arrival of a baby necessary to break barriers and advance it?

Plot and character development

For tips on how to approach these 'What' questions, refer to the 'Plot and character development' section of 'How to use this book' on pages 5–6 of this guide.

1. What can the reader infer from Meena's mother's experience of delivering Sunil?

Example responses:

- She decides not to tell Meena until 'much later on' (p. 132), possibly years, after her 'transformation from semi-divine icon to semi-detached confidante' (p. 132), perhaps to protect and shield her from the trauma and injustice.

- The birthing experience, life-changing as it is, is even more traumatising and isolating for racialised women who are othered when they are at their most vulnerable.

- Even though the distance between Meena and her mama grows after Sunil's birth, the relationship not only recovers in time, but perhaps grows stronger, as her mama looks back and shares her near-death experience, with her thoughts firmly focused on not wanting to leave Meena 'alone yet' (p. 132).

> **PIT STOP**
>
> **S-T-R-E-T-C-H**
>
> Ask learners to consider:
>
> - How important they think this revelation might be?
> - Is Syal's primary focus on social commentary by drawing attention to the stark disparity between the maternity experiences of women from ethnic minorities in Britain, or is it for the reader to recognise that there is still hope for Meena and her mama's relationship to be salvaged?

2. What does the reader learn about Deidre being in hospital?

Example response:

Just as Meena informs Anita about her mama in hospital, Anita too reveals that hers is well. What's interesting, however, is the lack of trust between Anita and her mother. She seems to doubt Deidre's version that her 'dad beat her up' and believes her father instead, that she 'pricked her arm with a dart' to make it look like abuse (p. 133). Meena decides that it must be because of the discovery of Deidre's 'lustful assignation with the Poet' (p. 133).

CHAPTER 6 OF ANITA AND ME

3. What does the reader learn about different types of customs and expectations in this chapter and what is their impact on Meena?

Possible quotations to start a discussion:

- The arrival of new baby: Auntie Shaila's 'interminable five-course breakfast' (p. 133); Mrs Worrall's 'ten exquisitely-embroidered matinee suits and several knitted woollies' (p. 134).
- Sam is seen peeing in the red telephone box and Hairy Neddy remarks: 'That ain't a crime. That's a bloody custom, ain't it?' (p. 136).
- Reference to gang culture: 'initiation ceremony'; 'whenever a stranger appeared, they had begun dividing themselves up into camps of differing loyalties'; earning of 'Wench Wings' (p. 137).
- Reference to popular culture: '*Jackie* was all about Boys; how to attract them, keep them, get rid of them (at least the ugly ones)' (p. 137).
- Reference to relationship customs: 'We did not have boyfriends, under any circumstances' (p. 133).
- Reference to identities: 'girls were always the same – pleasant, helpful, delicate, groomed, terrifying' (p. 149); 'So you think because you live here you can become like the gori girls? What's next? Boyfriends? Babies?' (p. 161).
- Reference to social customs: 'We kids, as usual, had been fed first' (p. 157); 'The Aunties and mama were lining up a battalion of plates for papa and the Uncles who hovered around the entrance of the kitchen like hopeful domestic pets at a banquet' (p. 157); 'cannot allow a guest to leave hungry' (p. 158).

Example response:

We see in this chapter how the pressure mounts on Meena to fit in with her peers, the 'Wenches Brigade' (p. 138), epitomised through the satisfaction she feels in earning her 'Wenches Wings' (p. 156), yet we also see her growing frustration with the divisive and increasingly harmful behaviour she is expected to be partisan to. To an extent, Meena does acquiesce, yet we also see the rise of a rebellion that she channels towards the perceived pressure to conform that looms above her. She was to stay away from 'swearing and urinating in telephone boxes […] like that Lowbridge boy' (p. 53), and she was always to be the 'pleasant, helpful, delicate' (p. 149) girl that even 'pensioners' would 'sigh and beam' at in 'approval' (p. 152). It isn't until later in the novel that Meena starts to move away from such polarisation and instead recognises the myriad of ways for her to be both English and Indian, with the freedom and agency to carve out her own identity once she realises she can claim any place as her own.

> **PIT STOP**
>
> **S-T-R-E-T-C-H**
>
> Ask learners to consider:
>
> - What Syal might be trying to suggest with the allusion to the similarities between Indian and English customs?
> - Why is Meena not positioned to celebrate these at this stage in the novel?

4. What does the reader learn about Tracey in this chapter?

Example response:

Consistently presented by Syal to juxtapose her rebellious and antagonistic older sister, we are able to contextualise in this chapter why she is presented as reclusive and emotionally vulnerable. Intimidated by Anita to join in the 'peeing contest', we discover abhorrent signs of abuse and neglect: 'the top of her legs looked like sticks of lard, thin without muscle tone, neglected' (p. 141). Tracey experiences unparalleled hostility and ostracism when she refuses to join in the 'peeing contest', eventually succumbing only to reveal a horrifying truth that she is a victim of abuse, the 'row of bruises' around her 'thighs' suggested to be sexual, and possibly by her father, as Meena notices the 'imprint of ten cruel, angry fingers' (p. 142).

> **PIT STOP**
>
> **S-T-R-E-T-C-H**
>
> Ask learners to analyse:
>
> - To what extent Anita's fascination with sex might be a reaction to her experiences within her own household?

5. What does the construction of the motorway symbolise to the villagers of Tollington?

Example response:

'Suspicion takes over' soon as the news of the new road 'linking up the industrial estate' to the 'motorway to Wolverhampton' is received (p. 143). The idea of a 'motorway extension which would cut through fields' is terrifying and threatening, even to the 'posh detached houses' (p. 143). Meena remembers this to be a fear that even precedes the arrival of the Kumars to the village, resulting in a protest march led by Uncle Alan. This was dismissed by the authorities, who don't even 'quake' (p. 143) at the expression of resistance. Instead, the 'promised Renaissance' takes a 'diversion' where nothing changes in Tollington, 'except children were

CHAPTER 6 OF ANITA AND ME

turning into teenagers, teenagers were getting married and quietly moving away to where the jobs were supposed to be' (p. 142). Therefore to the villagers, this road represents broken promises. It represents change that is unwelcome, change that is happening against their wills, and change that is not turning their fortunes for the better. This reminds them even more of their 'halcyon [mining] past' (p. 142) which at least brought with it livelihood and a sense of community.

> **PIT STOP**
>
> ### S-T-R-E-T-C-H
>
> Ask learners to consider the impact that such powerlessness, resulting from structural problems of industrialisation and unemployment, might have on the relationships within the Tollington community.

How?

Language

Narrative voice

Key quotations:

- 'When I say we talked, what I mean is Anita talked and I listened' (p. 138)
- 'I wanted to say, leave it, leave her alone, but she wasn't my sister, was she?' (p. 141).

The increasingly introspective and conversational nature of the narrative voice in this chapter affords the reader a deeper personal connection with Meena, especially at the time of key moments of transition in this Bildungsroman. It functions as a tool that not only invites them to witness, but also engage with Meena's inner thoughts, filled with layers of subtext. She is navigating through the complexity of a teenage friendship with an obvious power imbalance, and more importantly, a moral dilemma where the underlying desperation to alleviate her guilt forces the reader to shift from a position of passivity to one where they are invested, and full of concern.

Irony

Key quotation:

- Meena's mother expresses concern about Meena speaking like an 'urchin' and 'swearing and urinating in telephone boxes [...] like that Lowbridge boy' (p. 53).

In this chapter, we are reminded of her words, which resonate ironically as Meena begins her linguistic rebellion. Not only does Sam urinate in a telephone booth, but Meena too complies and participates in the 'pissing competition' too. Syal therefore uses irony as a vehicle for social commentary, highlighting the absurdity of Meena's mama's restrictions on her linguistic identity and how it in fact pushes her away instead. It also highlights the impact of being disenfranchised and its subsequent rebellion that is no longer exclusively associated with the youth of Tollington, but with Meena as well.

Use of dialect and accent

Key quotations:

- 'Even Pinky's voice set my teeth on edge […] lilt of Punjabi in it, the over-pronunciation of the consonants, the way every sentence rose at the end so everything became a question' (p. 151)
- 'Coz this ain't naff old Wolverhampton anymore' (p. 152)
- 'Anita mocked her in a bad parody of Pinky's accent' (p. 156)
- 'Yow'm a real Wench. That was bostin what yow did' (p. 156).

Syal's use of accent and dialect is skilfully rendered in this chapter to highlight not only Meena's active attempts at assimilation and need for acceptance, but also those of her rejection of a linguistic identity that makes her more 'Indian' than 'English'. She purposefully employs colloquialisms reflecting the working-class Black Country influences, experimenting with her 'Yard' accent to win Anita's favour, whilst also alienating and distancing herself from Pinky and Baby. What's interesting is how Syal uses Meena's reflections of the Indian accent to shed light on existing biases and prejudices, calling them into question as the reader is made uncomfortable with what could be perceived as Meena turning on her own. The irony, however, is unmissable, drawing a sharp contrast to how Meena's mama reprimands Meena on her linguistic accommodation in Chapter 3, banning even the use of the mere colloquialism to refer to a sandwich: 'Just because the English can't speak English themselves does not mean you have to talk like an urchin' (p. 53). Ultimately, Syal draws our attention back to the topic of identity, and its interconnectedness with Meena's linguistic transformation, a transformation that symbolises her need to belong in Tollington and her desperation to reject the idea of what she perceives as cultural conformity.

Character focus

Meena

Key quotations:

- 'Dear Cathy and Claire, I am brown […] Will this stop me getting a guy?' (p. 145)
- 'I wanted to shed my body like a snake slithering out of its skin and emerge reborn' (p. 146)

- 'Now I thought of myself, a hurried visitor to our dinner table […] like a long-suffering houseguest, and where I wanted to belong' (p. 148)
- 'Childhood, something I was desperate to wrap in rags and leave on someone's doorstep with a note, Take it Away' (p. 148)
- 'I knew I was a freak of some kind, too mousy, clumsy and scabby to be a real Indian girl, too Indian to be a real Tollington wench' (p. 150)
- 'I had earned my Wench Wings without even trying, and it had been so simple and natural, and what thrilled me most of all was that I did not feel at all guilty or ashamed' (p. 156).

Meena is crafted by Syal here as the epitome of someone pressured to assimilate, rejecting her perceived 'Indianness' in a desperate attempt to conform, and belong. Her growing intrigue with her body and physical intimacy is also reflective of the beginnings of her transition from innocence to experience.

Meena and Anita's relationship

Key quotations:

- changing dynamics: 'Anita and I were now officially "mates"' (p. 135)
- power imbalance: 'When I said we talked, what I mean is Anita talked and I listened' (p. 138)
- catalyst for transition from innocence to experience: 'Anita told me the facts of life' (p. 144)
- connection and belonging: 'My life was outside the home, with Anita, my passport to acceptance' (p. 148)
- absence of authenticity and depth: 'Sometimes when I looked into her eyes, all I could see and cling to was my own questioning reflection' (p. 150).

Syal's representation invites the learners to analyse this perceived 'friendship' as one that is undoubtedly superficial, forged out of Meena's desperation to conform and belong.

Meena and papa's relationship

Key quotations:

- 'Papa and I spent a few glorious mad weeks together […] sent to school in crumpled uncoordinated clothes' (p. 132)
- 'Best of all, papa never stopped me hanging around with Anita' (p. 132)
- 'You talked to me. Why have you stopped?' (p. 147)
- 'I felt wrong-footed and bewildered' (p. 147)
- 'Life isn't all ha-ha-hee-hee with your friends' (p. 150)
- 'The next morning he did not look at me, and when Anita came calling at the back gate, he picked up his newspaper and left the kitchen, slamming the door behind him' (p. 161).

Despite caring deeply and being well-intentioned, in this chapter we see papa's efforts to connect with Meena go in vain as he fails to recognise the source of her frustrations and the internal conflicts she battles with. Instead of resolving and reconciling through conversation, he resorts to being emotionally withdrawn, which does nothing to narrow the growing distance between him and his daughter.

Structure

Learners should explore the following examples from the opening and the ending of Chapter 6 and be invited to consider:

- Why Syal has chosen to begin and end with this focus on Meena and papa's relationship?
- What their predictions might be about key characters and plot developments within this chapter.

Opening: 'Papa and I spent a few glorious mad weeks together when we had tinned spaghetti hoops and biscuits for breakfast' (p. 131).

Ending: 'I could not sleep that night and apparently neither could papa' (p. 161).

Ask learners to consider:

- What Syal is suggesting about papa's parenting skills and abilities at the beginning of the chapter and to what extent do they matter to Meena's perception of him?
- In what ways papa's detachment from Meena at the end of the chapter is different to Deidre's detachment from Anita?

Motif of lying

Key quotation:

- 'Meena, I am going to ask you something and you had better not lie' (p. 158).

Ask learners to consider:

- In what ways is Meena's purpose for lying different to her decision to lie at the beginning of the novel? Can it be justified at all?
- In what ways is Meena's purpose of lying reflective of Anita's bad influence and the lengths she will go to for self-preservation?

Extracts

1. How does Syal use language to develop a vivid presentation of the different types of gangs in Tollington?

'We would all have liked to be part of Sam Lowbridge's Tollington Rebels, a group of affectedly bored bikers [...] Anita's contribution was a pile of back copies of *Jackie*, a teenage magazine which formed the basis of my sex education for years' (p. 136–7).

Example response planning, using topic sentence scaffolds:

Syal presents the different gangs as:

- victims of the lack of social mobility
- disenfranchised individuals seeking belonging
- keen to indulge in gratuitous expressions of violence
- building 'communities' on the premise of exclusion
- unafraid to exhibit unfiltered and pure hostility
- representative of 'mob' mentality
- evidence of the generational complexities and tensions.

Example response, unpacking quotations and language therein to support points:

Syal develops vivid descriptions of the different types of gangs in this chapter to highlight the concept of 'mob' mentality. The gangs, as a collective, epitomise teenage rebellion and mischief, whilst also representing the power of peer relationships in shaping individual decisions and behaviours. We see this through the use of the mental verb 'encouraged', as Anita plays a coercive role in pushing Meena to transgress. Moreover, the violent, dynamic verb 'ransack' demonstrates that the extent of this influence. It not only results in the exploitation of the individual, but also impacts the general community through this blatant insistence on absolute violence. It's a reminder of the challenges faced by adolescents when peer expectations clash with personal autonomy, serving as a microcosm of the broader pressures enforced on individuals to assimilate into the dominant culture.

CHAPTER 7 OF ANITA AND ME

At a glance

- **Chapter summary quotation:** 'But if Tollington was a footnote in the book of the Sixties, then my family and friends were the squashed flies in the spine' (p. 165)
- **Big Question:** How does this chapter explore the difficulties of living as a minority?
- **Significant plot event:** At the village fete, Anita and Meena have their fortunes told, and Sam Lowbridge challenges the decision to spend the fete's earnings in a racist outburst.
- **Character focus:** The Pembridges, Sunil, mama, Meena and Anita's relationship
- **Key themes:**
  - Racism
  - Othering
  - Friendship
- **Handle with care:**
  - Reference to a range of racially offensive terms in this chapter will need to be handled with sensitivity. Please refer to the 'Handle with care' guidance in the 'How to use this book' section for further support.
    - 'No Irish, Blacks or Dogs' (p. 165)
    - 'darkies' (p. 193)
    - 'wogs' (p. 193).

Why?

'Why' is important not only within the world of the text, but also when considering authorial intent and messaging.

- Why does this chapter begin with hope (the promise that spring brings, the reminder of the community hidden behind 'shut doors' (p. 162)) coming together at the Spring Fete against the romantic, 'mythical' notion of the Swinging Sixties (p. 164)?

- Why does Syal use the platform of community celebration to create even more dichotomies for the reader to critique? For example, the Mad Mitchells vs the Pembridges, Reverend Ince vs Uncle Alan, and those who are tolerant vs those who are not. Perhaps because we as readers need to see contrasts to appreciate disparities, and hidden within these contrasts are recognisable human attributes, seen across cultures and histories.

- Why does Syal bring our attention to the footnotes of the history books, to those ignored, marginalised and rendered voiceless? Is it meant to act as a reminder of the stories that are documented in history, and the stories that are not, and what it feels like to be made invisible when you don't belong in the dominant narrative? Is it to remind us what can happen when you disenfranchise a community, an identity, altogether, disregarding their frustrations and 'sensibilities'?

- Why does Syal choose to have Sam and his gang change and retaliate in the way that they do? Is it to bring our attention back to the victims like Auntie Usha whose 'revolutions were quieter and often unwitnessed' (p. 165), left to endure in silence, left to deal with their trauma in isolation, turned away from opportunities and barricaded with closed doors: 'No Irish, Blacks or Dogs.' (p. 165)?

In a time of a changing cultural, economic and political landscape, we are reminded through Meena what it feels like to be ignored. This allows us to consider Chapter 7's Big Question:

> How does this chapter explore the difficulties of living as a minority?

What?

What happens?

This chapter is about change, and the resistance to it, as we are ironically reminded by the motto on the Pembridge's house: 'Semper Eaden', meaning 'Always the Same' (p. 167). It begins with the promise of change and the hope that spring brings, that something 'clean and brand new was about to happen' (p. 163), yet reminds us of the darkness lurking in the corners. At the start, we see the Tollington community coming together from behind 'shut doors' (p. 162) and embracing spring 'with soapy red arms' (p. 163). The community are vigorously socialising and celebrating the arrival of change, yet the Mad Mitchells remain in their bubble of isolation, the target of all the 'tut-tut[ting]' (p. 163) and local gossip. Syal then walks us through iconic moments of the Swinging Sixties, amidst Meena's reflections on how Tollington seems to have bypassed it altogether. Here, minority communities like hers are 'squashed [like] flies in the spine' (p. 165), and the only representation she does see is 'someone else's version of Indian, far too exaggerated and exotic to be believable' (p. 165). Still, 'spring in the village' is a joyous occasion for her, a time 'always welcome and always celebrated with […] the Tollington Spring Fete' (p. 166). It is the only 'organised, communal' (p. 166) event that brings forth celebration and community, with the wholesome blossoming of relationships: Hairy Neddy proposes to Sally, and Uncle Alan has a reflective and inclusive conversation with papa. The event, however, is not without undercurrents of friction and even some animosity: Uncle Alan's visionary approach is at odds with the more restrictive and rigid stances taken by Mr Ormerod and the Reverend; the Pembridge family add to the tension with their internal dynamics and obvious discontent for each other; and Sam Lowbridge displays an aggressive demeanour and eventually disrupts the festivities; all culminating in racist vitriol.

In its exploration of change, this chapter also brings to light racism in its different forms, reminding us of unchanged mindsets. We see it through sweeping assumptions made about beliefs, microaggressions, prejudicial viewpoints aired without challenge and reminders of darker, more violent actions in the past. This is also a chapter where Meena and Anita fall out for the first time, almost foreshadowed by the fortune teller: 'You will lose everythink [sic] before you begin again' (p. 185). It is clear that despite beginning with Meena's love for the change that her 'favourite season in the village' brings (p. 162), she is starting to feel insecure. She has a 'feeling of fear and loneliness' (p. 197) towards the end of that chapter about the 'change [that] always strolled hand in hand with loss, with upheaval' (p. 197). This is a change that Tollington and her life seem to be headed towards.

Social, cultural and historical context

It is important for learners to fully understand, appreciate and be able to realistically envisage life in the fictional village of Tollington in 1972 for Meena. They may require pre-teaching activities on the following features of social, cultural and historical context so they can write about them confidently.

The following are some useful quotations to consider when discussing this context with learners.

- **The Swinging Sixties**: 'far off mythical country where laughing teenagers in sharp suits and A-line dresses drove around in psychedelic Minis, having sex in between chain-smoking and dancing lumpishly in the audience of Ready Steady Go!' (p. 164).
- **Dr Reita Faria wins Miss World 1966**: 'The reigning Miss India won the Miss World contest' (p. 166); 'The sense of excitement and pride it awoke in my parents and their friends obviously made a lasting impression' (p. 166); 'And she a doctor as well' (p. 166); 'Everyone's long-held belief confirmed that Indian women were the brainiest and most beautiful in the world' (p. 166).

CHAPTER 7 OF ANITA AND ME

- **Racist clashes in the Midlands in the 1960s**: 'Have we ever had trouble from people round here? You know, like Usha had over in Willenhall? Those shaved head boys shouting at them, pushing the kids around?' (p. 172); 'The image of Auntie Usha being shoved around by anonymous white fists stayed with me' (p. 173).
- **An alternative perspective of Winston Churchill**: 'If I can end up quoting a man I am sure is everybody's hero here, Sir Winston Churchill' (p. 175); 'Churchill is not particularly one of my heroes' (p. 179); 'no doubt he was a great leader [...] when Mahatma Gandhi came over to visit, your Mr Churchill described him as "that half naked little fakir"' (p. 179-180); 'Mr Kumar, he is not my Winston Churchill, and I thank God for that' (p. 180).

Vocabulary in context

The following vocabulary from Chapter 7 can be pre-taught to help with reading fluency and reduce cognitive load. What does each of the following words mean in context?

Word	Quotation	Definition
brandishing (v.)	'Mrs Keighly running out of her yard brandishing a garden hose' (p. 162)	waving something, especially a weapon, in rage or excitement
kitsch (n.)	'the Mad Mitchells next door merely chucked a few more bits of junk into their front garden, adding to their bizarre monument to kitsch' (p. 163)	borrowed from German, it refers to a show of art considered to be excessively garish and in poor taste, but at times appreciated ironically or in a knowing way
pestilences (n., pl.)	'Had there been a plague of serpents in Tollington, like those pestilences Uncle Alan had talked about in Sunday School?' (p. 163)	a plague; fatal epidemic disease
doffing (v.)	'Not all of them were wearing hats, but if they had been, lots of doffing would have been the order of the day' (p. 167)	raising a hat as a greeting or token of respect
naff (adj.)	'even though their uniforms of striped shirts and brown cords were rather naff' (p. 169)	unfashionable
Canute-like (adj.)	'As Mr Pembridge opened the gate, there was a slight swell forward which he stopped, Canute-like, with his upraised hands' (p. 173)	like Canute, Danish King of England (1017-35), remembered for standing in front of the sea to make the point that he was unable to turn the tide
double entendre (n.)	'Anything Uncle Alan said was taken as a saucy double entendre' (p. 177)	double-meaning; a word or phrase open to more than one interpretation, one of which is usually indecent/risqué

PIT STOP

Retrieval point

Return to this vocabulary in a later lesson, assessing if learners can link each key word to the relevant character(s). For a bonus point, develop each link into an analysis of how the writer's language choice presents that character.

Examples:

- What might the 'doffing' of hats represent and why might the residents of Tollington feel the need to continue this tradition?
- What does Mrs Keighley's reaction of brandishing a garden hose suggest to the reader about the general reaction to Sam Lowbridge's 'heavy petting' sessions, and why do you think Syal chooses to create humour through this imagery?
- What might the phrase 'double entendre' suggest to the reader about Uncle Alan's character and how has Syal used this detail to position him to juxtapose Mr Ormerod and the Reverend?

PIT STOP

Direct instruction point

Discuss the purpose of literary, cultural and religious allusions, and how they can be used to portray more symbolic viewpoints. Invite learners to consider the following allusions and the symbolic inferences that can be made as a consequence:

- the motto on the Pembridge's house – 'Semper Eadem' meaning 'Always the Same'
- the allusion to the Danish king in reference to Mr Pembridge
- the belief that 'charity should indeed begin at home' (p. 191).

PIT STOP

Academic writing point

Learning key vocabulary could be a practical, active step in answering the Big Question: **How does this chapter explore the difficulties of living as a minority?**

Vocabulary to explore the difficulties:

- disenfranchisement
- dismissal

- overlooked
- omitted
- forgotten
- invalidated
- vilified.

Vocabulary to potentially combat the difficulties:

- celebrated
- recognised
- commemoration
- memorialised
- validated
- acknowledged.

Discussion point: Ask learners to consider what Syal might be suggesting about the wider implications on a young person's identity when they don't see themselves represented in dominant narratives?

Plot and character development

For tips on how to approach these 'What' questions, refer to the 'Plot and character development' section of 'How to use this book' on pages 5-6 of this guide.

1. **What is stereotypical about the representation of spring in the opening of this chapter and its significance to a place like Tollington?**

    Example responses:

    - increased social interactions
    - promised hope and new beginnings
    - communal celebrations, such as a 'Spring Fete'.

2. **What does the reader learn about the 'Mad Mitchells'?**

    Example response:

    The extensive collection of broken and neglected items in their front garden suggests humble economic means and perhaps a combination of medical needs and deprivation. Meena, however, is intrigued and sees it as an art installation, a 'bizarre monument to kitsch' (p. 163). While her mama 'tut[s]' every time she walks past the 'grimy opaque windows, the tattered curtains and the peeling front door' (p. 163), Meena remains fascinated by the 'Mad Mitchell Collection' (p. 163). The family, known to live reclusively, are never seen to travel further than the 'town shops' (p. 163). They seem to be disturbed by the idea of journeys, queuing 'at least a half hour before the hourly bus', 'checking the horizon every few minutes' (p. 163) and easily losing sight of their daughter, Cara, who is often seen slipping onto the road, 'wandering down the white lines singing to herself' (p. 163). Despite the obvious signs of isolation, Mr Mitchell, who spends most of his time in the outside lavatory, always greets Meena with warmth and a 'cheery, 'Bloody noice morning, Meena duck!" (p. 164).

PIT STOP

S-T-R-E-T-C-H

Ask learners if they can remember any other examples of members within the Tollington community who are isolated or face prejudices for being different. What do they think Syal is trying to communicate by including such a wide range of examples?

Example responses:

- 'Launching immediately into anyone who started name-calling was the only way to stop it becoming day-to-day bullying, as I saw happened to other kids—the fatties, the spotties, the swots and naturally, the only other four non-white children at my school' (p. 118).
- 'Don't want the estate kids coming round here' (p. 162).

3. What does the reader learn about Tollington's Spring Fete?

Example response:

- The much awaited, 'only communal, organised event [...] held in the grounds of the grandest house in the village' (p. 166), the fete would draw crowds from neighbouring villages with 'stalls from all the surrounding villages' (p. 166) to raise money for 'local churches' and 'a chosen charitable cause' (p. 167).

4. What does the reader learn about the Swinging Sixties and how does Tollington's version appear different to Meena?

Example response:

- Meena reflects on reading about the 1960s later on in life and how it presented itself as a 'far off mythical country' with its 'laughing teenagers in sharp suits' and 'A-line dresses' driving around 'psychedelic minis' (p. 164). It was meant to be a celebration of primal and unrestrained joy, embodied by a 'sexual revolution', 'chain-smoking and dancing lumpishly in the audience' of the famous TV programme, *Ready Steady Go!* (p. 164). The 'only point of contact' Meena recognises in this representation of history is the questionable Mini they owned and Sam Lowbridge's 'heavy-petting sessions' on the park swings (p. 164). In fact, in Meena's Tollington, 'drugs' were what 'Mr Ormerod kept', 'parties were

CHAPTER 7 OF ANITA AND ME

what grown-ups had' and 'music would always be switched off at ten o'clock on the dot' (p. 164). The Tollington she remembers seems like a world away from the version of the history books, a mere 'footnote' (p. 165).

5. **What does the reader learn through Meena's observations and feelings about the representation of the Indian community in history and their treatment in Britain in the 1960s and 1970s?**

   Example responses:

   - Meena observes desperation to be validated and represented: 'I did not realise how starved we were of seeing ourselves somewhere other than in each other's lounges' (p. 166).

   - Meena observes the residents of Tollington perceiving ethnic minorities through a post-colonial, white lens: 'It's about giving them culture, as well as civilisation [...] They'll want fans next, radios, cookers' (p. 172). She also observes the emotive impact of such divisive narratives and condescending perspectives on the Kumars: 'Doesn't he know we were fitting bidets into our house when their ancestors were living in caves? [...] God Shyam, is that how they see us? Is it really?' (p. 172).

   - Meena recognises an aspect of reconciliation, and in some ways submission, in light of well-known racist tensions happening elsewhere in the Midlands: 'They have accepted us, have we ever had any trouble from people round here? You know, like Usha had over in Willenhall, those shaved head boys shouting at them, pushing the kids around?' (p. 172).

   - Meena observes fear and anger that 'just because it doesn't happen to us, does not mean it is not happening!' (p. 172), and frustration at the pressure of pretence and conformity that they live with: 'They leave us alone because they don't think we are really Indian. "Oh, you're so English, Mrs K!" Like it is a buggering compliment!' (p. 172).

   - Meena understands why her parents want to protect her from the realities of the friction of identities and racist vitriol: '[they] changed the subject quickly, as I knew they would' (p. 173).

   - Meena lives with the trauma. Even later in life, the impact of racist clashes stays with her 'for ages', making her feel powerless and enraged: she 'felt both impotent and on fire'(p. 173).

6. **What does the reader learn about Meena and Sunil's relationship in this chapter?**

   Example responses:

   - Meena feels a growing jealousy: 'Mama and papa played with him downstairs' (p. 169); Sunil stops Meena's 'midnight jaunts' to her parents' bed because 'inevitably [...] Sunil would be sleeping on her chest, a snuffling milky mouth of warm roundness, barring the way to her heart' (p. 170).

BLOOMSBURY TEACHER GUIDE: ANITA AND ME

- Meena notices a changing family dynamic, suggesting Sunil be given to Sunshine Orphanage in earnest: '[I] didn't think I was being too unreasonable' to 'drop' Sunil off for a trial period, resulting in mama's tears (p. 169).
- Meena feels an intrigue and fascination toward Sunil, recognising how he is not 'like most of the other babies that had passed through our doors' (p. 168) and starts to interact with him: 'I waved at Sunil [...] he flashed me a heart-stopping radiant smile' (p. 171).
- Meena feels guilty for her jealousy and doesn't want 'another emotional collapse' on her 'conscience', so changes 'tactic' with 'silly voices' and 'plasticine faces', performing the 'devoted sister' (p. 169).

7. What does the reader learn about the different couples in this chapter and their relationships?

Example responses:

Mr and Mrs Pembridge

- Marriage across social class: 'It was the strangest voice [...] never the voice I imagined she would have. It was a miner's daughter's voice, all tin and rust and under the earth' (p. 174).
- Power imbalance and absence of affection: 'beckoned Mrs Pembridge who came to stand dutifully by his side' (p. 173); 'She shot an imploring look at her husband who beckoned her again, becoming impatient' (p. 174); 'staring at Mr Pembridge with an expression that somehow contained both utter contempt and profound pity' (p. 190).

Hairy Neddy and Sandy

- Protection and support: On seeing Sandy struggling to sell and her 'stall already forgotten', Hairy Neddy steps in with a 'gallant gesture', drawing the crowds in with a fabricated story about Sandy's toys as 'Space Gonks', generating intrigue. He 'ostentatiously' waves his money to inspire others to join in and buy from her, saving her from humiliation on her 'first year as a stallholder' (p. 177).
- Display of love and romance: Sandy is so affected by his kindness that she is moved to tears, and with 'brimming' eyes, takes a note from Hairy Neddy as he proposes to her, which Meena lip reads 'in slow motion' and views as 'one of the most romantic moments ever', resulting in 'squeals and applause' and everyone joins in with them in celebration (p. 178).

Papa and mama

- Honesty in communication and security in a relationship: On hearing about the Ballbearings women flirting with papa, mama 'listened to those close encounters with a satisfied possessive expression' and soothed papa instead, 'They are harmless Shyamji, just having fun' (p. 180).

- Discomfort with public displays of emotion in light of cultural norms: 'how lucky he was to have his own Indian wife whom he knew would never display such loose behaviour in a public place', but instead show love in more private displays of affection: 'Papa would nod and kiss her cheek and she would wrap her delight close to her like a shawl' (p. 180).
- By showing the reader the different types of relationships, both secure and fickle, Syal not only dismantles the stereotype that the Kumars seem to believe about the lack of sincerity in relationships amongst the English, but also reminds the reader how different dynamics of relationships can exist across cultures.

8. What do the Pembridges symbolise in this chapter?

Example responses:

- The literal and metaphorical distance between the working-class community and the ruling elite: 'For the other three hundred and sixty-four days of the year, the Pembridge mansion remained out of bounds to us, as effectively as if it had been surrounded by electric fences and a shark-infested moat' (p. 167).
- The stereotype of the family of money that prioritises marriages within their community to secure financial security: Mrs Lowbridge remarks, whilst passing judgement on Graham Pembridge's physical features, 'Inbreeding's a terrible thing, ain't it?' (p. 168).
- The instability of a relationship that also reveals a power imbalance: 'He turned round and beckoned Mrs Pembridge […] to come and stand dutifully by his side' (p. 173); 'She shot an imploring look at her husband who beckoned her again, becoming impatient' (p. 174).
- The potential for marriage as a form of social mobility, represented by Mrs Pembridge: 'It was a miner's daughter voice, all tin and rust and under the earth' (p. 174).
- Social prejudices as a consequence of disparity in financial power: Mrs Lowbridge's comment on Graham's physical demeanour and Mrs Worrall's exclamation on learning that Mrs Pembridge is a miner's daughter, 'Blue blood, my arse!' (p. 174).

9. What does Hairy Neddy's speech symbolise (p. 178)?

Example responses:

- how impressionable the people of Tollington are
- how easy it is to redirect passions with persuasion and intrigue
- how there is always a possibility to inspire change and influence thought.

10. What does the motto on the Pembridge's house, 'Semper Eadem', symbolise to Meena?

Example response:

- The motto, which Meena is informed by papa to translate to 'Always the Same', reinforces the Pembridge's status to Meena as an 'island of grace, tranquillity, and unimaginable wealth' (p. 167). This exists as a stark contrast to the deprivation in Tollington, symbolised by the village school 'preparing to gradually close down' (p. 167), and the slow deterioration of the rural landscape as urbanisation began to take over: 'neon motorway lights began slowly appearing' (p. 167).

11. What do the fortune teller, Madam Rosa (alias of Mrs Goodyear), and her prophecies symbolise?

Example responses:

- How easy it is for someone to use religious code in a reductive manner.
- The pressure on young women in the time period to secure their fortunes through marriage: 'marrying into unimaginable wealth with a handsome upright Christian man' (p. 182).
- The pressure on young men in the time period to be a source of provision and stability, and the emphasis therefore on having sons: 'married men were reassured that next year would bring them promotion, status and a batch of sturdy sons' (p. 182).
- The racial prejudice and bias demonstrated through her hesitancy to serve Meena: 'clutch nervously at her upside down goldfish bowl' (p. 183).
- Reinforcement of stereotypes and racial prejudices: marrying a 'doctor' (p. 183); 'do well at school [...] in an office, or possibly on a bus [...] make a lovely home for your husband and five children' (p. 183).
- Unconscious bias generated from limited knowledge and interactions: 'in her limited terms of reference, Mrs Goodyear was only telling me what she thought I longed to hear' (p. 183).
- Prejudice against the prospect of interracial marriages: 'I see a tall man, coloured like yourself' (p. 183); 'the nearest she could come to imagining a mixed relationship was a Methodist marrying a Catholic' (p. 183).

CHAPTER 7 OF ANITA AND ME

> **PIT STOP** ▼
>
> ## S-T-R-E-T-C-H
>
> Ask learners to find an extract or a number of quotations in this chapter to illustrate the contrast between both fortune tellers and how Madam Rosa's replacement is positioned to appear more authentic.
>
> Example responses:
>
> - 'dressed as if she had looked up fortune teller in the dictionary and chosen her wardrobe accordingly' (p. 183)
> - 'shiny olive toned skin [...] looked Indian enough to be one of my Aunties and made me want to trust her' (p. 184)
> - when she senses troubles in Anita's future: 'Don't think I can read you, darlink' (p. 185)
> - when Meena apologises for her 'friend', Anita, she replies with insight: "Is that what you think she is, darlink?' She smiled' (p. 186)
> - 'tucked the sixpence away into a hidden pocket in her gown, a purple night studded with a million twinkling stars' (p. 186).

12. What can the reader infer about Reverend Ince's decision to spend the proceeds of the fair on the roof of the chapel?

Example response:

Even before this decision is made, it is evident through the exchanges with Uncle Alan that this is a decision he disapproves of and will not be one in the best interest of the village, as he stands by the Reverend's side with his 'lips drawn shut' (p. 191). The play on the religious allusion that 'charity should indeed begin at home' (p. 191) subtly foreshadows the resistance to spending money on charities abroad, which would have been an active campaign of compensation at the time as part of Britain's post-colonial relationships. Instead, the Reverend plays on the economic frustrations of the villagers, using inflammatory language, reminding them to consider 'what is happening to [their] village' and insisting on the need for 'blessing and light' to save the 'besieged Tollington' (p. 191). He shows a complete disconnect from their everyday grievances, dismissing their need for investment in their local school, the dire requirements for a 'shelter for the bus stop', a 'gate round the mine shaft' for safety, or even perhaps their desperation for more recreational activities like a 'bloody big party' with 'free booze' for both entertainment and escapism (p. 191). On the contrary, his decision to spend the collection on the roof of the chapel echoes many such decisions by people in power, showing an outright rejection of the true needs of the people and subsequently paving the way for 'mutters of discontent and resignation' (p. 192), before culminating in obstructive protest, as evidenced through Sam Lowbridge's 'barking' outburst: 'bloody church roof [...] wharra about us?' (p. 192).

13. What does the reaction of the crowd to Sam Lowbridge's outburst suggest to Meena and reveal about attitudes to racist and abusive behaviour in early 1970s Britain?

Example response:

Initially, Sam wins the favour of his audience with his authentic concerns about economic disillusionment and disadvantage. 'The sound of his own unchallenged voice' (p. 192) inspires him to continue to provoke and question, resulting in applause and support from the crowd. They seem desperate for their grievances to be aired and are almost relieved that someone has shown the courage to challenge them on their behalf. They look on with a 'collective intake of anticipatory breath', prepared and hopeful that 'something important was happening, epic even' (p. 193) as the status quo is challenged. However, it's interesting that when Sam takes a turn, using racist vitriol to use non-white people as a scapegoat for everyone's frustrations – 'yow'll do nothing but talk […] and give everything away to some darkies we've never met' (p. 193), echoing Peter's words from Chapter 1, and taking a territorial stance: 'this is our patch. Not some bloody wogs' handout' (p. 193) – the crowd remains silent and compliant.

This response is reflective perhaps of the influence of the dominant narratives of division propagated actively at the time in the Midlands, as some even join in, 'Go on lad! Tell him some more!' (p. 194), indicative of underlying racist beliefs that could exist unchallenged in communities and be aired publicly with support, as reflected through Enoch Powell's infamous 'Rivers of Blood' speech. Syal draws the reader's attention to the impact on Meena, representative of the real victims of such openly aired hostility, as she feels like she's been 'punched in the stomach' and her legs feel 'watery' (p. 193) at the thought of betrayal and contemptuous thoughts exist so freely around her. But then, of course, so is the resistance that comes through anonymously, 'yow don't talk for me, son! I'd be on my deathbed before that'd happen' (p. 194), which is also an important reminder that throughout history, there have always been those who have challenged injustices, and stood by the oppressed. This is echoed through the antithetical words from earlier in the chapter: 'these people can be so cruel […] some of these people are angels' (p. 166).

> **PIT STOP**
>
> ### S-T-R-E-T-C-H
>
> Ask learners to research the speech of austere shadow defence secretary, Enoch Powell, in 1968 in Birmingham and the classical allusion to Virgil's River Tiber foaming in blood. They should also consider the impact this would have had on policymakers, as well as the wider public at the time.

CHAPTER 7 OF ANITA AND ME

How?

Language

Narrative voice

Key quotations:

- 'The image of Auntie Usha being shoved about by white fists stayed with me for ages […] I felt both impotent and on fire' (p. 173)
- 'I could not understand this then, I simply divided the world into strangers and friends' (p. 173)
- 'Later on, when mama began to treat me like a grownup and had released nuggets of information about her and papa's experiences that would have given me nightmares as a child, this battle between desire and duty made perfect sense' (p. 181)
- 'I finally made the connection that change always strolled hand in hand with loss, with upheaval' (p. 197).

How does Syal position the audience to view Meena's transition from innocent to experienced?

PIT STOP

S-T-R-E-T-C-H

Ask learners to consider how it is more effective to see this transition from the lens of both the child and the adult narrator.

Example responses:

- increases both insight and empathy for both the child and the adult
- positions the reader to appreciate the trauma, even before it has been processed fully by the child
- makes the reader even more invested in understanding the lasting impact
- reflects the human condition and how time has the power to change perspectives and reopen old wounds.

Extended metaphor of gambling

Key quotations:

- 'But for papa, every win was tainted with the memory of all those other times he had gambled and lost' (p. 181)

- 'and I wondered why a man who had risked so much by setting foot in a foreign country with five pounds in his pocket and no friends to call on, could not simply throw caution to the wind and just let go' (p. 181)
- 'this battle between desire and duty made perfect sense' (p. 181)
- 'Papa courted chance like an old friend [...] however papa was not a recreational gambler' (p. 181-2).

Ask learners to consider:

- How Syal presents the process of migration as a gamble?
- How papa's guilt is presented and why it is significant?
- How Syal uses juxtaposition to emphasise papa's internal conflict?

Satire

Key quotations:

- 'You know that old trick, you ring up and get an interview in your best voice, then they see your face and suddenly the job is gone' (p. 165)
- 'inbreeding's a terrible thing, ain't it?' (p. 168)
- 'I was beginning to realise that truth counted for very little in the end' (p. 166)
- 'A ripple of excitement [...] Mr and Mrs Pembridge began the long walk from their oak panelled front door to the end of the drive' (p. 171)
- 'he did not seem keen in bringing the light to the darkest jungles of the Third World' (p. 171).

Ask learners to identify the way Syal uses satire for social commentary and discuss the prejudicial viewpoints and stereotypes that she challenges.

Example responses:

- As a literary technique to draw attention to various prejudices in society and their impact on individuals.
- To highlight long-standing racial and cultural clashes.
- To highlight both the absurdity and the ignorance.
- To position the reader to reflect on how prejudices often stem from misunderstandings and misconceptions.
- To draw the reader's attention to and encourage critique of upsetting biases through the lens of wit and humour.

Character focus

The Pembridges

Key quotations:

- 'The Pembridges lived at the posh end of the main road' (p. 167)
- 'The grandeur and elegance of the place affected us all, made even more desirable by its very inaccessibility' (p. 167).

The Pembridges have significant positional and influential power, created by Syal to represent a way of life that is aspired to as a cultural and social norm, providing hope and intrigue, yet remaining firmly out of reach of the local residents of Tollington. Their behaviour, serving as a mirror to societal prejudices and power imbalances, highlights the social hierarchy and cultural insensitivity that would exist in places like Tollington in the 1960s, and the significant disconnect between sensibilities. They also serve as a symbol of the larger community's expectations for assimilation and integration, and inadvertently impose pressures on immigrant families, such as Meena's, to subscribe to a way of living that is expected, even when it is far from reality.

Mr Pembridge

Key quotations:

- 'exquisite Tudor mansion owned by Mr Pembridge, a local Tory Councillor and businessman' (p. 166)
- 'always in a suit with a carnation as red as his face in his lapel' (p. 167-8)
- 'battled on, trying to win back his audience' (p. 175)
- 'still struggling through his speech' (p. 175)
- 'raised his pudgy hands' (p. 190).

Mrs Pembridge

Key quotations:

- 'She was a thin, bored woman with a head far too big and bouffant for her body, who would acknowledge our stares with a cursory flicker of a smile' (p. 168)
- 'edging forward clumsily' (p. 174)
- 'clicked her teeth nervously' (p. 174)
- 'it was the strangest voice, which did not at all go with her body [...] It was a miner's daughter's voice, all tin and rust and under the earth' (p. 174)
- 'swaying in the cavernous front porch of her mansion [...] cradling a wine bottle [...] staring at Mr Pembridge with an expression that somehow contained both utter contempt and profound pity' (p. 190).

Graham Pembridge

Key quotations:

- 'the horse was better looking' (p. 168)
- also known as 'Mr Plug-Face' (p. 168)
- 'his mother's skinny frame and his father's 'mardy' face' (p. 168)
- 'talked like he had a shilling's worth of gobstoppers in his mouth' (p. 168)
- 'he had obviously had something better to do this afternoon and looked like he just returned from safari somewhere, dressed in a mud-splattered tweed jacket and corduroys' (p. 190)
- 'did not seem bothered by his mother's obvious emotional state' (p. 190).

Sunil

Key quotations:

- 'He didn't yowl for hours on end [...] He did not throw food around or break ornaments or deposit curdy omelettes of sick on the furniture' (p. 168)
- 'But once in her arms, he would become the Sunil the rest of the world saw and loved, a smiling, dimpled, chubby, bite-sized morsel of cuteness, dispensing infant largesse from his throne, my mama' (p. 170).

Although Meena is intrigued by Sunil and drawn to his charm, there is still a feeling of detachment as she is yet to appreciate the permanence of his existence in their family. His overdependence on mama is what results in her eventual breakdown towards the end of the chapter as she appeals for help, 'I can't cope anymore, Shyam' (p. 196), which comes in the shape of 'Help from Overseas' (p. 198), Meena's Nanima.

Mama

Key quotations:

- 'seemed to exist in a self-contained world of nappies, cleaning, cooking and fitful twitchy catnaps' (p. 168)
- 'Sunil's need was so great that mama seemed to have disappeared under it' (p. 170)
- 'Keeping up an appearance of efficiency, but actually finishing nothing properly' (p. 170-1)
- 'Long exhausted silences or more frightening blank stares, where she would gaze at me and papa as if we were strangers' (p. 171).

Mama is clearly beginning to feel overwhelmed to the point of losing her sense of self, as Meena too reflects, 'Nothing was safe anymore; even my own mama had talked in an unknown poet's voice' (p. 196), suffering perhaps from a mixture of postnatal depression and intense loss. Her changing demeanour is a glaring cry for help, which eventually results in Nanima's arrival.

Anita and Meena's relationship

Key quotations:

- 'in a fit of uncharacteristic generosity' (p. 184)
- 'dark mood' (p. 186)
- Meena, fully aware of her 'tempers' and 'how to ride them', keeps a 'respectful distance behind her' (p. 186)
- 'awful murderous hatred' (p. 186)
- 'Meena's got to come too' (p. 188)
- 'bloody stupid cow sometimes' (p. 195).

On the surface, it appears that this relationship is strengthening, as Anita and Meena appear inseparable. Meena continues to follow her around, Anita shares a seat with Meena, and even tells Sherrie that 'Meena's got to come too' (p. 188) when they plan to go to her farm to ride Trixie. However, this chapter brings to light the disparity in their power dynamics, especially when Anita goes into a 'dark mood' (p. 186) following the fortune teller's prophecies. Meena shows maturity and insight in recognising that Anita's moods have the power and capacity to consume her, as evident through the metaphorical reference to the cyclone, yet the reader also recognises how Meena is getting dangerously close, finding herself 'inside her head' and beginning to share her hyperbolic 'awful murderous hatred' (p. 186). The conditional use of language also illustrates Meena's fear of 'retreat[ing] too far' (p. 186), as she is painfully aware of the capacity of Anita's wrath, and Meena appears determined to protect herself from the accusation of betrayal. Despite these dynamics, Meena knows deep down that she cannot rely on Anita, being fully aware that she 'would not hold' her or take her 'hand' (p. 193). This is exactly what happens following Sam Lowbridge's betrayal, resulting in Meena's first outburst at Anita and walking away without turning back.

Structure

Learners should explore the following examples from the opening and the ending of Chapter 7 and be invited to consider:

- Why Syal has chosen to begin and end with this focus on change?
- What their predictions might be about key characters and plot developments within this chapter.

Opening: 'Spring was always my favourite season in the village, and as the cuckoo sounded, almost every cottage door would swing open' (p. 162).

Ending: 'I had not imagined this, this feeling of fear and loneliness [...] change always strolled hand in hand with loss, with upheaval' (p. 197); 'my feet had suddenly gone icy cold' (p. 198).

Mirroring and foreshadowing

Anita was a bad influence, established in the previous chapter and reinforced by the fortune teller along with some ominous suggestions about her future. This symbolises how Anita may never be awarded the scope to evolve and transition and positions the reader to be fearful of her and the impact she may subsequently have on Meena.

Meena's decision to follow Anita from a distance is also reflective of their first day together. This is a stark reminder that their relationship has not evolved, but in fact remains stagnant, almost stunted. Even though Anita's gestures, such as buying Meena toffee apples at the fair or ensuring that she joins her for a horse ride can be seen as small acts of kindness, the reader begins to see that these are perhaps acts of manipulation instead.

Ominous foreshadowing of betrayal and violence

'Since joining Anita's gang, I had become more suspicious of how the familiar could turn into the unknown, and what happened at the Fete revealed how many strangers did indeed live amongst us' (p. 173).

The reader is positioned to be prepared for Sam and Anita's betrayal towards the end of the chapter, thereby increasing not only their empathy, but fear for Meena's wellbeing and safety.

Revelations and epiphanies

The revelation of Sam's true identity and the moment of climax:

- 'My legs felt watery and a soft panic softened my insides to mush' (p. 193)
- Meena's epiphany about Anita: 'I knew she would not hold me or take my hand' (p. 193); 'Anita Rutter, yow am a bloody stupid cow sometimes' (p. 195); 'I was not bothered that they seemed to have forgotten me [...] To my surprise, I did not care much' (p. 197).

Extracts

1. How does Syal use language to develop a vivid presentation of Sam's transformation and what does it represent?

'Somebody sniggered loudly behind us, all heads turned to see who was spoiling this ritualistic moment. Sam Lowbridge and various gang members [...] Mr Pembridge battled on, trying to win back his audience' (p. 174–5).

Example response planning, using topic sentence scaffolds:

Syal presents Sam, his gang and their transformation as:

- an act of defiance and rejection of the status quo
- a stark reminder of the real victims of Tollington's stagnancy
- representative of collective resistance

CHAPTER 7 OF ANITA AND ME

- brazen in their disruption and intrusion into the festivities
- exuding confidence and disinclination to compromise
- purposeful, and almost menacing
- unconcerned with their impact on the villagers.

2. **How does Syal use language to show the differences between Uncle Alan and Reverend Ince in the following extract?**

'Mr Ince, our church vicar, a thin erect man with a shock of fuzzy salt and pepper hair had a hands-off approach to his flock [...] almost unrecognisable' (p. 178-9).

Example response planning, using topic sentence scaffolds: 💡

Syal presents the difference between Uncle Alan and Reverend Ince as:

- holistic approach vs self-serving approach
- integrity and commitment vs cultivated facade and pretence
- reliability and sincerity vs insincerity and superficiality.

Example response, unpacking quotations and language therein to support points: 🔍

In this extract, Syal presents the differences between Reverend Ince and Uncle Alan as a contrast between true dedication and carefully cultivated performance. Whilst the Reverend is the face of the church leadership, Meena describes him satirically as having a 'hands off approach to his flock', only making himself visible for 'one sermon a week' and 'occasional outings' in 'hardly used robes'. This suggests to the reader that his role and commitment are mostly superficial and perhaps a critique of institutionalised religion, highlighting the disconnect between actions motivated by true holistic beliefs and those performed to maintain a facade of service. What's more, he is described as 'tak[ing] the credit' for Uncle Alan's 'back-breaking work' and relentless efforts in the background, from fundraising through 'sponsored events and door to door collection', to engaging with and encouraging locals to use the church hall, to the everyday maintenance jobs like sweeping the pews and arranging the flowers. These actions reinforce to the reader how Uncle Alan's dedication is unparalleled, his actions illustrating selflessness, driven by a moral purpose. This is further reinforced through Syal's antithetical positioning of both men: 'Uncle Alan got his hands dirty and Reverend Ince kept his clean to shake with various dignitaries', and therefore inviting the reader's disbelief and empathy when the Reverend refuses to award Uncle Alan any autonomy, disregarding his input on the charity collection decision.

CHAPTER 8 OF ANITA AND ME

At a glance

- **Chapter summary quotation:** 'It felt so strange to hear Punjabi under the stars. It was an indoor language to me' (p. 230)
- **Big Question:** In what ways do 'two worlds collide' with the arrival of Nanima (p. 204)?
- **Significant plot event:** Nanima arrives and relationships begin to change.
- **Character focus:** Nanima, Mr Topsy/Turvey, Uncle Alan, Meena and Sunil's relationship, Meena and mama's relationship
- **Key themes:**
  - Cultural identity
  - Othering
  - Change
- **Handle with care:**
  - Reference to racial othering in this chapter will need to be handled with sensitivity. Please refer to the 'Handle with care' guidance in the 'How to use this book' section for further support.
    - photographs from Black Hole of Calcutta reference 'like animals' (p. 211)
    - Nanima's reception by Ballbearings Women (p. 219) and Mr Ormerod (p. 223).

Why?

'Why' is important not only within the world of the text, but also when considering authorial intent and messaging.

- Why is Nanima's arrival so instrumental in bringing about the change that Meena has been waiting for?
- Why does Syal create a narrator-protagonist who provides us with such a candid view of connecting with emotions you've never experienced and relations you have never met; one who desperately resists attention, yet gives in immediately to the hedonistic celebrations?

CHAPTER 8 OF ANITA AND ME

- Are there, perhaps, unexpected identity dynamics revealed? Does this expose the power that one person can have to remind you of where you come from and make you feel secure in who you are? Is it possible to be 'junglee', yet also true to your identity?
- Why is this chapter important in instigating Meena's metamorphosis and the awakening of our protagonist to the possibility of embracing all aspects of her sense of self?

This allows us to consider Chapter 8's Big Question:

> In what ways do 'two worlds collide' with the arrival of Nanima?

What?
What happens?

As if in an ironic response to the chapter before, this one begins with the change that Meena dreads, only for the reader to realise how it is, in fact, the 'blessing' that the Kumars have been waiting for: Nanima's arrival. Nanima arrives amidst a fanfare celebration of 'laughing and crying', 'anointed [...] as a traditional gesture of welcome' and drawing the attention of not only the locals, but also 'someone in the grounds of the Big House', much to Meena's terror (p. 199). Symbolising everyone's 'beloved parent' she is immediately 'deif[ied]' (p. 201) by Meena's Aunties and Uncles, as their home begins to 'vibrate with goodwill and hope' (p. 203). Much to Meena's surprise and horror, the celebrations spill into their garden, 'reclaiming the Tollington night' (p. 203).

Meena immediately starts to observe change: in those around her, 'never seen the Elders so expansive and unconcerned' (p. 204), in her mama, 'so fresh and girlish' (p. 202), in Sunil, developing some independence and sitting on papa's leg for the first time, and in herself, finding herself 'doing jobs' she had previously 'run away from' (p. 209). It is Meena's blossoming sense of self, stemming from the mutual admiration between her and Nanima, which is the most transformative change. Meena starts to question the histories that she has grown up learning about, and begins to consider the alternative narratives brought to life by Nanima's stories. These are 'stories that never followed a pattern' (p. 209), fluctuating dramatically between the ordinary and the horrific, the absurd and the solemn, making Meena question existing representations and begin to realise how and why she 'always came bottom in history' (p. 211), and why her parents would want to choose a life in Britain despite living through the atrocities. She gets an answer in this chapter, an insight into the 'damn big mess' (p. 213) of post-colonial life, and what it meant to be 'poor and clever' (p. 212) in India.

The chapter also touches on the theme of education, the 'dreaded eleven-plus' (p. 213) as an avenue for social mobility and what it means not to have a choice, represented through the Rutters and the pressure of 'failure'. We also see new pressures emerging. The pressure to learn Punjabi so Meena doesn't feel 'left out' and can 'understand' her Nanima (p. 205) and the pressure that Meena puts on herself to ensure that her Nanima is not 'suddenly the entertainment' (p. 220). She is aware of the power dynamics of conversations, particularly those that do not resemble the 'meeting of equals' (p. 220), and she is therefore unprepared for the more wholesome interactions with Mrs Worrall, Uncle Alan and Mr Topsy/Turvey, whose Punjabi stuns her into 'silence'. This newfound protectiveness and confidence in her sense of self reaches a moment of climax when Meena misreads a situation and accuses Mr Ormerod of 'cheat[ing]' her Nanima (p. 225). Later, she also prevents Sam and his gang from 'having a huge laugh at Nanima's expense' (p. 228), channelling all her 'energy' and confidence into a stance that suggests that she is a force to be reckoned with.

Social, cultural and historical context

It is important for learners to fully understand, appreciate and be able to realistically envisage life in the fictional village of Tollington in 1972 for Meena. They may require pre-teaching activities on the following features of social, cultural and historical context so they can write about them confidently.

The following are some useful quotations to consider when discussing this context with learners. For more information, please refer to the contextual timeline.

- **The Maharaja of Patiala**: 'passing British soldiers once took away all the family's chickens [...] during a long march to visit the Rajah of Patiala' (p. 209).
- **The Black Hole of Calcutta**: 'The Black Hole of Calcutta was a popular image, angelic women and children choking on their own fear whilst yet more of my uncles and aunties in period clothes danced an evil jig of victory outside' (p. 211).

Vocabulary in context

The following vocabulary from Chapter 8 can be pre-taught to help with reading fluency and reduce cognitive load. What does each of the following words mean in context?

Word	Quotation	Definition
vindicated (v.)	'felt vindicated when I saw mama whispering their names to her' (p. 200)	justified; cleared of blame
rheumy (adj.)	'looking up into my mama's face, except it was darker and more wrinkled and the eyes were rheumy and mischievous '(p. 200)	watery, clouded eyes

CHAPTER 8 OF ANITA AND ME

surreptitious (adj.)	'punctuated by loud slurpings of tea and surreptitious massaging of her feet' (p. 201)	done secretively as it would not be approved or considered acceptable
servile (adj.)	'Whilst men who looked like any one of my uncles, remained in the background holding trays [...] their posture servile' (p. 211)	a demeanour that reveals an excessive willingness to serve and obey
benevolent (adj.)	'under the benevolent gaze of a statue of Queen Victoria' (p. 211)	kind-hearted, charitable
fracas (n.)	'fracas', made sense, the word sounded like a flurry of activity' (p. 212)	disturbance or quarrel
jaywalking (v.)	'Cara, the Mad Mitchells' daughter, doing her usual stint of jaywalking along the white lines in the middle of the road' (p. 219)	walking or crossing a street or road while disregarding approaching traffic
coup de grace (n.)	'And then my coup de grace' (p. 221)	finishing blow or shot

PIT STOP

Retrieval point

Return to this vocabulary in a later lesson, assessing if learners can link each key word to the relevant character(s). For a bonus point, develop each link into an analysis of how the writer's language choice presents that character.

Examples:

- What might the writer, Syal, be trying to show the reader about how people adore and respect Nanima and why might the surreptitious massaging of feet be of interest?

- In what way is the presentation of Indian men, looking like 'any of' Meena's 'uncles', problematic through their servile representations and positioning in the background? What is Syal suggesting through the impact on Meena?

- What is Syal suggesting through her reference to Queen Victoria's statue's gaze as benevolent?

PIT STOP

Direct instruction point

Learners can use the following to develop their understanding of the different variations of sentence structures and their use in this chapter. This will benefit their analysis skills for academic writing.

- **Asyndetic list**: 'I felt when we 'did' India at school [...] their eyes glowing like coals' (p. 211).

- **Anaphora**: 'gradually I got used to Nanima's world [...] in which the Land was revered [...] in which supernatural and epic events [...] seemed commonplace, in which fabulous wealth and dramatic ritual were continually upstaged' (p. 210-11).
- **Anadiplosis**: 'Before Nanima arrived, this urge to reinvent myself, I could see now, was purely driven by shame, the shame I felt when we 'did' India at school.' (p. 211)

PIT STOP

S-T-R-E-T-C-H

Ask learners to consider the impact of these sentence structures in their individual contexts and discuss the intended effect on the reader.

Example responses:
- generate tension
- communicate the intensity of thought and emotion
- exemplify the relentlessness of...
- emphasise/accentuate/reinforce the feelings of... .

PIT STOP

Academic writing point

Learning how to track key moments to understand why they are transformative could also be a practical, active step to answering the Big Question: **In what ways do 'two worlds collide' on the arrival of Nanima and how does this impact Meena?**

Key phrases to explore the impact of Nanima's arrival on Meena:
- Begins to feel that her rambunctious and rebellious nature is celebrated.
- Starts to accept that embracing her culture does not need to come at the cost of losing her identity as a teenager in 1970s Tollington.
- Realises her desire for love and responsibility is stronger than her desire to rebel.
- Begins to realise the significance of her mother tongue in connecting with her roots.
- Starts to make sense of the turbulence within her, in light of the stories of her heritage.

- Newfound desire to understand India better and resolve her own identity crisis.
- Lies, but this time for a cause, rather than a self-serving purpose: to protect her family and challenge racism.

Remind learners to use discourse markers to support them as they track key moments:

- Initially, …
- Then, …
- Finally, …
- Ultimately, …

Plot and character development

For tips on how to approach these 'What' questions, refer to the 'Plot and character development' section of 'How to use this book' on pages 5-6 of this guide.

1. What happens when Nanima first arrives?

Example responses:

- 'causing traffic to slow down and passing women to stop and squint curiously' (p. 199); 'patting their hair […] in case there were hidden television cameras' (p. 199)
- front step 'anointed' with oil as a 'traditional gesture of welcome' (p. 199)
- each of us 'shoved into her path to receive a blessing' (p. 199)
- 'handed Nanima a glass of water, one of our best glasses' (p. 200)
- received with 'reverence and adoration' (p. 201)
- celebrated and valued by all their family and friends: 'constant stream of visitors bearing gifts of sweatmeats and homemade sabzis' (p. 201).

Nanima's arrival is transformative, and the celebrations are both hedonistic and unparalleled. It's as if her arrival has been much-awaited, and has the power to fill a void that has existed not just for the Kumars, but for their friends as well.

2. What does the reader learn about Nanima's relationship with Meena?

Example response:

One of the most significant forces that binds this relationship is the mutual admiration they have for each other. Nanima understands and celebrates Meena's rambunctious personality, allowing her to recognise that embracing her Indian roots should not have to contravene her true self. She immediately brands her as 'junglee' (p. 200), the wild child. While this is not usually seen as 'a compliment', it is intended by Nanima as such. It is an acknowledgement and celebration of Meena's free spirit. She provides Meena with the security that she craves, both literally and metaphorically, as she drags her 'under her arm where it felt yeasty and safe. Tucking the quilt around' (p. 207) her with dexterity and expertise, to care for her, even in her sleep. Nanima tries to make herself useful in the house in whatever way she knows and understands, and Meena is full of admiration for 'this mad logic' (p. 208). We also see Meena beginning to mirror her, as the teachings and preachings start to become part of her child's vernacular: 'I must be getting soft in my old age' (p. 209).

Most importantly, we see through this relationship the blossoming of a sense of confidence and self as Meena starts to understand who she is, and how she can belong: 'Before Nanima arrived, this urge to reinvent myself, I could see now, was driven purely by shame' (p. 211).

3. What does the reader learn about the changes that start to take place in the Kumar household following Nanima's arrival?

Example responses:

- 'guests began to start spilling out into the garden' (p. 203)
- 'began reclaiming the Tollington night [...] guffawing Punjabi over fences and hedges' (p. 203)
- 'never seen the Elders so expansive and unconcerned, and knew this somehow had something to do with Nanima' (p. 204)
- 'had applied some ancient witchery to finally cut the umbilical cord that was slowly strangling both him and us' (p. 208)
- 'I found myself doing jobs I had run away from just a few weeks earlier' (p. 209).

From the superficial to the self-affirming changes, Nanima's arrival is transformative, bringing 'ancient witchery' that the Kumars have been in much need of, as they navigate through the challenges of living as a minority at a time of interracial friction, as well as steering through the minefield of welcoming and adjusting to the arrival of a new baby in the family.

4. What does the reader learn through Meena's reflection on history upon hearing Nanima's stories?

Example responses:

- Representation as victims and dehumanisation: 'hollow-eyed skeletons, barely recognisable as human beings' (p. 211).
- Disparity in power dynamics to create a hero vs victim narrative: 'blood of the brave besieged British' (p. 211); 'remained in the background [...] their postures servile' (p. 201).
- Missing narratives: 'a country that seemed full to bursting with excitement, drama and passion, history in the making' (p. 211); 'what happens when someone is deprived of education' (p. 212).
- Process of vilification through the creation of the foreign 'other' detailed in the contextual timeline (1756 and 1864): 'The Black hole of Calcutta was a popular image, angelic women and children choking on their own fear whilst yet more of my uncles and aunties in period clothes danced an evil jig of victory outside' (p. 211).
- Impact on sense of belonging: 'Of course if Britain had not left us in such a damn big mess' (p. 213).

5. What does the reader learn about why the Kumars had to leave India?

Example response:

We see Meena's confusion in this chapter, which stems from evident gaps in her historical understanding of the dynamics of post-colonial relationships. This is clear in her asking of questions like: 'Why, after so many years of hating the 'goras', had they packed up their cases and followed them back here?' (p. 212). The answer is an unsurprising reminder of the effects of the aftermath of the process of colonisation – being 'poor and clever, a bad combination' (p. 212) anywhere. There is a universal human dream of wanting a life with freedom of opportunity and choice, devoid of bureaucracy and corruption: Meena's mama reflects, 'at least in this country you can get to the top university without having to pay a thousand greedy officials to get there' (p. 212).

6. What does the reader learn from Nanima's stories about the Kumar's history?

Example responses:

- all of the family's chickens were stolen by 'passing British soldiers' to 'sustain them during a long march to the Rajah of Patiala' (p. 209)
- full of 'old and bitter family feuds where the Land was revered' (p. 211)
- suspicion that Nanima's grandmother's ghost lingers on top of their home in the village
- Nanima had a 'son [...] who died at birth' (p. 210)

- Meena's nana owned 'fleet[s] of village trucks' and had a 'terrible accident' in them, resulting in a 'leg so badly crushed' that his survival was questionable (p. 210)
- while he was on his supposed 'deathbed', Meena's grandfather's brother tried to 'flee with the family assets' (p. 210)
- Meena's nana was imprisoned by the British while he was 'still limping' because he 'would not fight in their army' (p. 210)
- no one heard from Meena's nana for four years until he 'limped back' into their courtyard, much to Nanima's shock and surprise (p. 210).

7. **What can the reader infer from the 'two very strange things' that happen in this chapter?**

   Example response:

   - 'For the first time ever [...] Anita burst into tears before fleeing down the nearest entry' (p. 206).
   - The cracks and undercurrents between Deirdre and Anita's relationship are emphasised, evident even through the manner in which Deirdre 'sags' (p. 206) on seeing her daughter, revealing how she feels restrained by her mere existence to live her life. This is juxtaposed in the same chapter by papa's unbridled celebration of Meena, calling her his 'jaan', his 'life' (p. 205). We also see the toll that Deirdre's misdemeanours are taking on Anita, successfully breaking her 'I Dare You stance' (p. 206) and unshaken resolve, generating 'anger and pity' (p. 206) in equal measures from not only Meena but also the reader, as the traumatic breakdown of a parent-child relationship unfolds.
   - 'There was someone in the grounds of the Big House and they were watching us' (p. 206).

   Once again, the Big House is a source of tension and suspicion, however, Meena's observation perhaps suggests that the appearance may not be what it seems. In a previous chapter, Meena stumbles across the statue of Ganesha in the Big House garden, and now we see that the Kumar's front garden party has drawn some interest, inviting the reader to consider the possibility that the residents of the Big House may be more familiar to Meena than she believes.

8. **What does Nanima symbolise to Meena's Indian friends?**

   Example responses:

   - 'the latest news from the Motherland' (p. 201)
   - 'a beloved parent' (p. 201)
   - 'a familiar symbol' (p. 201)
   - 'would deify her, their own guilt and homesickness would see to that' (p. 201)

CHAPTER 8 OF ANITA AND ME

- 'small vessel' expected to 'contain the ocean of longing' they 'stored in their bellies' (p. 201)
- 'house seemed to vibrate with goodwill and hope' (p. 203).

Ultimately, she reminds them how sacred their Indian roots and identity are to them, reminding them also of the difficulty of the choices they have had to face as immigrants, leaving their elders and families behind.

9. What does the Punjabi language symbolise to Meena?

Example responses:

- 'an indoor language to me, an almost guilty secret which the Elders would only share away from prying English eyes and ears' (p. 203)
- 'On the street [...] volume would go up when they spoke English' (p. 203)
- 'when they wanted to say something intimate, personal, about feelings as opposed to acquisitions, they switched to Punjabi and the volume became a conspiratorial whisper' (p. 203).

Embracing the Punjabi language feels like an act of defiance to her British roots, yet a necessary step in embracing her Indian heritage. Most importantly, though, it seems that Meena might not only lose her Indian culture but also her relationship with Nanima if she continues to avoid learning Punjabi.

10. What do Nanima's stories symbolise to Meena?

Example response:

Nanima's 'remembrances' seem too 'stretched' and 'removed' from Meena's perception of 'reality' (p. 210), yet symbolise to her the significance of the untold stories in history. They also represent 'secrets', and what happens to relationships when secrets are withheld, and when secrets are shared. Meena reflects on this and it allows her to rationalise her own relationship with her mother: 'everyone's mothers had secrets and kept them particularly from their daughters' (p. 210). The stories also symbolise a world Meena is told that she comes from, but one that she does not know, and listening to these stories inspires in her an 'urge to reinvent' (p. 211) herself. She begins to understand that perhaps it is this desperation for belonging that fuels the 'continual compulsion to fabricate' (p. 211), but Nanima's stories give birth to a new desire, as Meena begins to 'desperately' want to 'visit India and claim some of this magic' as her own (p. 211).

11. What do the various interactions in this chapter reveal about attitudes towards different races in early 1970s Britain?

Learners should consider:

- Nanima and the Ballbearings' Committee
- Nanima, Mr Ormerod and the Mean Man
- Mama and Deirdre.

Example response:

Meena is very quick to recognise that the interaction between Nanima and the Ballbearings Committee is 'not somehow a meeting of equals' (p. 220). The manner in which the Ballbearings women observe and comment on the minutest of details, such as Nanima's eyes and teeth, reminds Meena of the way Misty is 'check[ed]' (p. 219). This is indicative of their view of Nanima as a spectacle, an anomaly, someone so unfamiliar and othered that they are intrigued by the similarities and normalities of what they behold. Similarly, 'fascination' as well as 'distaste' in Mr Ormerod and the 'Mean Man's' glances makes her feel 'terribly guilty suddenly, protective', aware even as a child of the undercurrents of microaggressions, and angered especially by the looks of 'pity' (p. 223). We also see through Deirdre's and mama's 'icy exchange' (p. 215) the prejudicial assumptions that Deirdre makes, assuming Meena and her family are from Pakistan as well as the underlying 'disbelief' that anyone who is not white would consider themselves to be 'better than her' (p. 215), disregarding completely their level of education, morality or social contributions. Born out of a combination of limited cross-cultural interactions and an ignorant consumption of political diatribes, these conversations and interactions remind the reader of how casually such discrimination would take place and invites the readers to critique the impact they would have had on someone like Meena growing up in the 1970s in the Midlands: depicted as 'faceless hordes' in the television news, 'begging for sanctuary', 'confused, helpless', and reduced to being 'gesticulating wanderers', devoid of both personality and identity (p. 216).

12. What can the reader infer in this chapter from the way that Meena's parents are accepted in Tollington?

Example response:

We learn in this chapter that Meena's parents, who don't ask for 'approval or acceptance', get it 'nevertheless' (p. 216). They 'charmed people' (p. 216). What's interesting, though, is that the reason for this acceptance is that they are visibly seen to assimilate, with their 'new car' and 'parties' in their garden (p. 216). They are appreciated for being 'so English' (p. 172), an acceptance that is even admired by their own, as we observe through the Uncles' reactions to papa's conversation with the Ballbearings women, 'seemingly impressed' (p. 204) that he had associations with the locals. Yet, Meena's mama invites the reader to reflect on how problematic this is when recognition of assimilation is seen as a 'buggering compliment' (p. 172), and the subsequent impact it has on the identity and sense of belonging on a child-like Meena, already torn between two worlds.

> **PIT STOP**
>
> **S-T-R-E-T-C-H**
>
> Ask learners to consider who else in the text is not accepted and why that might be.
>
> Example responses:
> - the Mad Mitchells
> - Deirdre
> - Fat Sally.

How?

Language

Narrative voice

Ask learners to consider the unreliability as well as the vulnerability and innocence of the child narrator by considering the following examples:

- Meena's description and perspective of Mr Turvey
- 'Maybe I told Nanima about the blackberry bushes at the far end of the park at that point. Or maybe not' (p. 230)
- Nanima's use of 'dogs' as a euphemism for men and Meena's misreading of it
- 'I felt myself floating above them all, just like Nanima had risen up to the ceiling that first night with Sunil in her arms' (p. 228).

Hyperbole

Key quotations:

- 'How dare he steal my Nanima from me!' (p. 222)
- 'the old man [...] one of the church mafia and I was sure he was also one of the phantom hecklers who hid behind Mr Ormerod to spit his poison' (p. 223)
- 'I had been left in charge of my family and failed miserably; my baby brother was starving before my eyes and my aged granny was a helpless mute in front of two people' (p. 224)
- 'I was ten feet tall, I had a hundred arms, like the goddess on top of the fridge in Auntie Shaila's house' (p. 228).

As expected from a child narrator's point of view, Syal's use of hyperbole is not just for dramatic effect but also a reminder of how children perceive even the ordinary as extraordinary. It also heightens the perceived magnitude of any traumatic experiences. We see Meena experience these situations with amplified sensitivities, and our empathy thereafter increases for her.

Ask learners to consider:

- How the goddess Durga that Meena imagines herself turning into is significant. What does the goddess symbolise and how is Meena's association with her significant at this point in the text?
- How Meena's hyperbole is an adoption of the adult vernacular and perspective, and to what extent this might suggest that she is beginning to associate herself even more with her family, especially Nanima?

Character focus

Nanima

Key quotations:

- 'gnarled brown fingers' (p. 199)
- 'soft warm pillow which smelt of cardamom and sweet sharp sweat' (p. 200)
- 'jaunty monologue' (p. 201)
- 'loud slurpings of tea' (p. 201)
- 'let out an enormous rasping fart' (p. 207)
- 'the stories I knew Nanima owned and kept to herself' (p. 230)
- 'I went to school, my father insisted' (p. 231)
- 'Never did I think I was less than a man. More than a man sometimes, this I was' (p. 231).

Nanima is created by Syal as a symbol of self-confidence, exuberance and resilience.

Mr Topsy/Turvey

Key quotations:

- 'muscled into the group' (p. 221)
- 'voluminous trousers billowing with excitement' (p. 221)
- 'How dare this fat man with the ridiculous crimplene strides know more Punjabi than me!' (p. 222)
- 'I served in India. Ten years. Magical country. Magical people' (p. 222)
- 'We should never have been there. Criminal it was!' (p. 222)
- 'fond faraway look in his brimming eyes' (p. 222).

Mr Topsy/Turvey is created by Syal to remind both Meena and the reader, that appearances can be deceptive and how important, yet simple, it can be to make someone feel included and welcome.

CHAPTER 8 OF ANITA AND ME

> **PIT STOP**
>
> **S-T-R-E-T-C-H**
>
> Ask learners to analyse the unreliability of the narrative voice in Meena's representation of Mr Topsy/Turvey, and why Syal has emphasised this here.

Uncle Alan

Key quotations:

- 'in the middle of one of his jocular moral chats' (p. 226)
- 'Find out who the real enemies are, the rich, the privileged, not the other people trying to make a living like you, not people like you' (p. 226).

Uncle Alan is created by Syal as a symbol of what an ally looks like, and the impact they can have in combating racism, intolerance and injustice.

Meena and Sunil's relationship

Key quotations:

- Nanima's 'ancient witchery to finally cut the umbilical cord that was strangling' the Kumars (p. 208)
- 'Sunil was now anybody's, especially mine' (p. 208)
- 'mashing up boiled vegetables [...] for Sunil's meals, boiling water for his bottles and nappies and even carrying his stinky nappies out to the bicycle shed' (p. 209)
- 'I could not imagine how I ever resented him' (p. 209).

Meena starts to see her little brother for the person that he is, with a newfound lens of joy and intrigue, devoid of the previous emotions of jealousy. She starts to recognise this newfound bond with him. She begins to enjoy the evening 'activity called Entertaining Sunil' (p. 208) and starts to appreciate him as a younger sibling who offers her companionship.

Meena and mama's relationship

Key quotations:

- 'all of us the product of each other, linked like Russian dolls' (p. 201–2)
- 'how difficult it must have been for mama to leave Nanima and how lonely she must have been' (p. 202)
- 'I vowed then that I would never leave her, this wrenching of daughter from mother would never happen again' (p. 202)
- 'everyone's mothers had secrets and kept them particularly from their daughters' (p. 210).

Syal draws attention to this relationship through the ritual of picture-taking, encapsulating three different generations of women, each intrinsically connected, yet with their own inner conflicts and struggles. Meena's promise to protect and sanctify this mother-daughter bond reveals to the reader that her desire to rebel is not as strong as her conviction towards her family, and the sense of love and responsibility that she feels.

Structure

Learners should explore the following examples from the opening and the ending of Chapter 8 and be invited to consider:

- Why Syal has chosen to begin and end with this focus on the duality of Meena and her family's identities and lives?
- What their predictions might be about key characters and plot developments within this chapter.

Cyclical Structure

- **Towards the beginning of the chapter**: 'this unfamiliar scene where my two worlds had collided and mingled so easily' (p. 204).
- **Ending**: 'What is there to fear when you have already lived two whole lives? [...] Your mama is on her second one, here, over here. And you Meena...' (p. 231-2).

Dialogue is crucial to appreciate the moments of tension generated in this chapter. Consider, for example, the clipped dialogue between Deirdre and mama. It is especially powerful in its communication of the undercurrent tension between them – Deirdre's lack of respect for the Kumars and 'backhanded' stance juxtaposes mama's 'dangerously patient' control of her anger, masked with a maintained facade of politeness (p. 215). The 'icy exchange' simultaneously reveals one's power and composure vs the other's disrespect and 'disbelief', positioning the reader to appreciate not only the two characters but also what happens when their contexts collide (p. 215).

Extracts

How does Syal use language to demonstrate Meena's transformation in the following three extracts?

- 'Still, that evening our house seemed to vibrate with goodwill and hope [...] Never seen the Elders so expansive and unconcerned, and knew that this somehow had something to do with Nanima' (p. 203-4).
- 'It was all falling into place now, why I felt this continual compulsion to fabricate [...] had they packed up their cases and followed them back here' (p. 211-2).
- 'What was the matter with him? Didn't he understand what he had done? [...] I sank into the farty settee and gave in to the darkness' (p. 228-9).

Example response planning, using topic sentence scaffolds:

Syal presents Meena:

- Initially, ...
    - ashamed, conscious and resistant
    - weary of the Tollington community's feelings of racial superiority.
- Then, ...
    - intrigued and curious
    - beginning to feel validated
    - starting to see her inner turmoil reflected in the stories.
- Finally, ...
    - developing an urge to visit the place of her heritage and roots
    - beginning to resolve her identity crisis
    - succumbing to her anger and channelling her frustrations to assert herself
    - drawing strength and power from her spiritual heritage.
- Ultimately, ...
    - she is still unaware that she does not need to fight injustice and intolerance alone, and has allies within the Tollington community
    - she connects with her inner strength and recognises the power within herself.

Example response, unpacking quotations and language therein to support points:

Once Nanima arrives, Syal presents Meena's transformation as inevitable. We can see the immediate impact she has on Meena's sense of self and identity. Meena marvels at her, connects with her, admires her and respects her, which gives birth to an acceptance of her sense of self. We see Meena wanting to understand where she comes from and realise that she does not need to reconcile between two worlds. We see her marvel at the way her two worlds begin to 'collide'. Syal's use of present participles – 'reclaiming', 'guffawing', 'wafting', 'sprinkling' and 'twinkling' – emphasise the unashamed celebration of joy and identity that Nanima's arrival leads to. Meena, despite the temptation to run away indoors, is 'drawn to this unfamiliar scene', connecting with the 'whiff of defiance' and giving in to this freedom of expression that resonates with her own sensibilities. Nanima's celebration of the 'junglee' in her is significant. Not only does it connote the wildness and freedom of spirit that Meena relishes, but also reflects the rebelliousness brewing within her. It is precisely the validation she needs that she can be true to herself, as well as embrace her heritage and roots. She does not have to choose.

The final metamorphosis comes towards the end of the chapter when she feels threatened by Sam and his gang, yet empowered by Nanima, and is reminded of the impact of his words from the fete when he 'let the cider and his single brain cell do the talking'. The pain she still feels is evident as she reflects on how that one moment took away her 'innocence', and realises that nothing she can do to Sam will ever have the same profound effect. This epiphany is what gives rise to a power Meena finds within herself to retaliate, wanting to hurt him. She connects with her inner energy, evident through the religious allusion to the goddess Durga, channelling her symbolic bravery and protection, as well as hinting at her power of destruction. Meena's gaze stuns Sam and his gang into silence and we begin to see a hint of violence that Uncle Alan warns against. It is evident to the reader that something has awoken in Meena, and that her quest for self-discovery has only just begun.

CHAPTER 9 OF ANITA AND ME

At a glance

> **Chapter summary quotation:** 'I would no longer be Anita's shadow but her equal' (p. 237)
> **Big Question:** What does the death of Tracey's dog help Meena to realise?
> **Significant plot event:** Tracey's dog is killed.
> **Character focus:** Fat Sally, Anita, Meena and Anita's relationship
> **Key themes:**
> - Conflict and violence
> - Friendship
> - Neglect, bullying and abuse
>
> **Handle with care:**
> - Reference to a range of racially offensive terms and violent/traumatic incidents in this chapter will need to be handled with sensitivity. Please refer to the 'Handle with care' guidance in the 'How to use this book' section for further support.
>   - the name of Tracey's dog: Nigger
>   - the fight between Fat Sally and Anita: 'Fat Sally threw herself onto Anita with a strangled scream, grabbing handfuls of hair and pinning her squarely to the ground' (p. 240)
>   - the graphic death of Tracey's dog and how Anita has to end his life by dropping a rock on him with 'a heavy thud' (p. 244).

Why?

'Why' is important not only within the world of the text, but also when considering authorial intent and messaging.

- Why is it significant in this chapter that Meena gets reinstated as Anita's friend? Why does Anita accept her assertion without question? Is it to remind Meena that friendships can overcome conflicts, or so the reader can observe that Meena always had the power to influence the dynamic in their relationship?

- Why does Syal emphasise the fight between Sally and Anita, delving fully into the aggression and violence? Is it so we as readers can see what happens when pent-up frustrations explode? Or is it for Meena's benefit, allowing her to see that bullies can also be victims?
- Why does Syal create tension as Meena challenges Tracey on their dog's name, only to then build that tension further to its tragic demise? Are there, perhaps, bigger questions to consider about the dangers of losing one's morality and humanity? Or is it for the readers to see the impact the dog's death takes on Anita's body, even when she is desperate to curtail all emotions that make her human and vulnerable?
- Why is this chapter important, therefore, with its building tension, aggression and ultimate tragedy, in reinforcing Meena's metamorphosis and awakening her to the possibility of embracing all aspects of both her thoughts and biases?

This allows us to consider Chapter 9's Big Question:

> What does the death of Tracey's dog help Meena to realise?

What?

What happens?

The metamorphosis in Meena continues as she channels her newfound energy and confidence into walking back into Anita's life, like 'the prodigal returned' (p. 233). We see immediately her shift in perceived maturity, as the gang she was desperate to belong to is now a 'motley collection of toddlers and bedwetters' (p. 234), yet she still relishes the 'open-mouthed wonder and admiration' (p. 234) that encircles her. We see Meena extend compassion towards Tracey, inviting her along, and later we see her standing up to Anita for the first time, owning her decision and mirroring the defence that Anita put up for her previously by inviting her to the farm. We also see Meena standing up for her morals and unafraid to sacrifice her values in friendship, challenging Tracey on their dog's name and no longer unafraid to call out anything insulting. This character development is significant for Meena, who has previously equated being an 'individual' to being an 'outsider'.

At the farm, we see her extending sympathy on hearing of the impact of the slip road on the Palmers, unprepared for Mr Palmer's dismissal as he celebrates the economic benefits he has secured in its stead. This is where the possibility of social mobility, and the fear of not having this option hits Meena: 'Everyone was moving away, everyone except for me' (p. 237). However, there is a brief moment where Meena enjoys belonging and acceptance, even when it involves 'laughing at someone else' (p. 237). She hopes that she is about to see the beginning of a new relationship with Anita on her own terms, one where she 'would no longer be Anita's shadow but her equal' (p. 237). However, when the altercation between Fat Sally and Anita escalates quickly to a 'kicking, biting, scratching' (p. 240) fight, the different facets of Anita's personality start to dawn on Meena. She sees how Anita remains 'completely silent' against Fat Sally's 'constant impassioned monologue', and is 'troubled' by 'her quiet acceptance, her satisfaction at being pummelled' (p. 241). Meena's decision to turn a blind eye to Anita's aggression is interesting, even when she sees Anita channel 'all her energy' into hurting Fat Sally, causing 'a semi-circle of bloody indentations under each eye' and the subsequent sadistic pleasure she receives, her mouth twisting into a 'good-humoured grin' (p. 241). Instead, what Meena chooses to see is the 'victim' behind the 'bully', crossing the 'fine line between love and pity' (p. 242) and recognising that Anita needs her more. We see Meena try to dissipate the fight 'pathetically' (p. 241), aware of her inaction and hesitancy as the tension escalates beyond control and Tracey's dog breaks free. Her desperation to hold on to the fantasy of Anita that she's created for herself is even more pronounced when she tries to distract herself from the 'ugliness' (p. 242) she has witnessed. She instead admires the way Anita gets up nonchalantly 'in one easy motion' and proceeds to ride Trixie like a 'centaur' moving with 'joy' (p. 242).

Meena watches and relishes this moment as the 'antidote' she needs, before being brought abruptly back to reality with the 'screech' of a car, 'endless pause [...] punctuated by a shrill, inhuman scream' (p. 242). Tracey's dog has been hit by a red car, probably Graham Pembridge's Porsche (p. 168). What follows are a few tense moments of Tracey in distress, 'sobbing' in 'earnest' (p. 243), and Hairy Neddy trying to take charge of the situation. It is Anita, who proceeds to take the dog out of its misery, 'calmly' strolling over to 'the family pet' and dropping a rock on him with 'a heavy thud' (p. 244). It's interesting how her body, 'limp as a ragdoll' and falling 'heavily' (p. 244) on Hairy Neddy speaks more of her vulnerability than any of her words or actions ever reveal. For Meena, this moment is an epiphany, as she recognises that her anger towards the dog has been misplaced. She becomes introspective and aware of her own fallibility and biases, holding herself to account for blaming 'him for what he was called, not what he was' (p. 245). She recognises the similarity between her and Sam Lowbridge – their shared folly of making the innocent 'the focus' of their 'resentment' (p. 245). The chapter ends with Meena accepting herself with bravery and insight, determined to come out stronger: 'It was not your fault, I told myself' (p. 245).

Social, cultural and historical context

It is important for learners to fully understand, appreciate and be able to realistically envisage life in the fictional village of Tollington in 1972 for Meena. The following are some useful considerations when discussing this context with learners.

- **Biba**: A London fashion store of the 1960s and 1970s.

- **Industrialisation and the construction of the M6**: 'Bloody slip road. They never mentioned that in the original plans.' (p. 236); 'I shall be a rich man pretty soon. And then we're off [...] Lake District! [...] Buying a hotel... No slip roads for bloody miles!' (p. 236-7).

Vocabulary in context

The following vocabulary from Chapter 9 can be pre-taught to help with reading fluency and reduce cognitive load. What does each of the following words mean in context?

Word	Quotation	Definition
prodigal (n.)	'crowded round me like the prodigal returned and I was touched' (p. 233)	someone who is reckless, especially in their spending of money
motley (adj.)	'How did I ever think this motley collection of toddlers and bedwetters constituted a gang?' (p. 234)	assorted or varied in character or appearance
alabaster (adj.)	'her sharp alabaster features focused and confident' (p. 236)	typically white calcite, often carved into ornaments
imperiously (adv.)	'she was pointing at Tracey imperiously' (p. 238)	with arrogance or in a domineering way
haute couture (n.)	'pull against his haute couture leash' (p. 238)	marked by superior craftsmanship; expensive clothes produced by leading fashion houses

PIT STOP

Retrieval point

Return to this vocabulary in a later lesson, assessing if learners can link each key word to the relevant character(s). For a bonus point, develop each link into an analysis of how the writer's language choice presents that character.

Examples:

- What might Syal be trying to make the reader consider when Meena admires Sherrie's 'alabaster features'? Consider how this is a critique of the white-centred representations of beauty that Meena would be accustomed to and how she might be conditioned to consider these superior.

- In what way is Anita's 'imperious' manner of talking to Tracey reflective of the broken relationship between the two sisters? What might Syal be suggesting about their family dynamics in general?

- What is Syal suggesting through her reference to Fat Sally's 'haute couture' scarf? To what extent might this be an indicator of social class and its impact on the friendship dynamics within the group?

CHAPTER 9 OF ANITA AND ME

PIT STOP

Direct instruction point

Learners can use the following to develop their understanding of the different variations of verbs and their use in this chapter. This will benefit their analysis skills for academic writing.

Dynamic/material verbs

- 'We **ambled** past the park where I could see Sam Lowbridge and his gang **lolling** on the roundabout we called the Witches' Hat' (p. 235)
- 'Fat Sally **threw** herself onto Anita with a strangled scream, **grabbing** handfuls of hair and **pinning** her squarely to the ground' (p. 240).

Stative/mental verbs:

- 'I **hate** that stupid name!' (p. 235)
- 'I **wondered** briefly if Catholics were anything like Hindus' (p. 239).

Present participles

- 'Tracey dived straight into the tangle of **kicking**, **biting**, **scratching** bodies' (p. 240)
- 'The piddly poodle went mad, **yapping** hysterically and **jumping** up, **trying** to escape' (p. 240).

Past participles

- 'Fat Sally **moved** closer, her fists **clenched**' (p. 240)
- 'Sorrow **flooded** me until it rose up to my eyes and made them sting' (p. 242).

PIT STOP

S-T-R-E-T-C-H

Ask learners to consider the impact of these sentence structures in their individual contexts and discuss the intended effect on the reader.

Possible answers:

- generate an ongoing feeling of...
- magnify and heighten the building tension
- amplify the immediacy of the action
- illustrate the extent of the impact on the emotional/mental state...
- communicate the finality and intensity of thought and emotion

BLOOMSBURY TEACHER GUIDE: ANITA AND ME

- emphasise the permanence of the impact of...
- exemplify the relentlessness of...
- emphasise/accentuate/reinforce the feelings of...

PIT STOP

Academic writing point

Learning how to track key moments to understand why they are transformative could also be a practical, active step to answering the Big Question: **What does the death of Tracey's dog help Meena to realise?**

Learners should be encouraged to make references to Meena's behaviour towards Tracey's dog in other parts of the text too. They can follow discourse markers to track Meena's transformation:

- Initially, ...
- Then, ...
- Finally, ...
- Ultimately, ...

Plot and character development

For tips on how to approach these 'What' questions, refer to the 'Plot and character development' section of 'How to use this book' on pages 5-6 of this guide.

1. What does Meena have to do in order to go to Anita's house?

Example response:

Meena has to do what she does best – put on a facade. She needs to convince her parents that she has recovered from her fever so she forces herself to 'eat two aloo rotis' and asks for a glass of milk to assure them that her appetite is restored. She then puts on a performance as she feeds Sunil, blowing on his food loudly and 'making him laugh', before proceeding with an 'exaggerated routine' of tidying up and 'chirpily whistling' until mama is forced to comply: 'Go on, then. You're giving me a headache now' (p. 233).

2. What changes as Meena returns to her 'now defunct gang' (p. 233)?

Example response:

One of the most significant changes is how Meena is seen as an equal and an important, celebrated member of the gang who is 'mobbed' as soon as she arrives. Meena is 'touched' by the attention, enjoying the 'open-mouthed wonder' and 'admiration' that encircles her. She puts on a performance, emphasising her new role in caring for Nanima and exaggerating some of the 'responsibilities': 'I've been cooking for her, washing her and that'. Meena's perspective of this 'gang' changes dramatically, as she acts dismissively and starts to consider herself too grown up and mature for the 'motley collection of toddlers and bedwetters that constituted a gang' (p. 233-4).

3. **What does the reader learn about Tracey in this chapter?**

   Example responses:

   - Juxtaposes Anita and evokes the reader's empathy: 'pinched, wan features had rearranged themselves into a compact heart-shaped face of such sweetness and sorrow' (p. 234).
   - She is disappointed to learn that Meena isn't there to call upon her.
   - Lonely and regretful to miss out on companionship: "She's up at Sherrie's farm. She's always up there now…' she said wistfully' (p. 234).
   - Still full of innocence and hope: 'her eyes widened' (p. 234).
   - Neglected and vulnerable: 'hair unbrushed in a frilly summer dress' (p. 234).
   - Craves responsibility and purpose: "Gorra tek Nigger with us,' Tracey said proudly' (p. 235).
   - Determined to prove herself yet also reliant on Deirdre: 'But I'm not scared of ghosts. Mom says she'll buy it for me when I grow up' (p. 235).
   - Apologetic and desperate to appease: "It's just 'cos of his colour, honest!' Tracey said pleadingly' (p. 235).
   - Emotionally astute and does not want to harm intentionally, unlike Anita: 'Tracey suddenly linked her arm in mine and said reassuringly, 'Mom chose it." (p. 235).
   - Terrified of Anita and instinctively switches to self-preservation mode: 'holding up the dog to her face like a shield' (p. 237).
   - On edge with behaviour reflective of a victim of physical and sexual abuse: 'visibly jumped at Sherrie's command' (p. 238).
   - Compassionate: "I can't send him home! Not on his own! He's daft round cars!' she stammered' (p. 238).

4. **What does the reader learn through Meena's conversation with Tracey about the dog's name?**

   Example response:

   It is evident that Meena is distressed because of the overtly racist choice of the dog's name: 'I hate that stupid name!' (p. 235). The name is confirmed by Tracey as Deirdre's decision: 'Mom chose it' (p. 235). This is reflective of her racism. Tracey is immediately apologetic and tries to rationalise the decision, 'It's just 'cos of his colour, honest!' (p. 235), but immediately recognises the severity of the abuse as she shifts to a 'reassuring' stance (p. 235). Meena finds it difficult to initiate this conversation, yet when she does, it is evident that it has been simmering inside her, 'That did it' (p. 235), and that she has been projecting these feelings of disgust onto the dog. This is confirmed later in the chapter: 'I had blamed him for what he was called, not what he was' (p. 245).

5. **What can the reader infer from the way Meena describes Sherrie?**

    Example response:

    It is evident through Meena's description of Sherrie's 'blonde hair streaming behind her' and 'sharp alabaster features focused and confident' that she is in awe of Sherrie and the power and control she exudes. She admires how she 'seemed elegant and completely in tune with her rotund steed'. Syal draws our attention to how Meena sees her through the white-centric conditioning of what she expects of royalty: 'Sherrie looked just like a medieval princess, I thought' (p. 236).

6. **What can the reader infer from the exchange between Meena and Sherrie's father?**

    Example response:

    Despite working on the land potentially all his life, Mr Palmer, 'tall, blonde and sunburned, even in winter' (p. 236) represents one of those whose livelihoods were impacted when industrialisation took over. The landscape in the Midlands began to change, particularly through the construction of the M6 and the subsequent 'slip road'. Yet when Meena offers him sympathy, he is quick to dismiss it, reassuring her that he has already taken the case to court and will be a 'rich man pretty soon' (p. 236), securing a promising future for himself with the settlement – a hotel in the Lake District. He laughs 'loudly' as he leaves (p. 236), implying a self-centred approach and reminding the reader of the stark reality of class and economic disparity in a place like Tollington. His response makes the reader consider what it would have been like for someone who had the luxury of choice, who not only escaped unscathed but also profited from the upheaval experienced by those left behind.

7. **What can the reader infer from Meena's reaction to Mr Palmer's declaration?**

    Example responses:

    - 'his words were snatched away in the wind' (p. 236)
    - 'My feet felt heavy against the stony road. Everyone was moving away, everyone except for me' (p. 237)
    - 'the last few feet up to the paddock felt endless' (p. 237).

Although Meena has always fantasised about leaving Tollington for her acting career, the reader now observes desperation within her, almost a compulsion to get away. Previously, the thought of not passing the eleven-plus and going to school with Anita made her feel trapped. But now, we see a despondency as she begins to realise the significance of social mobility, as well as her need to escape her hometown where she has been othered and experienced racism, both overtly and through microaggressions.

8. What does Anita's treatment of others reveal to the reader?

Example response:

As soon as Tracey arrives, Anita's immediate annoyance and interrogation reveal her intolerance. This reinforces the absence of both companionship and trust between the two sisters. This dismissive treatment of her sister as a character trait is further heightened through her condescending treatment of Fat Sally. Anita coerces her to use her mother's expensive Biba scarf and crudely draws attention to the class disparity by suggesting that her mother is wealthy enough to buy her another.

9. What can the reader infer from Meena's observations of Fat Sally?

Example response:

It is evident that Meena is conditioned to be repulsed by Fat Sally's size and to view her superficially, as she doesn't think her 'soft features capable of anything but bad moods and wounded pride' (p. 240). However, when she sees her defending her Catholic roots fervently, she undoubtedly experiences a connection, wondering 'if Catholics were anything like Hindus' (p. 239) and reflecting on how Fat Sally was effectively 'repeating verbatim one of her parents' lectures' (p. 239). She notices how Fat Sally is different, but doesn't yet comprehend that this difference is mocked and ridiculed. There is a fleeting moment of Meena wondering if Fat Sally too has to contend with a world different to the likes of Anita and Sherrie, one that features an 'army of overpowering female relatives' (p. 239) and is governed by a community's set of beliefs. However, she is not yet ready to view Fat Sally as a victim of bullying which is perhaps why this connection dissipates just as quickly as it is experienced.

10. What does Syal emphasise during the fight between Anita and Fat Sally?

Ask learners to consider:

- The juxtaposition between Fat Sally and Anita's behaviour and description.
- Meena's emerging realisation that Anita is both a 'victim' and a 'bully'.

Fat Sally

- 'was pulling so hard that the skin on Anita's temples was lifted up from her scalp' (p. 240)
- 'kept up a constant impassioned monologue as she pulled harder and harder' (p. 240)
- 'Everyone says so' (p. 240)
- 'bashing Fat Sally on the back with her riding crop; it was like pinging an elastic band at a yeti' (p. 241)
- 'the Biba scarf dragging in the dust behind them' (p. 241)
- '"My scarf!' screamed Fat Sally' (p. 241).

Anita

- 'Anita did not even register these curses' (p. 240)
- 'had her fingernails sunk firmly into Fat Sally's cheeks' (p. 240)
- 'completely silent [...] did not utter one word, emit one moan' (p. 241)
- 'triumph glazing her eyes' (p. 241)
- 'quiet acceptance' (p. 241)
- 'a satisfaction at being pummelled' (p. 241)
- 'I couldn't work out if this made her a bully or a victim' (p. 241).

Example response:

The contrast in description between the two girls is reflective of the bullying and subsequent conditioning that has impacted even Meena. She doesn't see Fat Sally as a victim, nor is she treated as one. Fat Sally's 'Biba scarf' is forcibly taken from her and seen 'dragging in dust' (p. 241) with complete disregard for both her feelings and belongings. In fact, she is dehumanised to such an extent that Meena does not even appreciate the magnitude of the 'bubbles of bright red blood seeping' from under her eyes, or the riding crop 'bashing' on her as if 'like pinging an elastic band at a yeti' (p. 241). Even at this moment, it is Anita who Meena views with both marvel and empathy: 'I could not work out if this made her a bully or a victim' (p. 241).

11. **What does the reader learn about Anita through her reactions to Fat Sally and her actions after the fight?**

Example response:

We learn that Anita is perhaps so used to violence and abuse in her household that she is conditioned to receive it with 'quiet acceptance' (p. 241), and has been desensitised completely. She does not 'register' the 'curses', remaining 'completely silent', and seems to have developed some form of coping mechanism with her 'steady' breathing and 'relaxed' muscles (p. 241). In fact, what we see is not someone who has learned how to accept and take abuse, but someone who has learnt how to retaliate. We see a streak of evil in Anita, how she can be cruel to an irrational extreme as she channels all her 'energy' into the 'ends of her fingers' (p. 241) and relishes the pain she causes Fat Sally: 'triumph glazing her eyes and twisting her mouth into a good-humoured grin' (p. 241). We see a quiet insurgence of sadistic pleasure as her expression reveals 'satisfaction' (p. 241) in the power she has over Fat Sally at the moment. She will even go to the extreme of putting her wellbeing at risk, merely to humiliate someone else: 'I made you do this, I knew you would do it and I have been proved right' (p. 241). What's even more shocking is the manner in which she recovers, her face instantly 'calm' with a 'faraway' expression, and transitions immediately to a 'centaur' as she gets up in 'one easy motion', brushing the 'dirt and hay stalks off her back' and proceeding to ride Trixie with effortless ease (p. 242). We see her transform into another person, one capable of fearlessness, talent and epitomising beauty. She moves 'with joy, as if she possessed the best and deepest secret', riding 'better than anyone else because she truly had no fear' (p. 242).

12. What does the reader learn about Meena's changing perceptions in this chapter?

Example response:

Most evidently, the reader notices a shift in Meena's perception of Anita. Anita, who has always been on a pedestal in Meena's eyes despite her indifference and ill-treatment of others, is now falling from grace, lying on the ground with hair 'about her head like a broken halo' (p. 241-2). Meena begins to notice that she is conflicted, and can't decide whether she is a 'bully or a victim' (p. 241). As before, when Meena had to distract herself from Anita's bullying of Tracey after the peeing competition, we see Meena trying to find solace and comfort in the manner in which Anita rides fearlessly, in sync with the horse as if she's a 'centaur' (p. 242). The reader sees that Meena is still compelled by her and drawn to her, and will search for whatever 'antidote' she can find to overcome her 'ugliness' (p. 242). Yet, Meena's awe of Anita is now shifting, giving way to an emotion that she hasn't before experienced for Anita – pity: 'She needed me maybe more than I needed her. There is a fine line between love and pity and I had just stepped over it' (p. 242).

What's more, the reader also sees a growing sense of emotional awareness in Meena as she 'suddenly' realises that 'Deirdre had no intention, ever, of buying Anita a horse' (p. 242), and that Sherrie's family will move, wrecking the fantasy of spending 'all day riding and grooming' (p. 242). Meena's heightened awareness and insight are just the beginning of her personal growth and her journey to transcend above and beyond her peers in Tollington.

> **PIT STOP**
>
> ## S-T-R-E-T-C-H
>
> Ask learners to consider where else in the text Meena begins to realise truths about Anita.
>
> Example responses:
>
> - when Anita's mother deceives her at the fair by stealing 'Dave, the Poet' from her
> - when she sees Anita burst into tears after her mother is dismissive of her and shouts at her before driving away in a car
> - when she observes Anita wearing an oversized uniform the day after her mother runs away.

13. What does the death of Tracey's dog help Meena to realise?

Example response:

The death of the dog is symbolic, as it reminds Meena of the sanctity of life and how easy it is to allow biases and prejudices to cloud your judgement, compassion and empathy. She regrets how she had 'wished' him dead and 'blamed him for what he was called, not what he was' (p. 245). She projected the 'resentment and hatred' of other characters in the text towards the vulnerable, despite knowing they are powerless and 'in no position but to accept it' (p. 245). It is a moment where Meena examines her conscience, recognising the similarity in sentiment between her and Sam Lowbridge. She recognises that any intolerance can easily poison and dehumanise. Her moral honesty in this moment is a reminder from Syal of the importance of being introspective and willing and open to recognising lapses in conscience and humanity.

How?

Language

Narrative voice

Ask learners to consider the reliability and unreliability of the narrative voice by considering the following:

- Meena's description of Anita and Fat Sally during the fight and how she generates empathy for Anita, yet portrays Fat Sally as an unaffected abuser.
- Meena's introspection as she recognises what Sherrie and Anita do not know about their parents' intentions.
- Meena's moral examination following the death of Tracey's dog.

Character focus

Fat Sally

Key quotations:

- 'squealed and almost fell off the gate [...] the rest of us howled' (p. 237)
- 'looked like she was going to cry' (p. 238)
- 'That's a Biba scarf that is [...] My mom got it from London' (p. 238)
- 'gasped audibly, I could tell no one had ever dared criticise her mum's dress sense before' (p. 239)
- 'And we aren't... I mean we ain't rich. We just work hard and save hard' (p. 239)
- 'They are not bloody nuns. They are decent women who have given their lives to God' (p. 240).

Fat Sally is created by Syal as an important symbol of a vulnerable character who is rebelling after being bullied and controlled for too long.

> **PIT STOP**
>
> **S-T-R-E-T-C-H**
>
> Ask learners to analyse the dehumanisation of Fat Sally through Meena's description of her and what Syal is suggesting through this depiction.

Anita

Key quotations:

- 'Anita, the same skinny harpy who had just narrowly missed gouging out another girl's eyes, was now whispering lover's endearments into a fat pony's ears' (p. 242)
- 'Anita strode over to a rockery [...] picked up a footballsized rock and held it out with both hands towards Hairy Neddy. 'Kill him,' she said' (p. 244)
- 'Anita snorted, such a belittling noise that Hairy Neddy seemed to shrink a couple of inches' (p. 244)
- 'The rock fell to the road with a heavy thud [...] Anita went as limp as a rag doll and fell heavy against Hairy Neddy' (p. 244).

Syal draws attention to how Anita is the ultimate representation of a bully, driven to unkindness and retaliation after being a victim for too long. She puts on a facade of indifference, yet the impact of killing the dog evidently takes a toll on her physically as she collapses on Hairy Neddy.

Meena and Anita's relationship

Key quotations:

- 'I suddenly realised now, that Deirdre had no intention, ever, of buying Anita a horse. Sorrow flooded me until it rose up to my eyes and made them sting' (p. 242)
- 'She needed me maybe more than I needed her. There is a fine line between love and pity and I had just stepped over it' (p. 242).

Syal draws attention to the shifting power dynamics in this relationship as Meena's awe and unquestionable admiration for Anita is now giving way to a new emotion: pity.

Structure

Learners should explore the following examples from the opening and the ending of Chapter 9 and be invited to consider:

- Why Syal has chosen to begin and end with a focus on food?
- Why Meena's loss of appetite is significant?
- What their predictions might be about key characters and plot developments within this chapter.

Opening: 'I forced myself to eat two aloo rotis' (p. 233).

Ending: 'decided to add another word to my expanding vocabulary. 'Can I have something... vegetarian for lunch?"' (p. 245).

Dialogue is crucial to appreciate the moments of tension generated in this chapter. Consider, for example, the clipped and strained dialogue between Meena and Tracey. It is especially powerful in its communication of the undercurrent tension and fury that Meena has been bottling up about the name of their dog, juxtaposed with Tracey's genuine embarrassment and innocence of the impact of the racial slur.

Foreshadowing

Syal prepares her readers for both the tragic, and symbolic death of Tracey's dog.

Key quotations:

- 'A car zoomed past, quickly followed by Blaze, the mad collie, who yapped furiously at its back wheels [...] The piddly poodle watched this with interest and then swerved towards the road'(p. 235)
- 'One of these days... He don't have no road sense!' (p. 235)
- 'I did not want to go any faster; the birds had suddenly gone silent' (p. 243).

Parallelism

When Anita says, 'What the hell's she doing here?', referring to Tracey, Meena responds, 'I said she could come' (p. 237). For the first time, Meena has challenged Anita's authority, standing up for Tracey. This exchange parallels an earlier dialogue in Chapter 7, when Anita similarly stood up for Meena to Sherrie. When Sherrie invited Anita to her farm but didn't invite Meena, Anita demanded that Meena had 'to come too' (p. 188). This parallelism helps to reinforce Meena's claim that she might finally be Anita's equal, meaning she now has the same self-assuredness as Anita.

Beliefs in the supernatural

Syal uses these beliefs to draw parallels between Meena's two worlds and to demonstrate how some perceptions and beliefs are universal, spanning both time and place.

Key quotations:

- 'The Christmas house is haunted now' (p. 235)
- 'the roundabout we called The Witches' Hat' (p. 235)
- The allusion to Chapter 8 and Nanima's beliefs in ghosts: 'My grandmother's ghost lives at the top of our house in the village' (p. 210).

Extracts

1. How does Syal use language to demonstrate the importance of friendship?

'I said she could come. She was bored. [...] "She's gorrenough money, ain't she?' called Anita, who was striding purposefully towards Tracey' (p. 237–238).

Example response planning, using topic sentence scaffolds: 💡

- Companionship: Tracey's need for belonging and shift from visible sorrow to delight upon being invited.
- Power dynamics: Tracey cannot go until she is invited, Meena takes the risk of bringing Tracey with her without approval from Anita, Anita accepts Meena's rebellion, and Sherrie has power because of her secure socio-economic position.
- Belonging: School plays a role in creating belonging or division, Sherrie and Anita will be the 'cocks of the yard' in their school whilst Fat Sally's changing schools is received with initial surprise, then despised and ridiculed.
- Compliance: Anyone not complying can be vilified or coerced – the use of Fat Sally's scarf despite her pleas and Tracey's distress, yet compliance, in accepting that her dog had to be tied up.

2. How does Syal use language to create tension?

'Before anyone knew what was happening, Fat Sally threw herself onto Anita with a strangled scream [...] 'My scarf!' screamed Fat Sally and Anita let go of her hair' (p. 240–241).

Example response planning, using topic sentence scaffolds: 💡

Use of repetition

- Epimone: 'You bloody **slag**! Your mom's a **slag**! **Everyone says so**! You'll end up in the bloody gutter! **Everyone says so, slag**!'
- Mesodiplosis: 'She did not utter **one** word, emit **one** moan'.

Use of verbs

- Present participles: 'entangling', 'grabbing', 'pinning', 'kicking, biting, scratching bodies', 'yapping', 'screaming', 'barking', 'wailing'.
- Dynamic/material verbs: 'catapulted', 'screamed', 'shouted', 'ran'.

Use of sentence structures

- Exclamatives: 'You bloody slag!'; 'Stop them Sherrie!'.
- Syntactic parallelism: 'I made you do this, I knew would do it'; "Nigger!' screamed Tracey. 'Dad!' screamed Sherrie. 'My scarf!' screamed Fat Sally'.
- Asyndeton: 'What really troubled me was her quiet acceptance, her satisfaction at being pummelled'.

Use of sensory imagery

- 'molars grinding with each syllable'
- 'strangled scream'
- 'yapping hysterically'
- 'was pulling so hard that the skin on Anita's temples was lifted up from her scalp'
- 'tiny bubbles of bright red blood seeping'.

Use of juxtaposition

- 'I stood transfixed, not even daring to interfere'
- 'Anita's face, it was clearly visible'
- 'Fat Sally kept up a constant impassioned monologue [...] but Anita did not even register these curses'
- 'Whilst words poured out of Fat Sally [...] Anita remained completely silent'
- 'I could not work out if this made her a bully or a victim'.

Use of figurative language

- 'words poured out of Fat Sally like messages from a fairground medium'
- 'piddly poodle barking into a single wailing note of anguish'
- 'triumph glazing her eyes and twisting her mouth into a good-humoured grin'
- 'like pinging an elastic band at a yeti'.

Example response, unpacking quotations and language therein to support points:

The introduction of the physical threat of danger raises the stakes and intensifies the tensions.

CHAPTER 10 OF ANITA AND ME

At a glance

> **Chapter summary quotation:** 'Clash of the Titans' (p. 258)
> **Big Question:** How is the reader positioned to view Anita with some sympathy in this chapter?
> **Significant plot event:** Anita's mother leaves Tollington (abandoning her daughters) and Meena's family invite Anita for dinner.
> **Character focus:** Deirdre, Anita, mama and papa, Nanima
> **Key themes:**
> - Innocence
> - Neglect, bullying and abuse
> - Friendship
> **Handle with care:**
> - Reference to the following incidents and terms in this chapter will need to be handled with sensitivity. Please refer to the 'Handle with care' guidance in the 'How to use this book' section for further support.
>   - 'walked out' (p. 246) as a euphemism for abandonment
>   - 'lezzie' (p. 247)
>   - 'virgin' (p. 248).

Why?

'Why' is important not only within the world of the text, but also when considering authorial intent and messaging.

- Why does Syal show the reader Meena thinking about the contrast in how she would have reacted if her mother had walked out compared to Anita's relatively neutral approach?
- Why is it significant and poignant that Deirdre ordered the wrong-sized uniform for Anita?

- Why does Anita react so aggressively to Meena's physical tenderness and how does it foreshadow dark events to come later in the novel?
- Why does Syal show Meena's parents disagreeing about how best to offer support to Anita and Tracey now that their mother has 'walked out'?
- Why do Meena's parents allow her lie to Anita about 'all the top restaurants' (p. 254) to go unchallenged when they have reacted so strongly to untruths in the past?
- Why does Syal show us Anita and Meena enjoying one another's company over their shared interest in fabric and fashion over dinner?
- Why does Anita uncharacteristically acquiesce to mama's request that she return Meena's items to her room?

This allows us to consider Chapter 10's Big Question:

> How is the reader positioned to view Anita with some sympathy in this chapter?

What?

What happens?

Anita's mother, Deirdre, leaves Tollington (abandoning her daughters). Meena uses the sharing of this information to deflect her parents' disappointment and anger when she asks them what a 'virgin' is, and her family invite Anita to their home for dinner. The evening provides a lens through which Meena can appreciate the real cultural and moral differences between herself and Anita. Anita attempts to take home some of Meena's possessions without permission and is handled firmly by Meena's mother as she leaves.

Social, cultural and historical context

It is important for learners to fully understand, appreciate and be able to realistically envisage life in the fictional village of Tollington in 1972 for Meena. They may require pre-teaching activities on the following features of social, cultural and historical context so they can write about them confidently.

The following are some useful topics or terms to consider when discussing the context of this chapter with learners.

- **Comprehensive and grammar schools**: Most local education authorities moved to non-selective comprehensive schools in Britain in the 1960s and 1970s, with only a few remaining grammar (selective) schools which were privatised.

BLOOMSBURY TEACHER GUIDE: ANITA AND ME

- **The Virgin Mary**: In Christianity, Mary is often referred to as the Virgin Mary in accordance with the view that she was impregnated by the Holy Spirit and gave birth to Jesus, thereby conceiving miraculously.
- **Social graces**: In 1960s Britain, manners and etiquette were important to some sections of society, but not others. 'Correct' language and behaviours to accompany certain domestic and social rituals, such as mealtimes and conversations, needed to be adhered to by those with 'good manners'

Vocabulary in context

The following vocabulary from Chapter 10 can be pre-taught to help with reading fluency and reduce cognitive load. What does each of the following words mean in context?

Word	Quotation	Definition
metamorphosed (v.)	'metamorphosed completely' (p. 246)	changed shape/form
indolent (adj.)	'the same indolent walk' (p. 246)	without effort or care; lazy
tam-o'shanter (n.)	'a droopy tam-o'shanter' (p. 247)	a round woollen/cotton hat of Scottish origin
masticated (adj.)	'half-masticated fish finger' (p. 254)	chewed; eaten
Kirpan (n.)	'might have a Kirpan concealed' (p. 255)	short sword or knife with a curved blade; an important item in Sikhism
tarty (adj.)	'not allowed, tarty' (p. 256)	looking sexually provocative, usually to describe females

PIT STOP

Retrieval point

Return to this vocabulary in a later lesson, assessing if learners can link each key word to the relevant character(s). For a bonus point, develop each link into an analysis of how the writer's language choice presents that character.

Why might Syal use the metaphor 'metamorphosed' when describing how the children mature over the summer? What is it she might be suggesting about their transformation from childhood into adolescence?

Why does Syal choose a reference to a 'Kirpan' when communicating misconceptions and prejudices held about certain groups in Britain?

Whose words is the reader positioned to assume the adjective 'tarty' is? Our narrator's? A particular adult's?

PIT STOP

Direct instruction point

Meena swings between wanting to be loved and accepted by Anita in this chapter and wanting to protect and defend her family and heritage – a typical childhood struggle depicted beautifully by Syal.

Teach students about **speech accommodation** (where speakers move closer to or further away from the speech style of the person they are speaking to in order to ingratiate/distance themselves with/from them). Study the following examples to illustrate the point:

Regional dialect:

- Meena to Anita: 'Wow, yow look bosting!' (p. 246)
- Anita to Meena: 'Bosting clothes, Meena!' (p. 256).

Standard English:

- Anita to mama: 'I was borrowing them [...] Meena said I could!' (p. 257)
- Mama to Anita: 'Could you put them back please?' (p. 257). Note: the 'darling' has been dropped.

'Darling' is a term of endearment used for Anita by Meena's mama. Ask students to spot where it is used first, where it falls out of use and where it is reintroduced. What might the significance of this be?

PIT STOP

Academic writing point

Learning how to track key moments to understand why they are transformative could also be a practical, active step to answering the Big Question: **How is the reader positioned to view Anita with some sympathy in this chapter?**

Learners can use the following discourse markers to track the shift in the readers' response towards Anita:

- Initially, ...
- Then, ...
- Finally, ...
- Ultimately, ...

Discussion point: Ask the learners if they think that the revelation of Deirdre's abandonment is sufficient to redeem Anita when she attempts to steal Meena's belongings.

Plot and character development

For tips on how to approach these 'What' questions, refer to the 'Plot and character development' section of 'How to use this book' on pages 5-6 of this guide.

1. **What is different about Anita's apparent reaction to her mother's leaving and Meena's imagined reaction if her mother did the same?**

    Example responses:
    - Anita appears subdued
    - Anita appears to have been upset
    - Anita tries to appear matter-of-fact and nonchalant
    - Meena reflects that she would be hysterical
    - Meena would be driven to violence by her anger
    - Meena would swear vengeance.

2. **How does Anita respond to Meena's attempt to comfort her in a maternal way?**

    Example responses:
    - repulsed
    - aggressive
    - uses derogatory language.

3. **What does Meena use to deflect attention from her parents' disappointment in and anger with her for using the word 'virgin'?**

    Example response:
    - Meena quickly changes the subject, informing her parents that Anita's mother has left. She knows this will provoke a strong response, particularly from her mother, who will take a keen interest and want to provide support for both Anita and Tracey.

4. **What cultural differences are raised when Anita comes for dinner?**

    Example response:
    - bringing something for the host: Anita arrives 'empty-handed' (p. 252)
    - sitting at the table for dinner
    - expectations around polite conversation
    - etiquette and manners (no elbows on the table, not eating with one's mouth open and saying 'thank you')
    - eating with cutlery vs eating with fingers

- clothing
- burping.

5. **What is different about the way Nanima reacts to Anita to the way the rest of Meena's family treat her when she comes for dinner?**

   Example response:
   - Nanima does not pander to Anita or moderate her behaviour in any way. She is 'unimpressed' by her and pushes past her 'clumsily' rather than taking extra care around her and calling her 'darling' like Meena's mama does (p. 254). This might be the writer suggesting that Meena's grandmother is suspicious, and wise to be so.

6. **What aspects of her bedroom make Meena worried about taking Anita up there to spend time after dinner?**

   Example responses:
   - that it was a child's bedroom, rather than a 'proper girlie hang-out' (p. 256)
   - no 'cosmetics' or 'posters' (p. 256)
   - only one childish 'record' (p. 256)
   - 'no lock on the door' (p. 256)
   - doesn't contain that which Anita's 'teenage den' does (p. 255).

How?

Language

Foreshadowing

Key quotation:
- 'I thought this was a good idea and dropped several hints […] none of which Anita ever picked up' (p. 258).

How does this signal the beginning of the end for Anita and Meena's relationship?

Metaphor of transformation

Key quotation:
- 'metamorphosed completely from junior school grubs to the glittering butterflies' (p. 246).

Now they are all no longer children or 'junior school grubs', the promise and 'glittering' allure of adolescence may signal an independence of thought, particularly for Meena, which may see her break free from the crowd and the trappings of Anita's cruelty.

Adjectival antithesis

Child vs teen – 'bouncy' vs 'indolent' (p. 246).

No longer bounding energetically from one juvenile scrape to the next, our characters' gait may encode much about their maturation into adolescence as they cultivate a far more nonchalant exterior.

Character focus

Deirdre

Deirdre is presented as having planned her departure as Anita's uniform arrives, but ultimately her actions are selfish in putting her own needs first.

Anita

Anita is affected by her mother's walking out but tries to put on a brave face, calling her a 'silly cow' (p. 247). She steals Meena's possessions as there is no longer anyone to provide for her.

Mama and papa

Mama and papa are united in their disgust and disdain when Meena enquires about the word 'virgin' and whether she is one, representing their strong conservative values. Mama wants to care for Anita upon learning that she has been left alone by her mother. Papa fears that they will be perceived as interfering and that mama does not understand English cultural norms. Mama has the measure of Anita and will not let her take advantage of her family.

Nanima

Nanima is presented as an excellent judge of character – despite the language barrier, she will not tolerate Anita's rudeness.

> **PIT STOP**
>
> #### S-T-R-E-T-C-H
>
> Ask students to compare the different maternal approaches demonstrated by Deirdre, mama and Nanima in this chapter. Where do archetypal maternal characteristics shine through and why do students think Syal shows the reader different types of mothers?

Structure

Learners should explore the following examples from the opening and the ending of Chapter 10 and be invited to consider:

- Why Syal has chosen to begin and end with a conversation involving Anita?
- How this may contribute to the reader's sympathy for Anita's character?
- What their predictions might be about key character and plot developments within this chapter.

Opening: "'Me mom's gone,' Anita said flatly' (p. 247).

Ending: 'Of course, darling. See you soon' (p. 258).

Dialogue is crucial to appreciate the redrawing of boundaries in relationships between characters in this chapter. Consider, for example, how mama states that 'Meena should have asked' (p. 257) her first upon discovering Anita has concealed various possessions under her borrowed coat without asking. Mama represents a clear, firm, consistent boundary-setting adult which Meena is used to, but Anita has never experienced.

Extracts

1. How does Syal use language to communicate the impact of her mother's leaving on Anita?

'Sitting alone on the park swings [...] snail trails of moisture and dirt running to her mouth' (p. 246).

Example response planning, using topic sentence scaffolds:

Syal presents Anita as:

- broken
- lonely
- lost.

Example response, unpacking quotations and language therein to support points:

The use of the phrase 'snail trails' when describing Anita may make the reader picture a much younger child, particularly when referring to the area near her mouth and nose. This positions the reader to feel real sympathy for Anita. She, although not a small child, no longer has her mother to wipe away the tears caused by loneliness. She is presented as abandoned and alone, without care for the 'snail trails' that glitter down her face, lost in her own sad thoughts.

BLOOMSBURY TEACHER GUIDE: ANITA AND ME

> **PIT STOP**
>
> ### S-T-R-E-T-C-H
>
> Might there be a certain irony intended by Syal in describing Anita as looking momentarily like a 'little old lady'? Still a child, how has she always sought to be 'grown-up'? How has this now come to fruition? How could this link back to the tragic event with Mrs Christmas and her conspiratorial 'wink' at Meena?

2. How does Syal use language to convey the panic Meena feels at not knowing what a 'virgin' is?

"Am yow a virgin then?' [...] 'Yeah, I am one actually' I said confidently' (p. 248).

Example response planning, using topic sentence scaffolds:

- Presentation of Anita as a predator: 'Anita's eyes glittered dangerously'.
- Metaphor of physical impact: 'I swallowed a marble of anger'.
- Adverbs of manner: 'I racked my brains furiously'.
- Stream of consciousness: 'no obvious connection there'.
- Rhetorical question: 'did it sound like?'.
- Options: 'or a dreadful disease'.

Example response, unpacking quotations and language therein to support points:

Syal skilfully presents Meena's panic at being asked by Anita if she is a virgin through various language methods. It is very important to her that she get this answer right as it's the chance to not be viewed as a 'baby' in her friend's eyes. The metaphorical 'marble of anger' she feels in her throat is almost palpable to the reader as the anxiety begins and she weighs up her options.

3. How are language and imagery used in the following extract to convey the magical escape from reality the girls experience through a shared love of the clothes found in Meena's wardrobe after dinner?

'But Anita's boredom turned to amazement [...] There were at least ten suits she recommended that I should never wear again, and as I had no further use for them, it seemed natural to give them to her' (p. 256–7).

Example response planning, using topic sentence scaffolds:

- Anita's rapture at their discovery: 'shouted [...] immediately pulling [...] off their hangers [...] 'Oh, I love this one!' [...] She really liked [...]'.
- Polysyndeton: 'silks and satins and cottons of deep purple and sea green and saffron yellow and cinnamon brown'.

CHAPTER 10 OF ANITA AND ME

- Metaphor: 'unfurled in a world of possibilities'; 'a constellation of stars as a hat'.
- Personification: 'holding them up to the light, making them sparkle and breathe'.
- Fashion discourse: 'practising our catwalk style, giving each other marks out of ten for poise, charm and sexiness'.

Example response, unpacking quotations and language therein to support points:

The reader is presented with a different Anita for a 'few hours' up in Meena's bedroom. She is enraptured by the fabric she finds in Meena's wardrobe and becomes absorbed in their beauty and the possibility they hold. Syal uses polysyndeton to capture the excitement Anita feels on first seeing the vast array of different materials and colours, the repetition of 'and' helping to communicate the breathlessness the character might have felt at encountering each new shade and texture. This is a true luxury to someone who lives as Anita does.

4. How does Syal present Meena re-evaluating her understanding of lying in this chapter?

Example response planning, using topic sentence scaffolds:

- 'caught a lie' and 'threw it right back'
- 'one porkie' she could 'get away with'.

Example response, unpacking quotations and language therein to support points:

Syal positions the reader to view Meena's resolve to protect her family from Anita's judgement when she comes for dinner. In realising that Anita represents the first 'non-relative' and 'white person' to eat Indian food with her family, she 'educates' her as to the prestige of eating with fingers by telling a lie. Syal presents Meena as becoming more adept at using versions of the truth to protect people's feelings, rather than for her own gain in this chapter.

PIT STOP

S-T-R-E-T-C-H

Ask learners to consider:

- Meena's use of 'porkie' (a euphemism) to describe the 'lie' she tells Anita when translating for Nanima.
- What point might Syal be making here about the important life lesson and step towards adulthood Meena is taking by using 'porkie', rather than 'untruth', for example?

CHAPTER 11 OF ANITA AND ME

At a glance

> **Chapter summary quotation:** 'would [Tollington] ever truly be home again' (p. 275)

> **Big Question:** How does this chapter present Meena's many difficult realisations about human nature?

> **Significant plot event:** Meena learns that Sam has led a violent and racist attack on the Indian Bank Manager, and she impulsively rides Trixie, falling and breaking her leg.

> **Character focus:** Papa, Anita, Tracey, Meena

> **Key themes:**
> - Racism
> - Othering
> - Friendship

> **Handle with care:**
> - Reference to a range of racially offensive terms in this chapter will need to be handled with sensitivity. Please refer to the 'Handle with care' guidance in the 'How to use this book' section for further support.
>   - 'slitty eye' (p. 264)
>   - 'Nigger' (p. 273)
>   - 'let him touch yow' (p. 276)
>   - 'Paki' (p. 277)
>   - 'Paki bashing' (p. 277)
>   - 'fuck' (p. 279).

Why?

'Why' is important not only within the world of the text, but also when considering authorial intent and messaging.

CHAPTER 11 OF ANITA AND ME

- Why is it significant that Sunil's first words are in English?
- Why is Meena disappointed when she sees the reality of the Christmas party hosted for employees where her father works?
- Why is Bill's daughter such a key minor character in Meena's flashback and what does she represent?
- Why does Syal have Meena notice the Indian Bank Manager?
- Why does the media presence heighten the sense of trauma evoked by Sam and his gang's actions during the broadcast?
- Why does Tracey react so violently to Sherrie inspecting Anita's underwear and how does this echo Anita's reaction to Meena's care in the previous chapter?
- Why does Syal present Anita as excited as she relays the story of the 'Paki bashing' (p. 277) to Sherrie?
- Why does Meena mount the horse and take such a clear risk?

This allows us to consider Chapter 11's Big Question:

> How does this chapter present Meena's many difficult realisations about human nature?

What?

What happens?

Papa gets a promotion and Sunil speaks his first words. Meena enjoys a long, lazy summer in the company of her friends. She learns about horses but is too fearful to ride. Construction workers arrive to demolish the old school in Tollington and, whilst the media are covering the event, Sam leads his crew in a racist demonstration.

Anita aligns herself with Sam romantically and begins accompanying him whilst he and others commit acts of violence against non-white people. On hearing about this, Meena mounts Sherrie's pony without help or equipment before quickly falling and getting severely injured.

Social, cultural and historical context

It is important for learners to fully understand, appreciate and be able to realistically envisage life in the fictional village of Tollington in 1972 for Meena. They may require pre-teaching activities on the following features of social, cultural and historical context so they can write about them confidently.

The following are some useful quotations to consider when discussing this context with learners.

BLOOMSBURY TEACHER GUIDE: ANITA AND ME

- **Urbanisation and changing landscape**: 'And as I speak the machinery is moving in to raze the Primrose Primary School to the ground, a school that has been standing in this lovely spot for nearly a hundred years... for many of the local parents, who have been waging a ten-year campaign against the closure, who now have to send their children to another school some nine miles away, this is a sad, if inevitable day' (p. 273).
- **1964 election, reference to Conservative MP Peter Griffiths' campaign for the Smethwick seat**: Sam 'manoeuvred close up to the camera lens and yelled, 'If You Want A Nigger For A Neighbour, Vote Labour!' before hurtling away' (p. 273).
- **Articles of Sikhism**: 'Nanima was feeding Sunil a bowl of rice, sugar and milk as he played with her *Kara*' (p. 274). References are made to Kara, one of the five articles of faith or Kakars of Sikhism, associated with dedication to the religious order. The Kara is a bracelet made from steel or iron known to have originated as a protective ring worn by Khalsa warriors on their sword arm. It symbolises the totality of God in the Sikh faith and acts as a reminder that whatever actions are completed by a person's hand, they should always be in keeping with the principles of the faith and teachings of Guru Nanak. The Kara should be kept clean and only removed if necessary.

Vocabulary in context

The following vocabulary from Chapter 11 can be pre-taught to help with reading fluency and reduce cognitive load. What does each of the following words mean in context?

Word	Quotation	Definition
swaddled (adj.)	'other similarly swaddled children' (p. 260)	wrapped up
anaemic (adj.)	'an anaemic strand of tinsel' (p. 260)	lacking colour and vibrancy
brylcremed (v.)	'carefully brylcremed his few remaining strands of hair' (p. 261)	used the product 'Brylcreme' to style
confidant (n.)	'offered to his confidant as a gift' (p. 263)	someone to confide in and share secrets with
tacking (v.)	'learned [...] what tacking meant' (p. 265)	placing riding equipment on a horse
benevolent (adj.)	'my contentment had made me benevolent' (p. 265)	well-meaning and kind; thoughtful and considerate of others
scimitar (n.)	'perform their scimitar swoops of joy' (p. 266)	a short-bladed knife which broadens to a point
belligerent (adj.)	'remained as brassy and belligerent as ever' (p. 266)	hostile and aggressive; stubborn and immovable
baleful (adj.)	'fixed me with a baleful stare' (p. 268)	threatening; menacing

CHAPTER 11 OF ANITA AND ME

staccato (adj.)	'a buzzing staccato' (p. 269)	a rhythm with each note/beat sharply separated
boycott (v.)	'unsure of which of these two evils they ought to boycott' (p. 269)	to actively withdraw from; deliberately not support/attend
silverfish (n.)	'sent silverfish shimmying into corners' (p. 274)	a silvery, bristletail insect that lives chiefly in damp outbuildings

PIT STOP

Retrieval point

Return to this vocabulary in a later lesson, assessing if learners can link each key word to the relevant character(s). For a bonus point, develop each link into an analysis of how the writer's language choice presents that character.

Examples:

- What did 'swaddled' mean and how might it be a metaphor for the childhood Meena was feeling desperate to cast off?
- What are some synonyms for 'belligerent' that would be helpful when writing about Anita?
- What are 'silverfish' and what do they tell us about the place Meena retreats to in order to hide?

PIT STOP

Direct instruction point

Making links to elsewhere in the text is an essential skill. Use the 'think-aloud' method (see below) to model linking the description of Nanima as 'baleful' at Anita's visit to other times in the novel when she has shown herself to be a highly perceptive, intuitive, almost magical character:

- soothing Sunil and breaking his attachment to mama overnight
- recognising Meena's wildness and desire to be free
- understanding that Meena is involved in the disappearance of the necklace.

The 'think-aloud' method is a live teacher demonstration with accompanying metacognitive narrative writing, meaning the teacher verbalises what they are doing and thinking while completing a task. You might say something like, 'Right, I need to decide which words to focus my attention on when I'm summarising this really important quotation...'

BLOOMSBURY TEACHER GUIDE: ANITA AND ME

Plot and character development

For tips on how to approach these 'What' questions, refer to the 'Plot and character development' section of 'How to use this book' on pages 5–6 of this guide.

1. **What does Syal mean in the opening paragraph of Chapter 11 when Meena describes her childhood as 'ebbing away' (p. 259) that summer?**

   Example responses:
   - loss of childhood innocence
   - exposure to the realities and harms of the world
   - abuse of trust
   - personal and emotional attack on identity from which it is impossible to recover.

   > **PIT STOP**
   >
   > **S-T-R-E-T-C-H**
   >
   > Ask learners to re-read the opening paragraph once they have finished the chapter. How, without them fully appreciating the context, did it prepare and position them as readers to appreciate the traumatic events to come? Why might Syal have used nature metaphors such as 'current' and 'landscape' (p. 259) to convey this message?

2. **In the flashback to Meena's attendance at her father's work's Christmas party, what does the reader learn are sources of disappointment to her?**

   Example responses:
   - the party was not being held solely in her father's honour
   - it was held at a swimming bath but was not a swimming party
   - her father does not have an exciting job.

3. **What is the reader shown about 'othering' in the incidents with Bill's daughter and the fake nail set gift at the Christmas party?**

   Example response:

   Even as a five-year-old, Meena is presented as experiencing fierce frustration at the way she is excluded and viewed as different. When she is 'stroked' almost like a pet out of curiosity by another girl, she lashes out at the perceived 'ownership' with a bite (p. 261). She also rejects the 'pink, latex' (p. 262) fake nails gifted to her by the disappointing Father Christmas, which are so mismatched with her own brown skin. This

CHAPTER 11 OF ANITA AND ME

reminds the reader that children represented by Meena have sensed their differences throughout their formative years in this country and that the memories of these events remain vividly lodged for them.

4. **What does the difference in mama and Nanima's response to Sunil's first words position the reader to remember about Meena's family?**

   Example response:

   Mama is proud. She dismisses the doctor's concerns and telephones papa to celebrate. Nanima ties a thread around Sunil's wrist muttering a 'spell' to protect him from the 'evil eye' (p. 264) which may be brought on if people believe a child is too clever or too beautiful. The difference in reactions reminds the reader of the cultural difference: pride vs protection.

> **PIT STOP**
>
> **S-T-R-E-T-C-H**
>
> How is Meena's reaction to Nanima's thread tying typically inward-looking? Why does Syal present her in this way?

5. **What clues are there that Tracey is increasingly unsettled and anxious in this chapter?**

   Example responses:

   - she became 'shrunken, hollow-eyed and silent' (p. 266)
   - she stayed inside whenever her father was home
   - she shied away from conversation
   - she kept herself apart and appeared resentful
   - she kept her gaze trained on her sister.

6. **What response does the arrival of the 'diggers' provoke in Tollington?**

   Example response:

   The local community come together in their response to the arrival of the 'diggers'. Their disgust and distaste are made clear with Mr Topsy/Turvey seeing fit to spit 'on the pavement' as they pass and others (Anita included) respond aggressively. The united front in the face of the 'machinery' and destruction to come blurs the lines between the various Tollington groups momentarily (p. 269).

7. What is significant about the bank-manager-type man Meena spots and about Sam and his gang watching him depart?

Example response:

The man Meena spots is 'Indian' and there is a flash of 'recognition' and 'acknowledgement' between them (p. 271). Syal is communicating to the reader the rarity of observing a person from Meena's family's community in such a position. On the other hand, Sam and his gang 'paused' (p. 272) long enough to watch the man depart for the bus stop. This is a highly significant plot development and one Syal is keen for the reader to absorb. It will, of course, become a crucial part of the narrative and the climax towards the end of the chapter.

> **PIT STOP**
>
> ### S-T-R-E-T-C-H
>
> Ask learners to consider why 'the Bank Manager' remains nameless and why Meena does not have a conversation with him (like her father would have done). How does this contribute to the climax of the chapter?

8. What is significant about where Meena heads directly after Sam storms the TV report?

Example responses:

- it is where Meena forged an alliance and then a friendship with Anita
- it represents nostalgic memories of better times
- it represents when Meena felt more in control
- it feels safe and like a sanctuary.

9. What makes Anita's 'new bra' the catalyst for Meena's accident?

Example response:

Sherrie and Anita's discussion of their bras leads, ultimately, to an uncharacteristically aggressive reaction from Tracey. This is prompted by the idea of 'touching', to which she seems incredibly sensitive. The sisters appear to share a secret and Meena interprets it as Anita having a boyfriend, which leaves her feeling rejected. Upon leaving to check on Tracey, Meena unwittingly overhears Anita's hideous retelling of the racial violence she has witnessed and been a party to. Unable to cope with and process her feelings in reaction to what she is hearing, Meena mounts Trixie and is thrown off, injuring herself badly.

How?

Language

Cataphoric reference

How does Syal create tension and speculation at the climax of the chapter when Tracey emotionally declares 'Seen yow with him! Yow let him touch yow as well! I'm telling' (p. 276)?

The pronoun 'him' without an antecedent deliberately obscures the identity of the unnamed male. The reader is positioned to wonder: is it Sam?

Sound

What are the alternative interpretations as to why Syal uses increased volume and harsh sound to signal change in this chapter?

'Grumbling', 'mechanical symphony' and 'buzzing staccato' (p. 269) are used to herald the arrival of the diggers, and with it the destruction of the 'old' Tollington and life (and relative childhood innocence) as Meena knew it. Harsh sounds are also used to announce the arrival of Sam's gang on their scooters.

Poignant description

How does Syal position the reader to feel sympathy for Meena when she is described as 'retching quietly' (p. 278) in response to the revelation that Anita accompanied Sam to his racial attacks?

The physical impact of the news on Meena jolts the reader's sympathy. They are shocked to imagine the young protagonist vomiting in response to what she is hearing. It is powerful and poignant that Meena still feels the need to minimise and control herself by retching 'quietly'. It is genuinely moving that Anita wields such power over her and ignites such fear.

Graphic description

How does the literal detail, devoid of imagery, create a raw depiction of Meena's agony in the following quotation: 'awake for every awful painful moment [...] fuck, seen her leg... [...] smelt my own pee [...] no longer control my eyelids' (p. 279)?

Character focus

Papa

Key quotation:

- "Your mama,' said papa, tight-lipped, 'says too much sometimes." (p. 260).

Papa is presented to be ashamed in the flashback when Meena realises his position at work is less glamorous and high-powered than she had assumed.

Anita

Key quotations:

- 'took any opportunity to be out of her house' (p. 266)
- 'If Anita had heard me, she did not care' (p. 271)
- 'cracks appeared which would finally split open the china blue bowl of that last summer' (p. 274-5).

Anita increases the distance between herself and Meena. She starts wearing a bra. She develops a relationship with Sam and is party to violence against non-white people (partaking in risk-taking behaviour perhaps as a way of coping with her abandonment).

Tracey

Key quotations:

- 'managing to delegate her trauma workload to her little sister, Tracey' (p. 266)
- 'less like a sibling and more like a fleeting shadow attached to Anita's snapping heels' (p. 266)
- 'Tracey's voice was so intense, so vindictive, it made my neck crinkle' (p. 276).

Tracey tags along with the girls. She rushes home like clockwork and is increasingly anxious and overly protective of Anita.

Meena

Key quotations:

- 'her smile told me everything I needed to know' (p. 277)
- 'My best friend was sharing me with someone else' (p. 277)
- 'All that time I wasted waiting for something to happen' (p. 279).

Initially happy with her lot, Meena harbours some guilt regarding the lost necklace. She naively assumes Anita allowing her to spend time with her and the others is 'friendship'. She is staunchly opposed to being reconciled with Sam and is crushed by his words. Later, she is further crushed by Anita's allegiance with Sam and is jolted to the reality that she no longer means anything to her 'friend' and that her energies have been 'wasted', driving her to take a disastrous risk.

Structure 🗂

Learners should explore the following examples from the opening and the ending of Chapter 11 and be invited to consider:

- Why Syal has chosen to begin with this focus on the clear foreshadowing of the awful events to come?
- Why Syal has chosen to end with the harrowing denouement?
- What their predictions might be about key characters and plot developments within this chapter.

Opening: 'I treated time with my usual jaunty contempt' (p. 259).

Ending: 'I better let them know I'm not dead' (p. 279).

Dialogue is used to present intensely emotional and aggressive exchanges between key characters which move the plot along quickly, hinting at crucial details for the reader and piquing their interest: 'Yow let him touch yow as well!' (p. 276).

Flashback

Papa's promotion instigates a flashback to Meena's one and only trip to the work Christmas party.

Notice the recount of this incident, when the reader learns of papa's promotion and its significance for Meena as a child in terms of her identity, in terms of the structure of the novel. In particular, the exchange with the colleague's young daughter and the Christmas gift of false nails for Caucasian fingers is formative.

Turning Point

The missing diamond necklace sparks the turning point.

The assumptions made about the identity of a possible 'thief' are highly significant in the narrative. Notice how Syal sets up the story perfectly for mama to jump to this conclusion and whether the reader is inclined to agree with her or take Meena's side and defend Anita.

Extracts

1. How does Syal use language to show the effect of Sam's words on Meena?

'Afterwards, I could not find Anita anywhere and felt too tired and dispirited to bother to call at her house. Sam's words remained with me, I felt as if I had been spat at, that there were gobs of bile hanging off my cheeks [...] I had to be on my own to wipe myself clean' (p. 273).

Example response planning, using topic sentence scaffolds:

Syal presents Meena as feeling:

- fatigued
- hopeless
- scarred
- marred
- unclean.

Example response, unpacking quotations and language therein to support points:

Syal presents Meena as feeling spent and in need of time alone following Sam's televised racist outburst. Dysphemistic descriptions of 'gobs of bile' on her cheeks and in her hair graphically position the reader to feel her disgust and sense of physical unease as a result of the words used. Expressing the need to be on her 'own' makes the reader wonder if it is shame, anger or any other combination of intensely personal emotions our protagonist feels in the face of such senseless hate.

2. How does Syal use language to show the reality of the situation dawning on Meena?

'My best friend in all the world really did have a boyfriend and had never told me. [...] until the real thing came along to claim her.' (p. 277)

Example response planning, using topic sentence scaffolds:

Syal presents the reality of the situation dawning on Meena:

- as now abundantly clear
- as a battle lost
- as though she has been naive and used by Anita.

Example response, unpacking quotations and language therein to support points:

Syal presents the reality of the situation dawning on Meena as a battle lost, and perhaps doomed from the start. In the metaphor 'fought for this friendship' the protagonist's tone is bitter and resentful as she realises that all her energies and efforts have ultimately been in vain. Anita had no intention of being her 'best friend' but was simply biding her time until the 'real thing' appeared. When Meena realises that the friendship meant far more to her than it ever did to Anita, she feels foolish and hurt. As readers, we feel for her and desperately want her to be able to grow from this, rather than to punish herself or others. Syal has brilliantly vilified Anita and championed Meena up until this point.

CHAPTER 11 OF ANITA AND ME

3. How does Syal use language to position the reader to appreciate the seriousness of Meena's injuries at the end of the chapter?

'I should have been in a film; in a film everything would have dissolved into hazy lines [...] I smelt my own pee and the clover stalks tickling my nose' (p. 279).

Example response planning, using topic sentence scaffolds: 💡

Syal conveys the seriousness of Meena's accident when:

- parallels to the films her father might have been in are drawn
- snippets of dialogue delivering dreadful details are relayed
- sensory details relating to the loss of control of her bladder are shared
- memory minutiae such as the 'tickling' of clover stalks up Meena's nose show how the size of the world shrinks following a major life event.

Example response, unpacking quotations and language therein to support points: 🔍

Dialogue is used to great effect at the end of the chapter. It shows the reactions of other characters to Meena's dreadful injuries and their precise detail. It also demonstrates the impairment of her senses as she can only recall hearing her friends converse, not seeing them. The expletives in the young girls' dialogue provide a credible depiction of their shock and worry at seeing Meena's unnatural body position. The frequent trailing dots suggest that they are almost lost for words in the face of such a difficult sight.

CHAPTER 12 OF ANITA AND ME

At glance

> **Chapter summary quotation:** 'A true hospital love, sanitised and inevitably temporary' (p. 286)
> **Big Question:** How significant is it that Meena would meet and befriend Robert at this point in the narrative?
> **Significant plot event:** Meena and Robert meet, become friends and then Robert dies.
> **Character focus:** Anita, Robert, Meena
> **Key themes:**
>   - Friendship
>   - Belonging
>   - Change
> **Handle with care:**
>   - References to the following emotive topics including terminal illness, mental illness and sexual innuendo in this chapter will need to be handled with sensitivity. Please refer to the 'Handle with care' guidance in the 'How to use this book' section for further support.
>   - Robert passing away from cancer
>   - 'trying his luck for a grope' (p. 292)
>   - 'padded cell' (p. 295).

Why?

'Why' is important not only within the world of the text, but also when considering authorial intent and messaging.

- Why does Syal show Meena consumed with thoughts of Anita at the start of her stay in hospital?
- Why is the image of Meena erasing Anita from her life 'like a child's pencil drawing' (p. 282) so poignant?

- Why does Syal show various medical professionals referring to Meena as 'Mary'?
- Why is Robert separated from the other patients by a glass cubicle and how do he and Meena overcome this obstacle?
- Why does Meena exhibit false cheerfulness at the news that Nanima is returning to India?
- Why does the incident where Robert is depressed provoke a selfish reaction in Meena?
- Why is Meena and Robert's final in-person meeting different?

This allows us to consider Chapter 12's Big Question:

> How significant is it that Meena would meet and befriend Robert at this point in the narrative?

What?

What happens?

Meena is in the children's hospital. She reflects maturely on the need to use the time to get over Anita. She meets and begins a friendship with Robert, a fellow patient on the ward. During a family visit to the hospital, Meena learns Nanima will return to India.

Preparations for Christmas on the ward herald Meena's recovery and release. After experiencing some lows, Meena finally meets Robert in person and officially becomes his 'girlfriend'.

Meena returns to Tollington, finding it shabbier and more rundown than she remembers. She encounters Sam and Anita, and nothing appears to have changed between the two of them.

On returning to the hospital for a check-up, Meena can't find Robert. She receives a letter on returning home from Robert's parents informing her that he has passed away.

Social, cultural and historical context

It is important for learners to fully understand, appreciate and be able to realistically envisage life in the fictional village of Tollington in 1972 for Meena. They may require pre-teaching activities on the following features of social, cultural and historical context so they can write about them confidently.

The main topic to note is microaggressions regarding pronunciations/ mispronunciations of ethnic minority names: 'Can't say your real name so Mary will do' (p. 280).

Vocabulary in context

The following vocabulary from Chapter 12 can be pre-taught to help with reading fluency and reduce cognitive load. What does each of the following words mean in context?

Word	Quotation	Definition
cadence (n.)	'like the end of a chapter in a long epic book, a dying cadence, a full stop' (p. 282)	the rise and fall of the voice
cliches (n., pl.)	'greeting card cliches' (p. 286)	over-used expressions/phrases
leaden (adj.)	'it felt heavy and leaden' (p. 289)	dull; heavy; slow
liability (n.)	'this alien, useless liability stuck to the end of my body' (p. 289)	a thing whose presence is likely to put the bearer at a disadvantage
tousled (adj.)	'the top of his tousled head' (p. 290)	messed up; not neat
diaphragm (n.)	'the green mask over my mouth panted up and down like a diaphragm' (p. 292)	the muscle involved in breathing in and out

PIT STOP

Retrieval point

Return to this vocabulary in a later lesson, assessing if learners can link each key word to the relevant character(s). For a bonus point, develop each link into an analysis of how the writer's language choice presents that character.

Examples:

- Who was 'a dying cadence' as Meena was taken to the hospital?
- With whom does Meena strike up her first 'boyfriend/girlfriend' relationship in Chapter 12? How does it feel very far removed from the greetings card 'cliches' she had envisaged?
- The announcement of whose departure in Chapter 12 causes Meena to feel 'leaden'?

CHAPTER 12 OF ANITA AND ME

> **PIT STOP**
>
> ### Academic writing point
>
> Rehearsing alternative readings or interpretations of key moments in a pivotal chapter or scene is an effective way of targeting the upper mark bands. Try the following scaffold:
>
> Syal uses parenthesis (brackets) when Meena's narrative becomes particularly colloquial: '(I'd never been to a disco, but…)' (p. 292). On the one hand, this could be because… Alternatively, the desired effect may be…

Plot and character development

For tips on how to approach these 'What' questions, refer to the 'Plot and character development' section of 'How to use this book' on pages 5–6 of this guide.

1. **What about the opening of Chapter 12 helps confirm for the reader that Meena will be OK despite being in the children's hospital?**

   Example response:

   Meena deems the cartoon decorations on the children's ward 'annoying' and notes the 'peeling yellow walls' (p. 280) critically in the opening of the chapter. The reader is satisfied she will make a full recovery upon seeing her characteristically barbed comments and rejection of anything she considers too babyish and beneath her.

2. **What upsets Meena at the beginning of the chapter?**

   Example responses:
   - projected length of her stay in hospital (until Christmas)
   - staff calling her 'Mary'
   - prospect of mama teaching her
   - failing to prepare for eleven-plus
   - missing Sunil's first birthday
   - cancelling the trip to India
   - thoughts of Anita
   - relentlessly monotonous routine.

3. **What details on page 284 show the toll Meena's accident and hospital stay are taking on her parents?**

   Example responses:
   - mama lost weight

- differences in how mama's face looked (more angular)
- both parents had bags/dark circles under their eyes
- papa's complexion had changed from rosy to sallow.

4. What is remarkable about the message code Meena and Robert devise?

Example response:

The rate at which the pair adapt to the code (placing consecutive alphabetised letters between the letters of the target words) is remarkable. We are positioned to marvel at the speed and ease with which the two are able to begin predicting and finishing one another's sentences, suggesting true intimacy.

PIT STOP

S-T-R-E-T-C-H

Ask learners to consider:

- How Meena and Robert always appear to understand one another and share common ground? Even when they hear each other speak for the first time (in what turns out to be their last meeting), their difference is something to marvel at and celebrate, rather than manipulate.
- How does Syal use their relationship as a foil to that of Anita and Meena?

5. What is so important about Meena's declaration that she is 'a grown-up now' (p. 288)?

Example response:

The novel's narrative arc has tracked Meena's journey from childhood to early adulthood. Here, our protagonist acknowledges this for herself. She feels 'grown-up', imitating the suppression of emotion she has observed her parents perform so many times. Knowing when keeping the truth from another person is permissible is part of Meena's learning curve.

How?

Language

Light relief

How does Syal use language to present the hospital and the patients' treatment by medical staff in an almost comedic way?

By contrast to the pain (both physical and emotional) that Meena experiences at the beginning of her stay in hospital, the setting and antics of her caregivers and fellow patients provide light relief in this chapter as she comes to terms with her situation.

Key quotations:

- 'peeling yellow walls' (p. 280)
- 'Alright Mary?' (p. 280)
- 'runny mashed potatoes and gristly pies' (p. 282).

Vivid description and dialogue

How does Syal use language to position the reader to see Robert as Meena does?

Through a combination of vivid description and dialogue, Syal presents Robert as vital and bright, preparing us for the intensity of the loving, meaningful relationship that follows (in contrast with the rough, risk-taking nature of Anita and Sam's relationship).

Key quotations:

- 'energetic, electric blue eyes' (p. 283)
- 'curly brown hair' (p. 283)
- 'Is she driving you mad?' (p. 283).

Interior monologue

'He's bored, you're the nearest' (p. 283) – whose unkind words does this sentiment echo? How does this position the reader to feel sympathy for Meena? The reader wills her to break free of Anita in her own mind and to speak more kindly to herself.

English dialogue

How does Syal present Nanima's love for Meena as they part before she leaves for 'home'?

Nanima switches to hesitant English (rather than her usual Punjabi) in her dialogue as they part ways: 'Meena...jewel...precious...light...bless you...' (p. 288). Her parting gift is to use a few carefully selected words she knows Meena will understand and hold on to.

Language of childhood

How does Syal invoke the language of childhood to communicate the pure, delightful nature of the relationship between Meena and Robert, a far cry from the complicated, difficult one cultivated with Anita?

Robert's laugh is described as sounding like 'rude farty bubbles in a bath' (p. 291). This is a poignant reminder of how their relationship was one of innocence and endurance, enacted in silence and without physical contact. Pure joy is emitted from this description. There is an echo too of the 'farty' noises of the settee enjoyed when Nanima first arrived. A similar safety and lack of judgement is implied.

Character focus

Anita

Key quotations:

- 'Anita had merely looked bored' (p. 282)
- 'she did not even wave me off' (p. 282)
- 'she closed her face like the end of a chapter in a long epic book, a dying cadence, a full stop' (p. 282).

Anita 'looked bored' as Meena was rescued and taken to hospital. This presents her as immovable in the face of tragedy/trauma. The reader is positioned to harden towards her once more and to view Meena as resolute in her position to move on from Anita.

Robert:

Key quotations:

- 'infected by his soundless chortle' (p. 283)
- 'a dishy bloke' (p. 283)
- 'Pretty soon, we reached a stage where we did not even need to complete our unpronounceable sentences' (p. 286).

Physically isolated and compromised in his health, Robert is intelligent and kind. He makes a clear effort to boost Meena's spirits and cultivate a fun-based, genuinely warm friendship.

Meena:

Key quotations:

- 'after a while it took a huge effort simply to recall Anita's features' (p. 282)
- 'feeling something which was not boredom or pain or misery' (p. 283)
- 'a true hospital love, sanitised and inevitably temporary' (p. 286).

Meena matures significantly again in this chapter, recovering from initial despair and blame to swift resolve. She knows that Anita must be erased from her mind and her life. She finds genuine joy and comfort in her burgeoning relationship with Robert.

Structure

Learners should explore the following examples from the opening and the ending of Chapter 12 and be invited to consider:

- Why Syal has chosen to begin and end with this focus on the hospital?
- What their predictions might be about key characters and plot developments within this chapter.

Opening: 'I was in the Good Hope Children's Ward […] near the isolation booths' (p. 280).

Ending: 'We wanted to thank you for making Robert's time in hospital so happy. We know you will miss him too' (p. 296).

Extracts

1. How does Syal use Meena's return to Tollington to signal personal growth and her ability to move on?

'The whole village had aged behind my back, I decided […] a smell of urine and stale cigarette smoke hit me' (p. 294).

Example response planning, using topic sentence scaffold:

- Syal presents Meena as having outgrown Tollington…
- Syal presents Meena as now better able to appreciate the limitations and shortcomings of the village…
- Syal presents Meena as wiser and more astute on her return; she can now see the realities of Tollington…

Example response, unpacking quotations and language therein to support points:

Syal suggests that the distance (both physical and emotional) that Meena's hospital stay has afforded her allows her to see Tollington through new eyes and for what it really is. Where before she coveted more traditional British ways of living, she now sees them for what they are. She has grown up and knows to evaluate things at face value and to try not to romanticise as she did with Anita and the Tollington women more generally.

2. How does Syal prepare the reader for the inevitable as the chapter comes to a close?

'In the limbo days between Boxing Day and New Year's Eve […] when we meet next year. Meena. X' (p. 296).

Example response, unpacking quotations and language therein to support points:

The reader is poignantly placed to anticipate Robert's death and to sympathise greatly with Meena as the chapter draws to its conclusion. His absence when she visits the hospital for the final time and her optimism in her final written correspondence to him are truly moving. We genuinely wish otherwise, but know it is highly likely that Meena's own words about the 'temporary' nature of their relationship will come to pass. There is a satisfying circularity in the fact that she learns of his passing in a letter, too, this time from his parents. The use of letters is, of course, reflective of the time in which the novel is set. However, it is entirely befitting of the type of relationship the reader would like to believe Robert and Meena would have gone on to have had if he survived.

CHAPTER 13 OF ANITA AND ME

At a glance

- **Chapter summary quotation:** 'My days as a yard member were over' (p. 297)
- **Big Question:** How does this chapter explore the ways in which Meena finds true belonging?
- **Significant plot event:** Tracey almost drowns on the eve of Meena's eleven-plus.
- **Character focus:** Meena, Tracey, Sam
- **Key themes:**
  - Change
  - Belonging
  - Neglect, bullying and abuse
- **Handle with care:**
  - References to a range of offensive and derogatory terms and sexual references in this chapter will need to be handled with sensitivity. Please refer to the 'Handle with care' guidance in the 'How to use this book' section for further support.
    - 'Fucking bitch' (p. 301)
    - 'One day it would be FAT COW, the next day, NICE TITS, the day after, SILLY BITCH, and then SEXY LEGS' (p. 304)
    - 'SHITTY ARSE' (p. 305)
    - 'He's killing her!' (p. 308)
    - 'Bastard' (p. 311).

Why?

'Why' is important not only within the world of the text, but also when considering authorial intent and messaging.

- Why does Syal have Meena noticing the changes in Tollington?

CHAPTER 13 OF ANITA AND ME

- Why does Syal show Meena unable to focus wholly on her important exam? Why is she unable to escape some of the trappings of her 'old' life?
- Why is the identity of the residents and owners of 'The Big House' so significant?
- Why is it crucial that Meena does not have a final argument with Anita, but instead delivers her final message to her as she wishes to?

This allows us to consider Chapter 13's Big Question:

> How does this chapter explore the ways in which Meena finds true belonging?

What?

What happens?

Meena returns to Tollington and is taken aback by the changes she is now keenly aware of. The village is generally more run-down and unkempt; the local estate is spreading; the local school having closed, children have to commute to school and the rhythms of their days and their lives generally are altered as a consequence; teenagers congregate in the park at night; and Tracey is increasingly ghost-like.

Meena strives to focus on preparing for her grammar school entrance exam and distancing herself from Anita and her 'old' life. Unkind letters are a source of some distraction.

On the eve of her exam, she is left alone due to a family emergency and becomes unexpectedly embroiled in her 'old' life once more: Tracey leads her to the grounds of the Big House and they witness Sam and Anita having sex. In trying to reconcile with Meena, Sam inadvertently causes the situation to quickly get out of hand, culminating in a dangerous water-borne emergency for Tracey.

In seeking help to rescue Tracey, Meena uncovers the true identity of the incumbents of the Big House. Tracey is rescued. Meena breaks all final ties with Anita and Sam, the family moves away and Meena begins a new life.

Social, cultural and historical context

It is important for learners to fully understand, appreciate and be able to realistically envisage life in the fictional village of Tollington in 1972 for Meena. They may require pre-teaching activities on the following features of social, cultural and historical context so they can write about them confidently.

The following are some useful quotations to consider when discussing this context with learners.

- **Urbanisation and changing landscape**: 'all those children who used to have lazy hours to fill after lessons were finished [...] spent those same precious hours stuck in buses and cars, travelling from the new combined infants and junior school that had been built in the middle of the steadily growing Bartlett estate' (p. 297); 'Mrs Worrall told me about how the Bartlett estate had now spread as far as the edge of the cornfields and that 'all these townies get on the bus to come and sniff our fresh air''(p. 298).
- **Images reflective of the Manplan Project (1969)**: refer to the contextual timeline (page 201 of this guide). 'Now the cornfields were the only stretch of land separating us from the 'townies'' (p. 299); ' They also did not seem to notice the brand new building that had sprung up next to the Big House ' (p. 301–2).

Vocabulary in context

The following vocabulary from Chapter 13 can be pre-taught to help with reading fluency and reduce cognitive load. What does each of the following words mean in context?

Word	Quotation	Definition
niceties (n.)	'I [...] saw at once that she was beyond social niceties' (p. 300)	details; in relation to manners here
wayward (adj.)	'noticed that their wayward tomboy had suddenly become a walking cliche of the good Indian daughter' (p. 302)	stubborn; difficult to control
androgynous (adj)	'it was an androgynous voice too low to be a woman's, too knowing to be a man's' (p. 304)	having the physical characteristics of both sexes; unidentifiable as either
missives (n.)	'I don't know how my parents ever avoided discovering these missives' (p. 305)	a letter, especially long or official and often humorous

PIT STOP

Retrieval point

Return to this vocabulary in a later lesson, assessing if learners can link each key word to the relevant character(s). For a bonus point, develop each link into an analysis of how the writer's language choice presents that character.

Examples:

- In what ways has Meena changed from the 'wayward tomboy' that she was at the beginning?
- What is Syal suggesting about the change in Tracey if she has reached a point where she is beyond 'social niceties'?

CHAPTER 13 OF ANITA AND ME

> **PIT STOP**
>
> ## Direct instruction point
>
> It is essential to understand how to create, and the impact of, an extended metaphor. Use the following extended metaphor as a model, where Meena describes the 'siege' that she has been put under by Sam and Anita as she studies for the eleven-plus:
>
> - 'my two weeks of revision for the eleven-plus became a fourteen day siege' (p. 304)
> - 'started with catcalls' (p. 304)
> - 'Then came the stones' (p. 304)
> - 'a shower of pebbles would land on my books' (p. 304)
> - 'Then came the notes' (p. 304)
> - 'If the notes had been obviously threatening […] I would have taken action' (p. 305)
> - 'I knew they were merely the first course of some showdown […] And naturally when it came, it took me by surprise' (p. 305).
>
> Invite learners to consider why Syal creates an extended metaphor at this point in the text.
>
> Example response:
>
> Syal creates this extended metaphor, which is also an allusion to a famous rhetorical speech, to emphasise the monumental significance and ongoing nature of the resistance/attack she receives from Anita and Sam. This is done not only to cause her distress, but to obstruct her progress for the eleven-plus, the result of which could provide her with opportunities and lead to her eventual social mobility, something Anita and Sam cannot have.

> **PIT STOP**
>
> ## Academic writing point
>
> Learning and rehearsing synonyms for Meena's 'transformation' could also be a practical active step in answering the Big Question: **How does this chapter explore the ways in which Meena finds true belonging?**
>
> Examples:
>
> - metamorphosis
> - reinvention
> - self-actualisation.

> **PIT STOP**
>
> **S-T-R-E-T-C-H**
> To what extent do you feel this transformation is influenced by Meena's own personality and spirit?

Plot and character development

For tips on how to approach these 'What' questions, refer to the 'Plot and character development' section of 'How to use this book' on pages 5–6 of this guide.

1. What effect does the construction of the motorway have on community life?

Example response:

Syal draws our attention to the deleterious and hostile effects on community life:

- 'all those children [...] precious hours stuck in buses and cars' (p. 297)
- 'arriving home in weary groups, dragging school bags and shoes on the ground' (p. 297)
- 'defrosting in front of their television sets' (p. 297)
- 'without the children [...] the streets were empty and unloved' (p. 297)
- 'all these notes became indistinct and fuzzy when pitched against the constant low roar of the motorway traffic which now rose each morning above the fields and hung over our houses like an unwanted, stifling cloud' (p. 298)
- 'even the stars had changed' (p. 298)
- 'Only the most gaudy constellation survived the neon fallout, and against it, black was no longer a colour in its own right, but simply an absence of light' (p. 298).

2. What might Meena's reaction to learning that Anita is going out with Sam reveal about her?

Example response:

- Defensive yet insightful: "Yeah?' I said, a little too defensively I thought' (p. 301).
- Indifference yet hurt: "Was [her best friend],' I corrected her, annoyed that this word stabbed me somewhere soft' (p. 301).
- Determination to move on: 'I don't give a toss what your sister does, Tracey. You can tell her that from me' (p. 301).

Syal draws our attention to Meena's overall indifference, and therefore antithetical response to the pain she experienced losing Robert.

3. **What does Meena realise as she eavesdrops on her parents' conversation?**

   Example responses:

   - Her parents' love for her is unconditional and that she will always have their faith and support: 'She will pass it, no problem. She's my daughter' (p. 303).
   - Her father realises and respects how she is growing into adolescence: 'Papa's silence told me how much better he knew me than mama, at this point' (p. 303).
   - Willingness to open herself to accountability: 'I was reaping the karma of all those lies and longings' (p. 303).
   - The impact of losing two people she holds dearly and the emotional resilience she is able to show: 'I was content. I had absorbed Nanima's absence and Robert's departure like rain on parched earth' (p. 303).
   - Her self-worth: 'The place in which I belonged was wherever I stood' (p. 303).

4. **What might Meena's response to the harassment from Anita, Sam and Tracey reveal about her?**

   Example response:

   Meena's reaction to the harassment (no longer going out on her bike and losing concentration in her eleven-plus studies) may suggest that the reader is being positioned to view her as still under Anita's power. It is not the content of the notes that is threatening, nor the cat-calling, but the knowledge that this is only the beginning. Perhaps Syal wants the reader to question whether Meena's biggest fear is that someone she claims to have erased can still control her.

5. **What might Tracey's reaction to Sam and Anita having sex reveal about her own vulnerabilities?**

   Example response:

   Tracey's reaction to her sister having sex with Sam is to desperately seek help, label it 'killing her' (p. 308) and intervene with ferocious words. This may suggest that her own view of sex has been negatively influenced by her lived experience. The reader has been prepared for this previously with her gradual withering and her strong reaction to physical touch. We question whether Tracey's childhood has been characterised and shattered by abuse.

6. What makes Sam's scar the catalyst for Meena's epiphany about him?

Example response:

The infliction of the physical mark can be interpreted in several ways if one does not know the full story. Usually willing to see the best in people and give them the benefit of the doubt, life has now taught Meena about human nature. After briefly entertaining benevolent explanations, Meena realises what she has known for a long time – she is no longer a naive child and Sam is a criminal. She can't yet bring herself to use the word, but her shift in perspective and understanding is clear.

How?

Language

Narrative voice

Key quotation:

- 'After all, I had never promised to be good, had I?' (p. 304).

How does Syal use represented speech to position the reader and influence their perceptions of Meena?

Example response:

Syal uses represented speech here to create a narrative voice that is almost self-conscious but with a spark of mischief. It is a reminder that the narrator is, after all, a child. It allows the old Meena to position the reader to view the change as a positive trajectory, so they can continue to celebrate their beloved protagonist.

Literary allusions

Key quotations:

- 'The village turned into the Pied Piper's Hamelin' (p. 297)
- 'and then there are only freeze frames: Tracey appearing from nowhere, leaping at Sam like a terrier; Anita following her up towards the overhang; Sam backing towards the edge laughing at this absurd challenge [...] and then that terrible splash which sucked in half the night with it — and silence' (p. 314).

Why has Syal included the reference to the Pied Piper and what that might suggest about control?

Example response:

Perhaps Syal's allusion to the Pied Piper, the age-old moral of what happens when human beings lose their sense of individuality and start to conform, follow without questioning, is a foreboding reinforcement of how the nature of social interactions begin to change in Tollington. With the children spending a significant amount of their time commuting to school, they start to move away from social places, 'wreaking havoc' (p. 297) in the neighbourhood streets and interacting with the locals. Syal's allusion foregrounds the stark reality of what it means to be a child that is a victim of urbanisation, losing both their innocence and vitality.

What is the significance of the reference to the 'freeze frame' to emphasise both the action, as well as the intensity of this scene?

Example response:

Once again Syal employs the hyperbolic for dramatic effect, as the reader watches the horror unfold, powerless to prevent it. We witness the scene in slow motion, a freeze frame at a time, appreciating not only the juxtaposition between the laughter and the physical movement but also the impending doom, as Tracey plunges into the water, possibly to her death.

Zeugma

A literary device where one governing word is used to modify two parts of a sentence in distinct ways. In the example below, this word is 'lost'.

Key quotation:

- 'I had lost a Nanima, a soul mate and temporarily, a leg' (p. 303).

Why does Syal emphasise the physical and emotional losses Meena experienced through the use of this method?

Example responses:

- to emphasise the severity of the loss she has experienced
- to illustrate how profound the pain is
- to reinforce how vulnerable and dejected she feels
- to elucidate that the connection she found with Nanima helped her find herself, and how losing her has devastated her to the core
- to demonstrate how some losses can be healed while the impact of others can be felt more deeply, and for longer.

Polysyndeton

A literary device where conjunctions are repeated for emphasis. In the example below, this is 'and'.

Key quotation:

- 'I would be a traveller soon anyhow. I would be going to the posh girls' school where I would read and argue and write stories and if I wished, trample the mangy school uniform tam-o'-shanter into the mud' (p. 304).

Why does Syal draw attention to the range of skills and opportunities that Meena is looking forward to? How would opportunities and skills support her social mobility? How does Meena feel about the life she has the chance to leave behind, and why might she feel so emotive about it, wanting to 'trample' the school uniform in the 'mud'?

Example response:

Syal uses polysyndeton to list the skills and opportunities Meena can look forward to as a grammar school pupil: 'read and argue and write'. Meena may also begin to exercise her own choice as suggested by the verb 'wished'. Together, these language choices, along with the image of her 'trampl[ing]' part of her uniform as a form of protest and self-expression, project a future Meena who is far more self-assured, assertive and confident. Social mobility and breaking free of the mould she may feel she has, thus far, been confined to in Tollington, are now within her reach.

Character focus

Meena

Key quotation:

- 'this is what I realised [...] I was content. I had absorbed Nanima's absence and Robert's departure like rain on parched earth, drew it in deep and drank from it. I now knew I was not a bad girl, a mixed-up girl, a girl with no name or no place' (p. 303).

Syal draws our attention to Meena's ultimate victory, her metamorphosis. We now see a Meena who has made peace with who she is, has found herself, and acts with conviction. She no longer acts 'out of fear' (p. 305), but more so with the wisdom of someone who has insight. She is intrigued by the attempts made to obstruct her revision, rising above the petty. When Sam Lowbridge proceeds to kiss her, we see a Meena who makes a choice – she 'let[s] him' (p. 314). She celebrated feeling 'mighty and huge' (p. 314), recognising that she has the ultimate victory. This is not only because she has reached the point of self-assurance, but because she knows that she has left a lasting impact on Sam: 'every time he saw another Meena on a street corner he would remember this and feel totally powerless' (p. 314).

Tracey

Key quotations:

- 'On closer inspection, the thin white figure was Tracey [...] now she was nothing less than transparent [...] her body a cobweb hung out on bones' (p. 300)
- 'She just stared at me' (p. 300)
- 'beyond social niceties' (p. 300).

Syal draws our attention to the loss of innocence, breaking down of a spirit, and impact that social anxieties and pressures can ultimately have on the most vulnerable.

Sam

Key quotation:

- Sam grabbed me by the wrists and I sucked in air and held it. 'When I said them,' he rasped, 'I never meant you, Meena! It was all the others, not yow!' (p. 313).
- Syal draws our attention to the destructive impact that divisive and xenophobic narratives can have on the impressionable. This often gives rise to feelings of delusion where even extreme actions, as is the case in the horrifying, racially-motivated assault of the 'Indian man', are deemed justifiable.

> **PIT STOP**
>
> ### S-T-R-E-T-C-H
>
> Ask learners to consider the impact of the following revelations and whether they make the reader for pity for Sam:
>
> - 'I wanted to make people listen' (p. 313)
> - 'I never meant you, Meena! It was all the others, not yow!' (p. 313)
> - 'You can move on. How come? How come I can't?' (p. 314).

Structure

Learners should explore the following examples from the opening and ending of Chapter 13 and be invited to consider:

- Why Syal has chosen to begin and end with this focus on Meena as an independent figure, making her own decisions?
- How this heralds a new beginning for Meena and in what ways?
- How Meena is keen to trust her instincts and resist the manipulation and control of others?
- What their predictions might be about key characters and plot developments within this chapter.

Opening: 'I spent a lot of time on my own that year' (p. 297).

Ending: 'I opted for a gracious silence' (p. 328).

Cyclical structure and irony

Tracey was found near the 'Christmases' abandoned house' resembling a 'ghost' (p. 300). This is both ironic and tragic, as Tracey was told by Deirdre (Chapter 9) that she would buy her this very house.

Repetition of mantra

Meena repeats her mantra of, 'I have an exam tomorrow' (p. 310). How this is reflective of Meena's awakened sense of responsibility? How is Meena's newfound focus inspired by the realisation that her social mobility is connected with her performance in this exam?

Change

- Changing people: 'I began to notice more strangers hanging round Tollington now. The park, once the domain of the under-tens and curious stray dogs, became a hang-out for various groups of teenagers who took over the swings and roundabouts, smoking and flirting together in separate clans' (p. 298).
- Changing atmosphere: 'even the stars had changed' (p. 298).
- Changing seasons: 'Spring bloomed into an early hot summer [...] But the park was out of bounds after sunset [...] Everyone in the yard felt their privacy invaded' (p. 301) – a significant contrast to the communal ritual of Spring Cleaning and sharing of stories mentioned in earlier chapters.

Ask learners to consider:

- The significance of more strangers in Tollington and the impact on the already disillusioned community.
- Why Syal emphasises the 'groups of teenagers' in 'separate clans' (p. 298) and how that might create further tension and division?
- The significance of the symbolic references to the stars and changing seasons and what Syal might be suggesting about hope and destiny.
- The cyclical nature of change.

Extracts

1. How does Syal use language to develop the tension in this extract?

'I was already running, cracking my head on branches... A witch's voice, strangely accented and croaky' (p. 315).

Example response planning, using topic sentence scaffolds: 💡

- Syal uses present continuous here to convey the urgency with which Meena desperately tries to find help...
- Syal lists anxious concerns to mirror the breathless concern Meena feels...
- Syal makes various references to witchcraft reminding us of Meena's childish fears...

Example response, unpacking quotations and language therein to support points:

Syal presents Meena's panic and fear reaching fever pitch here as she races to find help for Tracey: the tension is heightened through the character's internal monologue whereby the reader can hear Meena's galloping thoughts: 'phone the police somebody, which was the way out… I Have An Exam Tomorrow…'. They are jagged and jump around out of control. The reader is positioned to empathise with Meena, worrying simultaneously about the girl who can't swim in the freezing water and the biggest day of her life tomorrow.

2. How does Syal finally reveal Meena's self-actualisation relative to her 'relationship' with Sam?

'Sparks of recognition momentarily flew between us… the knowledge he would never have the character to cut the wires made me furious, for the waste, for his cowardice, for both of us' (p. 313).

Example response planning, using topic sentence scaffolds:

- Syal uses rhetorical questions to convey the disbelief Meena feels when she realises…
- Syal uses metaphors linked to sorcery such as 'illusion', 'sleight of hand' and 'sparks'…
- Syal conveys Meena's anger when she realises the truth about Sam…

Example response, unpacking quotations and language therein to support points:

Syal presents Meena's dawning realisation that Sam is as much under Anita's spell as she was through an extended metaphor linked to illusion and magic: describing Sam as a 'puppet' who will 'never have the character to cut the wires' (presumably from puppeteer Anita) powerfully conveys her disgust towards him and, arguably towards herself for ever having had feelings towards him or hopes for him.

CHARACTERS

A note on teaching characters

It is easy for students to fall into the trap of exploring characters as one-dimensional: Meena as the heroine, Anita as the villain and Sam Lowbridge as the criminal. However, if there is one thing we have learned from Syal's depictions, it is that every character is multifaceted with fears, vulnerabilities, desires and vices. In order to teach learners to identify and analyse these pivotal idiosyncrasies that make each character resonate fully with the human condition, it might be useful to provide a scaffold to both facilitate and encourage independent note-taking and tracking of the characters as the study of the text progresses. Learners could also use the analytical prompts curated for different characters in the 'How' sections of each chapter as a basis for their own investigations.

Scaffolds and worksheets

The following is an example of a scaffold that can be adapted to suit learner needs. It can be found in our downloadable resources.

Name of Character:			
Key quotations:	Tracking the character:	Key moments of weakness or vulnerability:	Key moments of juxtaposition:
	Initially, ... Then, ... Finally, ... Ultimately, ...		
	Tier 2 Power words:	Key moments of transition or change:	Contextual links:

Next, provide learners with a scaffold to synthesise their findings, analyse methods and evaluate authorial intent. This might look something like this:

CHARACTERS

> _____ **symbolises** _____. When we are **initially** introduced to _____, _____ is described by Syal as _____. **Perhaps** Syal uses _____ to emphasise _____. **It is interesting to note that** this description of _____ is juxtaposed with _____ that informs us _____. Syal may have **juxtaposed** _____ to **elucidate** _____. **It is clear through Syal's presentation** that _____ cannot _____. In this case, the presentation of _____ is similar to the presentation of _____. All _____ needs is _____, **yet** this is clearly not enough for _____. Syal's **use of** _____ **in particular, connotes/reveals/portrays** _____. **Suggesting**, _____. **The fact that** Syal has highlighted _____ about _____ **reiterates** _____.
>
> **Later** we see _____ **develop/ change** into someone who _____. Syal describes how _____ is now _____, someone that is _____, **unlike** _____. This _____ is a **turning point** for _____ as the **reader finally realises** _____.
>
> **Ultimately**, although _____, we see _____ represent _____. _____ ends up with _____, which, despite _____, is _____. Syal reminds us that _____.

Finally, there are a series of analytical worksheets included in our downloadable resources. 🖱 These have been adapted from Stuart Pryke's character analysis overviews for *A Christmas Carol*, original source unknown. Their purpose is to provide learners with analytical models that they can reduce into their own words, transform into dual-coded images to aid memory and magpie from to develop their academic writing abilities. There are also evaluative statements to extend and challenge higher attainers and encourage conceptualised debate. Learners should be invited to create similar overviews for some of the other characters independently to measure their understanding and techniques.

Character overviews
Meena Kumar

Meena Kumar, 'too mousy, clumsy and scabby to be a real Indian girl, too Indian to be a real Tollington wench' (p. 150), a girl 'stuck in between various gangs' (p. 25), symbolises a child at the cusp of adolescence. She is made to feel like she has to choose between identities and worlds, just so she can prove that she belongs. When we are first introduced to nine-year-old Meena, she is immediately presented by Syal as someone who has a desire to rebel and fabricate truths, a desire for which she finds an outlet in 13-year-old Anita Rutter, who gives 'voice' to all the 'wicked' things she has 'often thought but kept zipped up' (p. 138). Perhaps Syal uses Meena's desire to challenge societal and cultural boundaries to emphasise her inner conflict, highlighted especially by the restrictive metaphorical adjective 'zipped', amidst the external reality of living as a first-generation immigrant in 1970s Tollington, facing both overt ostracism as well as ignorance and microaggressions. It is interesting to note that Meena, who 'never wanted to be anyone else except [her]self only older and famous' (p. 146), starts to feel ostracised for her ethnic identity. She wants to 'shed [her] body like a snake' and emerge 'reborn' (p. 146), just so she can fit in. This simile in particular reveals not only the compulsion for a complete transformation but also alludes to the revulsion she starts to feel for who she is and what she stands for. It is Nanima's arrival that serves almost as a moment of anagnorisis when she realises that this 'urge to reinvent' is driven by unfounded 'shame' (p. 211). We then see Meena begin to reclaim her sense of confidence as well as identity. She decides that she will no longer be Anita's 'shadow', but her 'equal' (p. 237), and starts to see Anita for more than who she projects herself to be, stepping over the 'fine line between love and pity' (p. 242) in a moment of remarkable emotional maturity.

Although presented as a morally insightful person, Syal also reveals moments of weakness in Meena through some of her reckless choices. This includes lying, stealing, falsely accusing others of her misdeeds as well as resistance to stand up to injustices committed by the Wenches Brigade. Yet we also see Meena's fierce desire to protect her family and friends, empathise with the voiceless and demonstrate unwavering courage in standing up to bullies, to fight both racism and discrimination.

Finally, we see Meena emerge victorious, making peace with who she is, 'heal[ing]' both 'mind and body' and recognising that she was never a 'bad girl, a mixed-up girl, a girl with no name or place', but someone who could indeed be empowered by their cultural hybridity to 'belong' wherever they 'stood' (p. 303). Syal's message is clear through Meena's affirmation – belonging is arbitrary and shouldn't come at the cost of conformity. It is a 'choice' more than anything else, and one which can result in true empowerment and contentment.

Anita Rutter

Known as the 'undisputed 'cock' of our yard' (p. 38), Anita symbolises an extreme consequence of neglect, abuse and social deprivation. When we are first introduced to Anita, she is presented by Syal as the solution to Meena's need for liberation. Anita, like Meena, is keen to rebel, enjoys adventure and loves the outdoors. What's interesting is how Anita doesn't begin the friendship until she tests Meena, and how quickly Anita, with her 'foghorn voice, foul mouth and proficiency at lassoing victims' (p. 38–9), reveals the cruel and domineering aspects of her personality and propensity to both intimidate and dominate. The use of this metaphor in particular illustrates the power and control she has over those around her. It's as if she imprisons them under her spell, despite her offensive demeanour. Anita's fury is so 'powerful' that it is even described as 'almost tangible' and her 'wordless seething tempers' (p. 186) clearly terrify those around her. Perhaps Syal uses Anita to remind the reader of how dangerous it can be when brutish behaviour is unchecked, and how quickly it can escalate. This includes Anita's coercion and control of her friends, tormenting of her own sister, bullying of Mr Christmas, instigating Meena's stealing, attacking Fat Sally in a violent but composed way, and brazenly supporting and celebrating Sam's brutal and racist assault.

Despite Anita's facade of bravado and indifference, Syal brings our attention to how she also succumbs to vulnerability on more than one occasion, and how she may be a 'naughty girl but not a wicked one' (p. 268). She too, has a 'fear of ostracism' (p. 142), revealed through subtle fabrications like pretending to wear a bra or bursting into tears in response to her mother's condemnation. She also shows child-like ignorance that 'Deidre had no intention, ever, of buying Anita a horse' (p. 242), yet rides one with unparalleled expertise and affection. Furthermore, she collapses after putting their injured dog out of its misery, demonstrating the physical and emotional toll the act has on her body. It is no surprise that Meena begins to pity her and Meena's mama also feels sorry for the 'poor poor girl' (p. 250). Meena recognises that Anita is more in 'need' of her than the other way around, yet is sadly incapable of accepting kindness when she is given it.

Ultimately, we see Anita reduced to someone without choice. She is friendless and motherless, and shows no growth or insight, even when Meena writes to her before leaving Tollington. Anita's future looks bleak and without ambition, one where, according to her own sister, she may turn out just like their mother. Syal is possibly trying to suggest that Anita's dishonesty, cruelty and inaction on some occasions are unforgivable. Anita may have had power and influence throughout the narrative but ultimately loses to Meena on moral grounds.

Mama (Daljit Kumar)

Mrs Kumar, or mama, symbolises grace, resilience and moral fibre. She is the type of woman whose 'serenity masked backbones of iron and a flair for passive resistance' (p. 110), who has lived more than one lifetime. When we are first introduced to mama, she is described by Syal as someone who comes from a 'small Punjabi village' (p. 34) and is proud of her heritage. She carves out a brand new identity, driven by the pressure to assimilate felt by immigrants in 1960s Britain. She learned that 'she would get fewer stares and whispers if she had donned any of the sensible teacher's trouser suits', practised 'discretion' in her attire and spoke 'English without an accent' (p. 25). Perhaps Syal uses these sibilant verbs to emphasise the pressure that looms over people like mama. It reminds us of how life-changing it can be for a person's sense of self, as well as their understanding of what it means to truly belong. It is the latter that fuels mama's desire to educate and guide Meena with firm affection, instilling purpose and ambition: 'You prove you are better. Always' (p. 45). It is therefore unsurprising that Meena sees this duality within her: 'To everyone else, she was the epitome of grace, dignity and unthreatening charm', treated with 'deferential respect', yet to Meena, there is a 'monster beneath the mother' (p. 28). It is interesting to note that this juxtaposition is also reflective of the theme of mother-daughter relationships and generational conflict. Meena feels misunderstood, and often finds it difficult to connect with her mother, admitting that she is not a 'Yard Mama' (p. 53), and that the only time she can relate to her is when she sees any hint of fiery passion within her.

Mama is uncompromising when it comes to matters of morality. This is evident in her decision to deny Deidre the benefit of her 'impeccable manners' (p. 90) upon learning her racist name for their dog. She is fully devoted to her family and dedicates her time and efforts to educating Meena about her past, regularly drawing parallels between her life now with the world she came from, with orchards and peacocks and 'rainy monsoon nights' (p. 35). Mama recognises sacrifice and what it means to be 'intelligent but poor' and live frugally: 'My mother never ate out, never' (p. 26). Although mama's adherence to cultural traditions and beliefs occasionally causes friction between her and Meena, she is still determined to make Meena feel a sense of belonging and establish a grounding in her cultural identity. She takes her to a gurdwara to connect with her religious heritage and attempts to teach her 'rudiments of Indian cuisine' (p. 61).

As the text progresses, Syal draws our attention to mama's flaws and biases as well. For example, her assumptions about 'English' familial practices and an occasional sense of righteousness about her own cultural values: 'She never sees her own grandchildren [...] Her kids should be shot' (p. 135). However, mama is seen to be receptive and occasionally changes her stance. This is especially true as her interactions with the Ballbearings women increase and become more meaningful, revealed as she stands in the 'doorway, rapt' (p. 217) observing Mrs Worrall's kindness to Nanima. It is also evident when she realises that Deidre has been 'seeking approval all her life' (p. 216), softening her stance towards her, and when she learns that 'that Anita Rutter' is in fact a 'poor poor girl' (p. 250) who is both neglected and abandoned.

What remains consistent, however, is mama's compassion and faith in Meena's character and capabilities. She is described by Meena to be 'regularly' found 'in front of the television news with tears streaming down her face' empathising with 'those poor children [...] those poor miners [...] those poor soldiers' (p. 52). Mama's solicitude is unparalleled: 'enough heart for the rest of the world' (p. 52). It is therefore no surprise that as Meena matures, she begins to admire her for her integrity, as mama too starts to believe that her daughter shares her strength and will succeed: 'She is my daughter. She will pass it, no problem' (p. 303).

Papa (Shyam Kumar)

Shyam Kumar, or papa, encapsulating both 'vulnerability and pride' (p. 11), symbolises the struggle to balance cultural values and heritage with a desire to adapt to Western traditions for the sake of a family's wellbeing and integration. Papa is a dedicated father, affectionate husband, conscientious provider and, at times, a fierce protector. When we are first introduced to papa, we see him enforcing strong morals and integrity as he attempts to hold Meena accountable for her lies. He shares with her the parable of the boy and the tiger to instil life-long lessons that he continues to impress upon her throughout the narrative. He is described by Syal with a 'sensitive' face and a 'generous' mouth (p. 81), someone 'tasty enough to flirt with' (p. 180), yet desperately 'uncomfortable' (p. 179), partly because of his cultural sensibilities, with the attention he receives from the Ballbearings women.

Papa, of course, has his vices and indulgences. We learn that he 'loved gambling' (p. 181) and often won, but Syal draws our attention to this seemingly frivolous aspect of his personality to reveal a history that is deeper and profoundly tragic. We learn that he is someone who has 'courted chance like an old friend' (p. 181) because he knows all too well what it is like to take a gamble in life when the stakes are stacked against you: 'a seventeen-year-old in a refugee camp who owned what he wore' (p. 181–2). Papa is someone who understands vulnerability and sacrifice, who has 'lived and breathed and smelled' poverty (p. 182), for whom the past is not a 'mere sentimental journey' but 'a murky bottomless pool full of monsters and the odd shining coin' (p. 75). It is therefore unsurprising how he alternates between composure and outbursts of anger when he sees what he perceives as Meena digressing as she experiments with aspects of her identity and projection.

Papa is generous and charitable and loves to host 'mehfils' that are 'legendary' (p. 71), bringing friends together. This is perhaps in an attempt to create a community and support system to replace the one he, like many other immigrants, would have left behind. But it is when papa sings that Syal illustrates the emergence of his true being: 'Papa became himself when he sang. My tender papa, my flying papa, the papa with hope and infinite variety' (p. 83). The repeated use of personal pronouns demonstrates not only Meena's protectiveness of her father, but also her love and admiration for seeing his uninhibited, true self. Perhaps Syal wants the reader to empathise with papa here – the present participle 'flying' reminding us how his creative expression is what makes him soar, and how tragic it was that he was denied an acting career: 'offered a contract' when he was younger but 'refused' (p. 82) by Dadajee, a communist. However, papa's sense of duty is unparalleled, as he remains committed to provide for his family, going to an 'office everyday' and returning with 'a bulging briefcase full of papers' (p. 83). Syal invites the reader's empathy when Meena makes the 'connection' that if her 'singing papa' was the 'real man', how trapped he must feel 'the rest of the time' (p. 83).

Despite his personal compromises, papa shows on many occasions that he recognises and values integrity and kindness. This is evident through his candid conversions with Uncle Alan and Mr Topsy/Turvey, his quiet 'revolutions' (p. 165) though defiant comments about Churchill, 'not particularly one of my heroes' (p. 179), and his important reminders to Meena to always speak up against injustice. Papa's protection comes in many guises and he plays the role of the immigrant parent like a trained veteran. It is no surprise, therefore, that despite their disagreements, Meena values him for his love and dedication. He too shows growth in his understanding and acceptance of his daughter's emerging sense of self towards the end: 'Papa's silence told me how much better he knew me than mama' (p. 303).

Nanima

- Meena's maternal grandmother, who arrives from India to support her daughter following the birth of her grandson, Sunil
- immediately bonds with Meena and embraces and celebrates her for her freedom of spirit
- surprises Meena by visiting Mrs Worrall and interacting with confidence, buying chocolate at Mr Ormerod's shop and conversing with Mr Topsy/Turvey in Punjabi.

Key quotations:

- 'the eyes were rheumy and mischievous' (p. 200)
- 'I knew Nanima was going to be fun when she rolled backwards into the farty settee and let out a howl of laughter' (p. 200)
- when Nanima calls Meena a 'junglee' and papa explains: "It is not a compliment, you know!' But Nanima's expression told me it was exactly that' (p. 200-1)
- 'a beloved parent, a familiar symbol' (p. 201)
- 'I had never seen the Elders so expansive and unconcerned' (p. 204)
- 'Nanima had applied some ancient witchery to finally cut the umbilical cord' (p. 208)
- 'stories never followed any pattern' (p. 209).

Sam Lowbridge

- son of Glenys, a single parent
- considered to be Tollington's rebel
- had a criminal record since the age of 16
- expresses racist vitriol and takes part in a violent and racist attack
- is Anita's boyfriend later in the novel but also kisses Meena.

Key quotations:

- 'Sam Lowbridge was generally considered the Yard's Bad Boy [...] managed to acquire a criminal record by the age of sixteen' (p. 55)
- 'he'd always been polite, even kind to me' (p. 56)
- when Butch bites Sam Lowbridge, Mrs Povey says: 'Any dog that takes a chunk out of that bugger is alright by me' (p. 89)
- 'Bloody church roof? What's that gonna do for us, eh? Wharra about us?' (p. 192)
- 'high on the sound of his own unchallenged voice' (p. 192)

- 'Yow don't do nothing but talk, "Uncle". And give everything away to some darkies we've never met [...] This is our patch, Not some wogs' handout' (p. 193).

Deirdre Rutter

- Anita's mother, who betrays her by sleeping with Dave, the Poet
- decides not to invite Meena for tea, potentially discriminating against her because of her ethnicity
- racially discriminates and names their dog using an offensive, racial slur
- neglects her daughters and runs away with a butcher from Cannock.

Key quotations:

- 'tottered into the yard on her white stilettos, her pointy boobs doing a jive under a very tight white polo neck sweater' (p. 54)
- 'always on the edge of a sneer' (p. 55)
- 'Deirdre looked me up and down as if making a decision, then turned on her heel and tip-tapped into her yard' (p. 55)
- 'an air about Deirdre that prevented the gossips' (p. 90)
- 'Deirdre's face sagged when she saw her daughter waiting for her on the corner' (p. 206)
- 'I had always been a little afraid of Deirdre, with her scarlet gash of a mouth and her backhanded conversation' (p. 215)
- 'but now I could see something else, something unexpected in her face – she was frightened of us' (p. 215)
- 'Deirdre had been seeking approval all her life in this village' (p. 216).

Tracey Rutter

- Anita's younger sister who is bullied even by her own sister
- neglected, physically fragile and implied to be sexually abused by her father
- lonely and desperate for attention, forming a strong bond with their family dog and left devastated when he is tragically killed in an accident
- slaps Sherrie's hand away, reacting emphatically, when Sherrie admires the material of Anita's bra
- is very distressed when she finds Sam and Anita having sex, believing that he's 'killing' her, possibly impacted by her own experience of sexual abuse
- has a near-death experience and lies that Sam and Anita threw her in the pond.

Key quotations:
- 'Tracey threw herself at Deirdre's legs but she pushed her off, irritated' (p. 54)
- 'legs looked like sticks of lard, thin without muscle tone, neglected' (p. 141)
- 'row of bruises around Tracey's thighs, as purple as clover heads, two bizarre bracelets perfectly mimicking the imprint of ten cruel, angry fingers' (p. 142)
- when realising what their dog's name means: "I... I didn't know. Sorry. [...] suddenly linked her arm in mine and said reassuringly, 'Mom chose it.'" (p. 235)
- 'Whilst Anita grew taller, browner and louder, Tracey became shrunken, hollow-eyed and silent' (p. 266)
- 'Tracey began to prefer alcoves, entries and staying inside whenever her father was home' (p. 266)
- 'She stood apart from us resentfully, a silent, wet blanket ready to douse our flames' (p. 266).

Roberto Rutter

- Anita and Tracey's father
- suggested to abuse Tracey.

Key quotations:
- 'He had his blue Dunlop tyre factory overalls on and was dragging deeply on a butt end' (p. 18)
- 'a row of names in blue fuzzy ink ran up his arm like a roll call, Brenda, Deirdre, Janice, Gaynor, just legible under unsuccessful attempts to cross them out' (p. 18)
- 'He tugged the sleeve up further to reveal the name perched on top of an undulating muscle, still pristine and untampered with, three letters set in a faded red heart, MUM. 'That's who I miss, chick. No one could replace her.'' (p. 18).

Uncle Alan

- Sunday school teacher and youth leader of the local Methodist church
- proactive and progressive, taking part in social causes such as charity drives and coaching youths such as Sam Lowbridge
- shows solidarity with the Kumars following the racist incident at the fete.

Key quotations:
- 'the nearest thing we had to a sex symbol in a ten mile radius' (p. 41)

- 'ancient, at least twenty-eight' (p. 41)
- 'chestnut brown curly hair, a huge smile, an obscene amount of energy' (p. 41)
- 'trying to whip up solidarity for a protest march which he had christened Tollington In Turmoil!' (p. 143)
- 'Uncle Alan got his hands dirty and Reverend Ince kept his clean' (p. 179)
- 'Papa [...] always seemed to relax in Uncle Alan's company' (p. 179)
- 'a bitter smile twisting his lips, 'Mr Kumar, he is not my Winston Churchill, and I thank God for that." (p. 179).

Mr Ormerod

- owner of the village tuck shop
- avoids Uncle Alan all day when he questions the charitable drive led by the church to give Bibles to Africans, instead of respecting their decision to follow the religion of their choice.

Key quotations

- 'No one instigated conversation with Mr Ormerod if they wanted to get home before their next birthday' (p. 21)
- 'hyperactive in the local Wesleyan Methodist church' (p. 21)
- 'closed his eyes and began muttering a prayer but no one bothered to join in' (p. 77)
- 'having a moral crisis [...] his desperation to be the most holy and charitable man in Tollington with the strong desire he now felt to smack Anita Rutter' (p. 153)
- seen 'laughing and chatting' with someone who Meena believes to be 'one of the phantom hecklers' from the village fete 'who hid behind Mr Ormerod to spit his poison' (p. 223)
- 'had developed a grumbling, if not a bloody angry appendix' (p. 302).

Sherrie

- one of Anita's friends who owns a pony, Trixie, and lives on a farm
- following a court case about the motorway and unbeknownst to Sherrie, her father sells the farm once development starts and buys a hotel in the Lake District with the money that he wins
- Anita tells Meena that she has plans with Sherrie to share a flat in London.

Key quotations

- 'Sherrie was shivering in a short denim skirt and high heels, and had applied mauve eyeshadow all the way up to her eyebrows' (p. 103)

- 'Sherrie looked just like a medieval princess, I thought, her blonde hair streaming behind her, her sharp alabaster features focused and confident' (p. 236)
- 'elegant and completely in tune with her rotund steed' (p. 236)
- 'cocks of the school' (p. 239)
- 'flicked open her fag packet expertly' (p. 187).

Fat Sally

- Anita's friend, who belongs to what seems to be a financially stable family, but masks this fact to fit in and be accepted
- overweight and conscious of how she looks and the impact that has on her perceived attractiveness
- distressed when Anita forces her to hand over her expensive Biba scarf that her mother got for her from London
- has a violent and physical fight with Anita where she maintains a strong grip on Anita's hair, pulling it with force as Anita continues to attack her
- very upset when Anita mocks her for going to Catholic school.

Key quotations:

- 'Fat Sally was squeezed into a psychedelic mini-dress with a shiny scarf tied around her waist, and lips looked wet and shimmery, like a gold fish' (p. 103)
- 'she ate like she wanted to choke herself, without pleasure or pride [...] and when I saw her mother, I understood why' (p. 189)
- 'I had not liked Fat Sally up until this point, but I knew what it was like to live inside a body you did not feel was yours' (p. 189)
- 'I could tell no one had ever dared criticise her mom's dress sense before' (p. 239)
- "'It's not a slags' school,' shouted Fat Sally, trembling now. 'It's Catholic! So there! And we aren't... I mean ain't rich. We just work hard and save hard, we make sacrifices so I can have a good education!'" (p. 239).

Mrs Worrall

- offers to create a rota when Meena's mama is taken to hospital.

Key quotations:

- 'a few drops of spit fell onto his chin which Mrs Worrall expertly wiped away with her pinafore hem' (p. 65)

- 'Mrs Worrall was attempting to kneel, her fat knees cracking, and I suddenly saw what the last twenty-two years of her life must have been, this endless uncomplaining attendance of a broken, unresponsive body' (p. 66–7)
- 'Mrs Worrall's big treat was an extra lemon puff in front of *Crossroads*, whilst her husband dozed off' (p. 67)
- 'We'll have to do a rota. For Mr K. Mek sure him and the littl'un eat and that' (p. 130).

Mr Worrall

- married to Mrs Worrall
- a war veteran who gets life-changing injuries from getting too close to a shell and needs constant care
- expresses his affection for Meena through non-verbal gestures when she holds his hand.

Key quotations:

- 'the smell of a sick room, unaired and lonely [...] A shape took form before me, thin useless legs in clean striped pyjamas' (p. 65)
- 'Mr Worrall's face, wide blue-blue staring eyes and a mouth permanently open, asking for something, wanting to talk, with the bewildered, demanding expression of an unjustly punished child' (p. 65)
- 'his fingers seemed to rustle like dry twigs but, amazingly, I could feel the pump and surge of his heartbeat throbbing through his palm' (p. 65–6)
- 'It was the shells. In the war. He got too close' (p. 66).

Uncle Amman

- the first person that Mr Kumar meets on arriving in the UK
- shows Mr Kumar kindness and supports him in getting accustomed to life in the UK
- more subdued and self-effacing than his wife, Auntie Shaila
- suffers a heart attack towards the end of the novel that results in Meena's parents leaving her on the night before the eleven-plus exam.

Key quotation:

- 'Uncle Amman would finish with a flourish, as if it were perfectly natural to meet a total stranger and within ten minutes, find him a meal, a home and a list of Situations Vacant' (p. 31).

Auntie Shaila

- married to Uncle Amman and regularly supports Meena's mother in disciplining her
- vocal about her views on religion, traditions and upbringing
- cares for the Kumar family when mama is in the hospital for Sunil's birth.

Key quotations:

- 'Your mama is in a delicate way, you should be pressing her feet and asking for forgiveness' (p. 108)
- 'bursting with optimist and unsolicited advice' (p. 110)
- 'fed-up with Auntie Shaila's constant clucking, her re-organisation of mama's spice rack and her interminable five-course breakfast' (p. 133)
- 'Auntie Shaila had radar built into her sari blouse and she collared papa soon afterwards in a corner, demanding to know what had gone on' (p. 160).

Pinky and Baby

- Uncle Amman and Auntie Shaila's daughters
- Meena falsely accuses them of stealing to avoid the blame.

Key quotations:

- 'They were in matching outfits again, pink jumpers with hearts and daisies around the neck, jeans with a carefully ironed crease running down the legs, long black hair in bunches' (p. 151)
- 'Pinky was my age, Baby a year younger, and they looked to me like infants' (p. 151)
- 'Even Pinky's voice set my teeth on edge, a soft plaint whine with a lilt of Punjabi in it, the over-pronunciation of consonants' (p. 151)
- 'they were too easy a target, mere hors d'oeuvres for Anita's appetite' (p. 151)
- 'to my annoyance, I could feel the pensioners sigh and beam at my cousins in approval, uplifted by this vision of pretty little sisters in matching separates and coordinated dimples' (p. 152)
- 'Pinky finally spoke, she sounded so calm and grown up […] 'The man in the shop. He will soon find out you have taken the tin. Then what will you do, Meena?"' (p. 156).

Mr Topsy/Turvey

- has served in the British army for 10 years and knows Punjabi
- well-meaning towards Meena and welcoming towards Nanima

- demonstrates that understanding people's backgrounds builds intercultural trust and respect.

Key quotations:
- 'muscled into the group, his voluminous trousers billowing with excitement' (p. 221)
- 'yanking at my bangs. Last year I thought this was cute, now I wanted to poke him in the eye' (p. 221)
- 'Mr Topsy/Turvey watched her with devoted eyes. 'I served in India. Ten years. Magical country, Magical people. The best'' (p. 222)
- 'We should never have been there [in India]. Criminal it was! Ugly' (p. 222)
- 'Mr Topsy/Turvey spat on the pavement as the diggers rumbled past his gate' (p. 269).

Mrs Christmas/Connie

- a charitable and kind member of the Tollington community who shows affection towards Meena and gives her a sweet
- dies of cancer but is preserved in her house by her husband for weeks.

Key quotations:
- 'always dressed like it was midwinter' (p. 40)
- 'face rosy pink' (p. 42)
- 'surprisingly sparkling and deep blue eyes' (p. 42)
- When donating to charity: 'I shan't be needing it, chick. Not where I'm going' (p. 42)
- referring to Meena: 'You've always been a smashing chick, you have' (p. 44)
- 'I saw her…like in front of the telly…no face left. Gone. Eaten away' (p. 77).

Mr Christmas

- dedicated to his wife
- devastated and disturbed after losing her, keeping her dead body for months.

Key quotations:
- 'emerged in his vest and braces, his face blue with fury' (p. 44)
- 'Connie needs her medicine first' (p. 45)
- 'a gently smiling Mr Christmas, still dressed in his tank top and vest. He paused to wave shyly at everyone before being carefully helped into the police car' (p. 77)

- 'he always doted on her' (p. 78)
- 'Three weeks later, having just returned from a short spell in hospital, Mr Christmas died in his sleep. He was buried with Mrs Christmas' (p. 79).

Sandy

- Hairy Neddy's neighbour and tries desperately for his attention
- sets up a stall at the village fete and is ridiculed for her creations until Hairy Neddy generates interest in her 'Space Gonks'.

Key quotations

- 'Sandy was making monumental efforts to impress him [...] her dressing gowns become shorter and fluffier by degrees, her hair changed colour every few days' (p. 51)
- 'Sandy, who was doing her lipstick in the wing mirror, paused with her hand up to her mouth' (p. 243)
- 'Sandy smiled at him gratefully, thrilled that someone cared enough to think for her, and sat down again with a pleased, resigned sigh' (p. 243).

Hairy Neddy

- Meena's neighbour, who has a rock band and embraces the nickname that has been given to him by Tollington, naming his band 'Hairy Neddy and his Cool Cucumbers'
- stands up for Sandy and supports her at the village fete using his charisma to generate attention for her homemade toys, presenting them as desirable and unique
- protective of Sandy and becomes romantically involved with her, before marrying her towards the end of the book
- despite his facade of bravado, he finds it difficult to physically put Tracey's dying dog out of his misery but still supports Anita when she does and catches her as she collapses.

Key quotations:

- 'the yard's only bachelor' (p. 46)
- 'blokey kind of face topped with a sort of bouffant hairdo' (p. 47)
- "Stay inside, chick!' he called to her in the tone of a fire chief faced with a towering inferno. 'Yow'll only get upset." (p. 243)
- 'Anita snorted, such a belittling noise that Hairy Neddy seemed to shrink a couple of inches' (p. 244)
- 'I'm gonna miss me warm-up now. I hate playing be-bop without me finger exercises... Must be getting soft.' (p. 244).

Rajesh Bhatra

- works for the men responsible for the motorway
- Meena feels an instant affinity with him
- robbed and brutally injured in a racially motivated assault by Sam and his gang that Anita supports too
- serves as a catalyst for encouraging the Kumars to move out of Tollington.

Key quotation:

- 'It was all the others, not yow [...] You mean the others like the Bank Manager?' (p. 313).

The Mad Mitchells

- a couple and their young daughter, Cara, who demonstrates signs of mental illness
- Meena's neighbours ('The Mad Mitchells' is the name used by Meena to refer to Cara's parents)
- of humble economic means
- live in a cluttered house
- Cara is sent to a psychiatric institution against her parents' wishes – this surprises Meena who believes that Cara will thrive in an open space, as opposed to an enclosed cell.

Key quotations:

- 'Mr and Mrs Mitchell were a middle-aged brother and sister who lived with Cara, a moon-faced dopey woman, who, it was rumoured, was their incestuous daughter' (p. 113)
- 'Cara sang to herself, swaying with the chill wind' (p. 130).

CONCLUSION

Reasons NOT to study this work of literature:

- because you have been told you need to diversify or decolonise your English curriculum
- because you need an author who isn't another 'old/dead, white man'
- because it's what your head of department has told you to teach.

Reasons to study this work of literature:

- to immerse children in a witty, vivid, sharply observed world full of rich characters they will root for and love to hate
- to open your students' eyes to the past – in many cases, their past
- to ask your students to feel and to light a fire in their hearts
- to remember why you chose to teach our subject.

On the surface, this book is a classic Bildungsroman; a coming-of-age story of a nine-year-old girl, caught between two cultures and growing up in a 1970s Britain that is on the cusp of industrial and political change. But this text represents a lot more than that. While it celebrates the warmth and humour of communities existing with one another, for friendships and alliances, of judgements and disconnect, it does not hold back from exposing the darker narratives of histories and the way they continue to shape Britain's identity in the present. Syal's creation of characters who are not stock representatives of good and evil, but instead flawed, as humans tend to be, with their vulnerabilities as well as their moral depravity, is a refreshing take on social problem fiction.

Learners deserve deliberately crafted, safe opportunities to think critically and to discuss difficult topics openly. To do justice to *Anita and Me*, we believe that this thinking and discussion can be best facilitated through dialogic conversations (or 'talk for learning', if you prefer). This approach positions learners to consider how the questions Syal raises are still relevant to Britain today, how nationality is still equated with ethnicity, how diversity is still viewed with scepticism and how belonging is still translated to conformity. It is only when we set up and rigorously maintain safe environments with fictional references that learners can interrogate and debate without the fear of 'getting it wrong'. It is then that we can truly foster a culture that allows our learners to take lessons from Britain's past and use them to positively influence the course of the future. To set up dialogue that is truly meaningful, memorable and led by the learners, we recommend using the principles of Socratic debating – discussed at length by Mary Myatt and Yamini Bibi in a *Listen In: Myatt & Co* podcast (Bibi and Myatt, 2022) – as well as the framework set out by Peter D'Sena in the introductory chapters to support learners in their conversations about the taboo language used.

Ultimately, though, this is a text about a tweenager wrestling through the complexities of adolescence. To a young person, it validates and speaks to the various frustrations of communicating with parents, navigating through friendships, and coming to terms with the universal physical and emotional changes of this age and stage. It is, therefore, a text which is timeless and one which leaves the reader feeling, by the end of it, that they know more than they did.

APPENDIX: A CONTEXTUAL TIMELINE

Teaching a set text in relation to authorial intent requires the careful teaching of socio-historical context. Since context is a separate assessment objective in the English Literature GCSE course, it is no surprise that some teachers choose to front-load this information so their learners can make inferences from a place of knowledge. Context, however, only elevates reader-response when it can be contextualised. There are strong arguments for teaching it as and when relevant to minimise the impact on working memory.

To give teachers flexibility, we have included a contextual timeline at the back of our guide and included it as a downloadable resource, so that teachers can make pedagogical decisions appropriate for their students and teach context as and when they need to. Whilst some contextual events have been exemplified and explained in this timeline, others are mere dates, intended as a build-up to provide the necessary prerequisite knowledge for students to understand the implications of various events. We have also included brief references (in **bold italics**) to explain the significance of some of the key events to support learners in making more nuanced and informed interpretations, rather than turning contextual links into a tick-box exercise for accessing marks.

1599: The East India Company

Explains the build up to 'The Black of Hole of Calcutta', referenced in the text.

To counteract the Dutch monopoly of the spice trade, Queen Elizabeth I signed an official charter to a group of the City of London merchants, conferring the monopoly of English trade to what was now going to be known as The East India Company. Its business resulted in affordable tea, cotton textiles and spices to reach the shores of England, while its London investors were awarded returns 'as high as 30 per cent' (Roos, 2020). Although initially set up for the purposes of trade, Erikson (quoted in Roos, 2020) refers to it as the 'de facto emperor', with a private army of 260,000 soldiers, two times the size of the British army at the time.

1690: East India Company established a trading base in Calcutta, building Fort William as a defensive measure

The motives and role of the Company began to change almost immediately and in 1696 'the Company was given permission to fortify the settlement and

APPENDIX: A CONTEXTUAL TIMELINE

in 1698 actually purchased the towns of Sutanati, Govindpur and Calcutta' (AMP Ltd., n.d.).

1702: Fort William was constructed in Calcutta by The East India Company

Explains why The East India Company was being seen as a threat and contextualises 'The Black Hole of Calcutta', referenced in the text.

1707: Calcutta raised to the status of presidency by The East India Company

1756: 'The Black Hole of Calcutta'

When the British garrison began strengthening Fort William's defences, the Nawab of Bengal, newly succeeded to the throne, sent orders to the British Governor of Calcutta to cease fortifications. Upon the Company's refusal, the Nawab marched on the city, which fell following a short siege. On the night of June 20th 1756, according to survivor John Zephaniah Holwell, 146 British prisoners of war, including one woman and several wounded men were herded into an 18 feet by 14 feet dungeon in Fort William in Calcutta (Holwell, 1758). What followed was an incident that left a cultural imprint, and was cited regularly as validation for British imperialism. Possibly imprisoned for one night before a suitable place for incarceration was to be found, it is thought unlikely that the prisoners were intended for death. However, a combination of extreme heat, dehydration, humidity and insufficient air took its toll and according to Holwell, only 23 prisoners survived. Historians have debated the accuracy and scale of the event, with some outlining that a number of Indian, Dutch and Portuguese civilians were also imprisoned. Historians, such as H.H. Little who conducted a notable study, published in *Bengal Past and Present* (The Calcutta Historical Society, 1916), cast doubt on the accepted vision, querying whether the 'Black Hole' was as small and deadly as originally portrayed in British accounts, arguing the possibility of exaggeration for propaganda purposes.

1757: Battle of Plassey – Nawab of Bengal Siraj-ud-Daula defeated and replaced with Mir Jafar by East India Company

1765: The East India Company was granted Diwani – the right to collect revenue – in Bengal and Bihar

Explains the change from the economic to the political role of The East India Company and contextualises the growing disconnect.

1841: The first recorded use of the term 'Black Country', referring to a region in the West Midlands, known for its heavy industry and coal mining heritage. The name is assumed to have originated from the thick coal seam found in the area and the black soot that emerged from its factories.

1857: Indian Mutiny

1857: 'Divide and rule' policy of the British

Contextualises the growing disconnect and challenges some of the misconceptions voiced by members of Tollington within the text.

1858: Britain's official rule begins in India

1864: Colonial Empire and the process of 'Othering'

Explains one of the key themes in the text and contextualises the comments made by various members of Tollington, both consciously and sub-consciously.

In the mid-1860s, British politics saw a shift in focus from colonisation to race politics. Whilst addressing a meeting at the Royal Anthropological Institute, James Hunt, President of the Institute, declared that: '...the brain of the Negro had been proved to be smaller than the European' (Hunt, 1864, p. xv) [concluding amongst other things] '...that the Negro is inferior, intellectually, to the European' (p.xvi). His colleagues lauded him on his 'excellent paper' (p. xvii).

Historian Linda Colley, while writing about the role played by the 'Empire' on the emerging ideas of British nationalism writes: 'Britons could feel united in dominion over, and in distinction from, the millions of colonial subjects beyond their own boundaries' (1992, p. 325). And in a country that was already made up of distinct nations with unique identities, defining 'Britishness' against the backdrop of 'Others' could generate an identity that was 'superimposed over an array of internal differences' (Colley, 2003, p. 6).

1928: William Hicks as Home Minister

Contextualises Meera Syal's stance for writing a text that challenges the dominant colonial discourse and contextualises the relationship of mistrust between Meena's Indian friends and relatives and the members of Tollington.

The home minister in the Conservative government said this about India in 1928: 'I know it is said in missionary meetings that we conquered India to raise the levels of Indians. That is cant. We conquered India as an outlet for the goods of Britain. We conquered India by the sword. And by the sword we shall hold it' (Stanley, 1938).

1942: 'Quit India' Movement

Explains how the disconnect and exploitation resulted in resistance. Contextualises the partition of the Indian subcontinent.

1947: Partition of India

Contextualises the partition stories shared amongst Meena's family and friends, and explains the impact on her parents' and grandparents' values and identities.

In August 1947, British colonial rule in the Indian subcontinent came to an abrupt end, 10 months earlier than planned. Britain's last Viceroy to India, Lord Louis Mountbatten, announced and led the British exit, partitioning the subcontinent into two independent nation states: Muslim-majority Pakistan and Hindu-majority India. The new borders were drawn up by Sir Cyril Radcliffe, a British barrister who had infamously never travelled further east than Paris before being tasked with drawing up the lines of partition in a mere 40 days. The final drawing was announced two days after India's Independence.

What followed was one of the greatest forced migrations in human history, resulting in an unprecedented and unexpected outbreak of terrifying violence and mass genocide. Communities that had coexisted for almost a millennia – Hindi, Muslim, Sikh, Zoarastrian, Jewish, Jain – were driven apart by fear and paranoia as the once syncretic society was brutally torn apart, giving birth to inveterate hostility. Fifteen million people were uprooted, between 1 and 2 million presumed dead, and 80,000 thousand women known to be abducted. American photojournalist Margaret Bourke-White, witness to the opening of the gates of a Nazi concentration camp just a year earlier, described how Calcutta's streets 'looked like Buchenwald' (Dalrymple, 2015).

1948: British Nationality Act

Explains the significance of the theme of belonging and contextualises the comments made by various members of Tollington, both consciously and sub-consciously about ethnic minorities.

This Act introduced the concept of British Nationality by virtue of citizenship of the United Kingdom and its Colonies. Although the UK Government could not legally restrict immigration from the Colonies or Commonwealth nations, the government nevertheless began implementing strategies to deter potential immigrants and indirectly restrict non-white immigrants. Several 'artificial limits' that were not 'publicised' were taken, (Spencer, 2002, p. 53). Campaigns included the distribution of pamphlets and posters, warnings of economic challenges and housing shortages, inhospitality, bland food, harsh climate, and the threat of intense labour that awaited the immigrants in the UK.

1954: Henry Hopkinson, the Minister of State at the Colonial Office

Contextualises how the policies and narratives on immigration shifted and were subsequently exploited by politicians, referenced on numerous occasions in the text.

During a debate at the House of Commons, Hopkins declares: 'As the law stands, any British subject from the colonies is free to enter this country [...] We still take pride in the fact that a man can say *civis Brittanicus sum* whatever his colour may be and we take pride in the fact that he wants and can come to the mother country' (Spencer, 2002, p. 28).

1955: *The Dam Busters*

Contextualises the racist name of Tracey's dog, and how it was a well-known choice at the time, influenced by popular culture.

This British epic war film was based on the true story of Operation Chastise (1943) where RAF squads attacked dams in Nazi Germany. The iconic black dog in the film, belonging to RAF bomber pilot Guy Gibson, was named after a racist slur, the N word. The Wing Commander even used his dog's name as a codeword to indicate when the dam had been breached. In 2020, the RAF altered the gravestone in Scampton, replacing the dog's name with a picture of a black dog. The naming of the Rutter's dog in *Anita and Me* not only reflects the Rutters' ignorance, but also such unfortunate informality around derogatory language that would have been normalised further through the release of *The Dam Busters* in 1955.

1962: Commonwealth Immigrants Act

Contextualises how the policies and narratives on immigration shifted and were subsequently exploited by politicians, referenced in numerous occasions in the text.

An act to temporarily control the immigration of Commonwealth citizens, introducing limits and application requirements.

1964: Peter Griffith elected as Smethwick's (West Midland) Conservative MP

Griffith won the seat with arguably the most racist electoral campaign in history. When interrogated by Panorama journalist James Mossman, Griffith maintained that he hadn't 'exploited' the building resentment around inter-racial communities, claiming he was the 'only political leader in the town [...] prepared to face up to the problems' (Woods, 2016).

1964: First issue of *Jackie* magazine

Contextualises the popularity of Jackie magazine and explains the subsequent influence on Meena and her sense of ethnic, gender and sexual identity.

This was an influential teenage magazine with sales reaching 600,000 regularly in the 1970s, covering themes of fashion, beauty, romance and pop-culture, featuring the likes of Donny Osmond and David Cassidy. Also known for its infamous advice section under the guise of 'Cathy and Claire', but led and produced by a traditional, male-led company, DC Tompson, who did not have a female editor till at least a decade later.

1966: Dr Reita Faria (Miss India) wins 16th Miss World competition

Contextualises the significance of Dr Faria's win to Meena and her family and friends.

A culturally historical and significant moment, Dr Reita Faria was the first woman of Asian descent to win such a title. Breaking stereotypes prevalent at the time, she demonstrated that beauty could coexist with intellect and ambition, subsequently inspiring an entire generation of women from the Indian subcontinent, and beyond. As Miss World, Dr Reita Faria served as a cultural ambassador and represented India at various international events and forums. Her role helped foster goodwill and help in challenging the stereotype of an 'Indian woman' at a global scale.

1966: *Smethwick: A Straw in the Wind*

Contextualises how the policies and narratives on immigration shifted and were subsequently exploited by politicians, referenced in numerous occasions in the text.

APPENDIX: A CONTEXTUAL TIMELINE

As nearly 75,000 immigrants arrived every year in the 1960s, many to work in the factories and support the rebuilding of postwar Britain, a BBC documentary *Smethwick: A Straw in the Wind* by James Mossman reported on the subsequent racial tensions in the West Midlands (1966). The report found that immigrant families were being turned away from churches, refused haircuts by barbers and were used to seeing signs that read, 'No Blacks. No Irish. No dogs'.

1968: Enoch Powell's 'Rivers of Blood' speech to a meeting of the Conservative Political Centre in Birmingham

Considered to be one of the most inflammatory and controversial speeches made by a British politician in modern history. In 1968, anti-immigration Conservative politician, Enoch Powell, made his now infamous speech where he strongly criticised Commonwealth immigration and the proposed race-relations bill using vitriolic language, suggesting that if the number of immigrants continued to rise, there would be an implosion of violence. Even though Powell was dismissed from his Shadow ministerial position as a consequence, the reverberations of the speech were felt.

1968: Commonwealth Immigrants Act

An amendment to the Commonwealth Immigration Act of 1962 passed by the Labour Government, this act restricted the future right to UK citizenship to those born in the UK or those who had at least one parent or grandparent born there. Those living in the ex-colonies without a direct family connection to the UK were no longer entitled to enter the country.

1969-1970: The Manplan Project

Contextualises the changing rural landscape as a result of Industrialisation and its subsequent impact the villagers of Tollington.

Commissioned by the *Architectural Review*, these were a series of photographs by Patrick Ward designed to capture ordinary British citizens against the changing landscape of Britain in the Swinging Sixties (Manplan, 1969). Aptly titled 'Frustration', this was a 70-page magazine issue that contained a series of images without the expected focus on architecture, shocking its readers as well as advertisers. Instead, it featured juxtaposing images that encapsulated hard-hitting realities and grim backdrops against the human beings most impacted by the change around them, giving a face to those who seemed to have missed the 'Swinging Sixties' altogether, or as Meena reminds us, places like Tollington.

1970–1979: Virginity Testing

Contextualises the mistrust and resentment alluded to in the comments by Meena's Aunties, as many immigrants at the time would have been subject to some form of racist interrogation or personal violation upon entry to the UK.

The UK Home Office tested women, predominantly of South Asian origin, for their virginity as a means for immigration control – a practice that doctors believe evolved from a gross misunderstanding of the female body and misconceptions of 'purity'.

Balraj Purewal, director of Indian Workers' Association in the UK was first informed of these violations when a young Indian man came to the Southall Youth Movement in 1979, seeking assistance. He explained that his fiancée, a school teacher from India, had undergone the invasive test to establish her virginity. The abuse received national attention when the news story was covered by the *Guardian* (Phillips, 1979). At least 80 women from the subcontinent are known to have undergone these 'tests' in the late 1970s (Travis, 2011).

2021: Virginity Testing became a Criminal Offence in the UK

REFERENCES

AMP Ltd. (n.d.). *EAST INDIA COMPANY FACTORY RECORDS: Sources from the British Library, London, Part 5: Calcutta, 1690-1708.* [online] Available at: http://www.ampltd.co.uk/collections_az/EIC-Factory-5/highlights.aspx#:~:text=In%201696%20the%20Company%20was%20given%20permission%20to [Accessed 15 Dec. 2023].

Beck, I.L., McKeown, M.G. and Kucan, L. (2013). *Bringing Words to Life: Robust Vocabulary Instruction.* 2nd ed. New York: Guilford Press.

Clark, R.C., Lyons, C. and Hoover, L. (2004). Graphics for learning: Proven guidelines for planning, designing, and evaluating visuals in training materials. *Performance Improvement*, 43(10), pp.45–47. doi:https://doi.org/10.1002/pfi.4140431011.

Bibi, Y. and Myatt, M. (2022). *6. Socratic debate with Yamina Bibi - Listen: Myatt & Co podcast.* Available at: https://podcast.myattandco.com/1525270/9952500 [Accessed: 09 Feb. 2024].

Calcutta Historical Society. (1916). *Bengal, Past & Present: Journal of the Calcutta Historical Society, 1916, INDIAN CULTURE.* Available at: https://indianculture.gov.in/bengal-past-present-journal-calcutta-historical-society-10 [Accessed 09 Feb. 2024].

Colley, L. (1992). 'Britishness and otherness: An argument. *The Journal of British Studies*, 31(4), pp. 309–329. doi:10.1086/386013.

Colley, L. (2003) *Britons: Forging the nation, 1707-1837.* London: Pimlico.

Collins, K. (2021). Foreword. In: Quigley, A. and Coleman, R. (p. 2021). Improving Literacy in Secondary Schools Guidance Report. [online] Education Endowment Foundation. Available at: https://educationendowmentfoundation.org.uk/education-evidence/guidance-reports/literacy-ks3-ks4 [Accessed 14 Dec. 2023].

Dalrymple, W. (2015). The mutual genocide of Indian partition. *The New Yorker.* Available at: https://www.newyorker.com/magazine/2015/06/29/the-great-divide-books-dalrymple [Accessed: 09 Feb. 2024].

Department for Education. (2013). *English Literature: GCSE subject content and assessment objectives, GOV.UK.* Available at: https://assets.publishing.service.gov.uk/media/5a7ca069e5274a29d8363d20/GCSE_English_literature.pdf [Accessed: 09 Feb. 2024].

D'Sena, P. (2023). Interviewed by Zara Shah, November 2023.

Erikson, E. (2020). *How the East India Company Became the World's Most Powerful Monopoly.* [online] Yale MacMillan Center. Available at: https://macmillan.yale.edu/news/how-east-india-company-became-worlds-most-powerful-monopoly [Accessed 15 Dec. 2023].

FFT Literacy (2019). *Reciprocal Reading: A structured approach to teaching reading comprehension strategies.* [online] Education Endowment Foundation. Available at: https://educationendowmentfoundation.org.uk/projects-and-evaluation/projects/reciprocal-reading [Accessed 14 Dec. 2023].

Holwell, J.Z. (1758). A genuine narrative of the deplorable deaths of the English gentlemen, and others, who were suffocated in the black-hole in Fort-William, at Calcutta, in the Kingdom of Bengal, in the night succeeding the 20th day of June, 1756 by John Zephaniah Holwell. *Open Library.* Available at: https://openlibrary.org/books/OL17944636M/A_genuine_narrative_of_the_deplorable_deaths_of_the_English_gentlemen_and_others_who_were_suffocated [Accessed 09 Feb. 2024].

Hunt, J. (1864). 'On the Negro's place in nature'. *Journal of the Anthropological Society of London*, 2, pp. xv–xvii. doi:10.2307/3025197.

Jalal, A. (2013). *The Pity of Partition: Manto's life, times, and work across the India-Pakistan divide.* Princeton, N.J.: Princeton University Press, Cop.

Jones, K. (2019). *Retrieval Practice: Research & Resources for Every Classroom.* Suffolk: John Catt Educational Ltd.

Khan, Z. (2021). Ethnic health inequalities in the UK's maternity services: a systematic literature review. *British Journal of Midwifery*, 29(p. 2), pp.100–107.

Myatt, M. (n.d.). *High challenge, low threat.* [online] Mary Myatt Learning. Available at: https://www.marymyatt.com/blog/high-challenge-low-threat [Accessed 14 Dec. 2023].

Paivio, A. (1969). Mental imagery in associative learning and memory. *Psychological Review*, [online] 76(3), pp.241–263. doi:https://doi.org/10.1037/h0027272.

Quigley, A. (2018). *Closing the Vocabulary Gap.* London: Routledge.

Roos, D. (2020). *How the East India Company became the world's most powerful monopoly. History.com.* Available at: https://www.history.com/news/east-india-company-england-trade [Accessed 09 Feb. 2024].

Manplan (1969). 'Frustration', *Architectural Review.* photographs by Patrick Ward.

Mossman, J. (1966). *Smethwick: A Straw in the Wind.* BBC.

Phillips, M. (1979) 'Airport virginity tests banned by Rees'. *The Guardian*, 3 February.

Spencer, I.R.G. (2002) 'British immigration policy since 1939. *British Immigration Policy Since 1939: The Making of Multi-Racial Britain* [Preprint]. doi:10.4324/9780203437032.

Stanley, S. (1938). *Problems of colonial India I, S. Stanley: Problems of Colonial India I (April 1938).* Available at: https://www.marxists.org/history/etol/writers/judd/1938/04/india.htm [Accessed: 09 Feb. 2024].

Syal, M. (2004). *Anita and Me.* London: Harper Perennial. First published in Great Britain by Flamingo, 1996.

Travis, A. (2011). Virginity tests for immigrants 'reflected dark age prejudices' of 1970s Britain. *The Guardian.* Available at: https://www.theguardian.com/uk/2011/may/08/virginity-tests-immigrants-prejudices-britain [Accessed: 09 Feb. 2024].

Willingham, D. (2006). Ask the Cognitive Scientist: How Praise Can Motivate—or Stifle. *American Educator, Winter 2005-2006.* [online] Available at: https://www.aft.org/ae/winter2005-2006/willingham [Accessed 14 Dec. 2023].

Woods, R. (2016). England in 1966: Racism and ignorance in the Midlands. *BBC News.* Available at: https://www.bbc.co.uk/news/uk-england-birmingham-36388761 [Accessed: 09 Feb. 2024].

Young, M.F.D., Lambert, D., Roberts, C.R. and Roberts, M. (2014). *Knowledge and the Future School: Curriculum and Social Justice.* London: Bloomsbury Academic.

INDEX

A

abandonment 142, 145, 148
abuse 48, 74, 81, 131, 133-4, 185, 190, 207
abusive terms *see* offensive language
academic writing 8, 29-30
accent 77-8, 83
accessibility 4-5
adjectival antithesis 147
anaphora 55
assessment 7, 12-13

B

belonging 37, 84, 86, 114, 116-17, 125, 138, 172, 185, 199, 204
bias 37, 73, 83, 97, 126, 135
Bildungsroman 11, 36, 82, 199
bird imagery 21-2
Black of Hole of Calcutta 109, 201
British Nationality Act 1948 204

C

cataphoric reference 158
change 88-9, 95, 108, 113, 181
character analysis 7, 183-4
Anita Rutter 23, 56, 84, 104, 136-7, 147, 159, 169, 185-6
Auntie Shaila 195
Deirdre Rutter 46, 147, 190
Fat Sally 136, 193
Hairy Neddy 197
Mad Mitchells 198
Mama (Daljit Kumar) 35-6, 103, 120-1, 147, 186-7
Meena Kumar 34-5, 57, 72, 83-4, 104, 120, 137, 159, 169, 179, 184-5
Mr Christmas 196-7
Mr Omerod 23, 192
Mrs Christmas/Connie 196
Mrs Worrall 193-4
Mr Topsy/Turvey 119, 195-6
Mr Worrall 194
Nanima 119, 147, 189
Papa (Shyam Kumar) 56, 71-2, 84-5, 147, 158, 187-8
The Pembridges 102-3
Pinky and Baby 195
Rajesh Bhatra 198
Robert 169
Roberto Rutter 191
Sam Lowbridge 180, 189-90
Sandy 197
Sherrie 192-3
Sunil 103, 120
Tracey Rutter 46, 159, 179, 190-1
Uncle Alan 120, 191-2
Uncle Amman 194
character development *see* plot and character development
child narrator 15
chunking 5
Churchill, Winston 90
Colley, Linda 203
Collins, Kevin 4
colonialism 15, 27
comedy 57, 167-8
Commonwealth Immigrants Act 1962 205
Commonwealth Immigrants Act 1968 206
contextual timeline 4
corporal punishment 21
cultural context 15-16, 27, 40, 51, 63, 76, 89-90, 109, 126-7, 142-3, 152-3, 172-3, 201-6
cyclical structure 180

D

Dam Busters 204-5
dance imagery 45-6, 70-1
dialect 83
dialogic teaching 3
dialogue 7, 23, 55-6, 121, 137, 162, 168
didactic approach 2
disclaimers 2
discriminatory language 2, 14, 21, 37, 65, 76, 124, 130-1, 151, 153, 204-5
D'Sena, Peter 2
dual coding 6, 9
dynamic verbs 128, 139

E

East India Company 201-3
economic change 15
epiphanies 105
exclamatives 55

F

facades 26–7
figurative language 140
flashbacks 21, 58, 155
flipped learning 5
foreboding 43
foreshadowing 98, 105, 137, 142, 146
friendship 66, 80, 104, 137, 138

G

gambling metaphor 100–1
gangs 75, 80, 86, 88
gender 15
guilt 50, 57, 59

H

historical context 15–16, 27–8, 40, 51, 63, 76, 89–90, 109, 114–15, 126–7, 142–3, 152–3, 172–3, 201–6
hyperbolic language 34, 118–19

I

identity 27, 29–30, 80, 108
imagery
birds 21–2
music and dance 45–6
nature 33–4
sensory 139
sound 22, 158
immigration 15, 31, 204–7
industrialisation 76, 127
innocence 23, 47
interior monologue 168
intertextuality 61, 71
irony 82–3

J

Jackie magazine 76, 205
Jones, Kate 7
juxtaposition 46, 73, 139

K

kamasutra 41
key themes 10

L

labels 2
language
of childhood 168
dialogue 7, 23, 55–6, 121, 137, 162, 168
discriminatory and offensive 2, 14, 19, 21, 37, 65, 76, 99, 124, 130–1, 151, 153, 171, 204–5
literary devices 34, 55–6, 71, 100–1, 118–19, 146–7, 158, 167–8, 177–9
narrative voice 21, 33, 70–1, 82, 100, 118, 135, 177
see also imagery
Lee, Harper 11
linguistic reclamation 2
literary allusions 71, 177–8
lying 14–15, 21, 85, 150
see also truth vs lies

M

mantra 181
marginalisation 62, 65–6
metamorphosis 108, 123, 125, 179
see also transformation
metaphor 100–1, 146, 174
microaggressions 2, 19, 89, 164
mirroring 105
Miss World competition 89, 205
morality 15, 18, 51
motifs 7, 22, 28, 71, 85
motivation 9
music imagery 45–6, 70–1
Myatt, Mary 7, 9

N

narrative voice 21, 33, 70, 82, 100, 118, 135, 177
nature imagery 33–4

O

offensive language 2, 14, 19, 21, 65, 124, 130–1, 151, 153, 171, 204–5
othering 61, 65, 155–6, 203

INDEX

P

Paivio, Allan 9
parallelism 138
Partition of India 1947 27–8, 50–1, 54, 63, 203
past participles 128
personal growth 170
personification 22
plot and character development 5–6, 7
  chapter 1 17–21
  chapter 2 30–2
  chapter 3 43–5
  chapter 4 53–5
  chapter 5 66–70
  chapter 6 79–82
  chapter 7 92–9
  chapter 8 112–17
  chapter 9 129–35
  chapter 10 145–6
  chapter 11 155–7
  chapter 12 166–7
  chapter 13 175–7
polysyndeton 178–9
post-colonialism 94, 108, 114
Powell, Enoch 99, 206
power dynamics 39–40, 45, 96, 104, 114
prejudice 37, 61, 83, 89, 97, 135
present participles 128, 139
Punjabi language 109, 116

R

racism 61, 65, 89–90, 94, 97, 99, 205–6
racist language 2, 14, 19, 21, 65, 99, 124, 130–1, 151, 153, 204–5
regional accents 77–8, 83
religion 15, 63, 67–8, 153
repetition 139
retrieval practice 7–8, 16, 29, 41, 52, 64, 77, 91, 110, 127, 143, 154, 165, 173
revelations 50, 57, 105, 158

S

satire 101
scaffolding 5–6
self-actualisation 182
sin 19, 54, 59
Smethwick: A Straw in the Wind 205–6
social context 15–16, 27, 40, 51, 63, 76, 89–90, 109, 126–7, 142–3, 152–3, 172–3, 201–6
sound imagery 22, 158
speech accommodation 144
stative verbs 128
stereotypes 17, 73, 92, 96, 97
stigma 2

structural analysis 7, 11–12
  chapter 1 23–4
  chapter 2 36
  chapter 3 47
  chapter 4 57
  chapter 5 72
  chapter 6 85
  chapter 7 104–5
  chapter 8 121
  chapter 9 137
  chapter 10 147–8
  chapter 11 160
  chapter 12 169–70
  chapter 13 180–1
supernatural 138
Swinging Sixties 88–9, 93
Syal, Meera 11

T

taboo language 2, 14
tension 139, 181–2
testing effect 7–8
themes 10
think-aloud method 17, 42
To Kill a Mockingbird (1960) 11, 61
transformation 121–3, 134, 146
trauma 50
truth vs lies 14–15, 21

U

urbanisation 153, 173

V

verbs 128, 139
violence 53, 105, 125, 126, 133
virginity testing 206–7
vocabulary in context 4–6, 16, 28, 41, 51–2, 63–4, 76–7, 90, 109–10, 127, 143, 153–4, 165, 173

W

Willingham, Daniel 9

Z

zeugma 178